Henry Giles

Sketches of Celebrated Irishmen, Irish Character, etc

Henry Giles

Sketches of Celebrated Irishmen, Irish Character, etc

ISBN/EAN: 9783744713672

Printed in Europe, USA, Canada, Australia, Japan

Cover: Foto ©ninafisch / pixelio.de

More available books at **www.hansebooks.com**

SKETCHES

OF

Celebrated Irishmen,

Irish Character, etc.,

By HENRY GILES.

———

NEW YORK:

P. J. KENEDY,

EXCELSIOR CATHOLIC PUBLISHING HOUSE,

5 BARCLAY STREET

1896.

Entered according to Act of Congress, in the year 1862,

By D. & J. SADLIER & CO.,

In the Clerk's Office of the District Court of the United States for the

Southern District of New York.

PUBLISHERS' PREFACE.

The Lectures and Essays here given to the public are among the finest efforts of the genius of HENRY GILES. None of the contents of this volume have ever before been published in book form. The many thousands who had the privilege of hearing Mr. Giles discourse on "Spirit of Irish History," "Irish Wit and Humor," "Irish Character, Mental and Moral," "Ireland and the Irish," "Irish-born Citizens," "Irish Emigration," "Daniel O'Connell," or "John Philpot Curran," will be glad of the opportunity of having those noble Lectures by them for frequent perusal. So, too, with the Essays on "Doctor Doyle" "Oliver Goldsmith," "Gerald Griffin," and "Wit and Humor in Scotland," written for a Boston periodical; many will be pleased to have them in a more permanent form.

The beautiful Lecture on "Catholic Art and Protestant Culture," new to most readers, will be found one of the most admirable essays ever written on a similar subject. It is probably one of the finest specimens in our language of that particular style of writing. "The Cost of War," written during and in relation to our own disastrous but, happily, successful war, was read in New York and other cities by a friend of Mr. Giles, after the gifted author had become unable to travel or to appear in public. This Lecture was, we believe, the last production of his brilliant and prolific mind.

This volume is invested with a mournful interest, from the fact of its being revised by the author in his sick room, if not in his sick bed. Some of its contents have already delighted thousands, as they are destined, we trust, to delight thousands and tens of thousands in the after time, when the bright spirit from which they emanated shall have winged its way to other spheres. They are among the latest flashes of a genius that may shine no more as once it shone—of a mind prostrated by much suffering, and darkened by much tribulation. Nevertheless, they will be found not unworthy of the brightest days of their author's earlier life.

CONTENTS.

GILES' LECTURES.

SPIRIT OF IRISH HISTORY.

It is now some years since I began to speak in Boston.
Among the first of my efforts, Ireland was my theme.   I
endeavored, as best as I could, to tell her story.   I was
heard with generous interest, but it was the story, and not
the teller, that inspired it.   It was called for throughout the
length and breadth of New England ; it was repeated in city
halls and in village lyceums.   Old and young, grave and gay,
listened to it with open ears and with eager hearts ; and to
many of them it seemed a new, and wild, and strange recital.
It is no longer novel.   It is now, not a story, but a drama ;
a black and fearful drama, which civilized nations gaze upon
with a terrified astonishment, that has no power to weep.
It was then gloomy and sad enough, and to those who know
life only in its general comforts, it appeared a condition
which it would be hard to render worse.   But the presump-
tuousness of man is constantly rebuked by the vicissitude
of events.   It is but too surely so in this case.   There was
yet the vial of a deeper woe in store, and that vial is now
open.   Tragic as the story of Ireland was, when first I
tried to tell it, it might yet be given with those flashes of

mirth and wit, those outburstings of fun, and drollery, and
oddity, and humor, which can be crushed in the Irish heart
only by the heaviest load of sorrow. Of such weight is
now the burden that lies upon it.

Ireland, now, is not simply a place of struggle, of want,
of hard work, and of scanty fare, it has become a wilderness of starvation. The dreariest visitation which humanity can receive, rests upon it—not of fire, not of the sword,
not of the plague ; but that, compared with which, fire, and
sword, and plague, are but afflictions ; that is, Hunger—
hunger, that fell and dreadful thing, which, in its extremity,
preys more horribly on the mind, even than the body;
which causes friend to look on friend with an evil eye, and
the heart of a maiden to be stern to her lover ; and the
husband to glare upon the wife that nestled in his bosom,
and the mother to forget her sucking child. Such, though
we trust never to come to this awful extremity, is the nature
of that calamity which lately has been preying upon Ireland. It is not, indeed, at this awful extremity, but far
enough towards it, to spread over that beautiful island a pall
of mourning ; far enough towards it, to quench the joy of
childhood, to bow down the strength of men, to wither the
loveliness of women, to take away the comeliness of the
young, and to cover the heads of the aged with a sorrow
darker than the grave. We cannot think of it with other
thoughts than those of grief. We cannot refer to it with
other speech than that of sadness. For my own part, I
cannot hear of this terrible affliction ; I cannot read of it ;
my imagination, of its own accord, transports me into the
midst of it, and, for the time, I dwell in the company and
throngs of the wretched. The necessity that compels me
to think and speak of it, bows down my soul to the earth,
and I am almost prompted to exclaim, in the words of the
prophet, "O, that my head were waters, and my eyes were

fountains of tears, that I might weep day and night for the slain of the daughters of my people."

Multitudes are perishing; that fact admits neither of doubt nor of dispute. Multitudes are perishing ; that fact is as certain as it is terrible. It does not signify what they are or where, the fact is still most horrible and most appalling. Were they savages in the depths of an African wilderness, our common humanity would urge us to send them succor. Were they the most utter strangers, foreign to us in every mode of thought and habit, that can render nations alien to each other, they would still be within the embrace of that common humanity, and its voice would plead for them. Were they most base and worthless, both in character and condition, their misfortunes would give them dignity, and win from us compassion. Were they enemies, and had done us the worst of injuries, not only the precepts of the Gospel, but the sentiments of magnanimity, would impel us to help them in the hour of their agony. But they are none of these. They have given to civilization some of its most quickening elements ; some of its most brilliant genius ; some of its fairest ornaments ; some of its most heroic minds. Numbers of us, here, are bone of their bone, and flesh of their flesh ; the fathers who supported our youth, live above, or lie below, the green sward of Erin ; the mothers who sang our infancy to sleep with its plaintive melodies, are still breathing its air, or gone to mingle with its saints in heaven. To all of us, of whatever nation, they are kindred in the ties of that solemn existence, which we feel the more intensely, the more it is afflicted. They are a people, too, whose own ears have been always open to the cry of the distressed. They have ever been willing to give, not merely of their abundance, but even of their want ; a people whose hospitality is free as the wind upon their mountains, and generous as the rain upon their valleys ; the fame of it as wide as the earth, and as old as their history. This people are now in grievous troubles. They are in the midst of famine, and we are in the midst of plenty. Out of this great plenty we are sending them support, and with support our pity and our prayers. Let us most gratefully and humbly bless God, who has put this most blessed privilege in our power; the privilege of saving those who are ready to perish, and of causing thousands of breaking hearts to sing for joy; to change mourning to gladness, and the spirit of heaviness for the spirit of praise.

I am not here to excite an interest; for that is already excited, and has been working bravely through the land with a passionate emotion. It has been shaking the hearts of this great people to the utmost verge of their dominion; agitating, not their cities alone, but piercing the sympathies of those who dwell in shanties on the open prairie, and by the half cleared forest; melting into tenderness, not the women of the land alone, but subduing the hardy men of the woods, of the camp, of the ship, and of the battle-field. I would not insult your sympathies by appealing to them; I would not insult your generosity by praising it; I am not here to plead a cause. Humanity in millions of hearts have effectually pleaded that cause already; and hands are lifted up, while now I speak, to thank Heaven, and the good humanity in which Heaven lives on earth, for the sympathy with which it has responded to the cries of afflicted brotherhood.

I will not therefore enlarge on the present distress; I will not, and I cannot, go into its technical detail; neither will I vaguely ascribe this great suffering to Providence. I will not seek the sources of it in the clouds above, or in the earth beneath; I will try, so far as my light leads me, to seek those sources in directions where they may be intelligibly accounted for. I would lay no blame on the present generation; I do not speak of them. I am not insensible to the great exertions of the Government of the British nation to meet the tremendous crisis now existing ; nor would I speak otherwise than in heartfelt, enthusiastic sympathy of those huge manifestations of kindness in the British nation, which show forth those sublime charities, that vindicate the divine and God-imaged character of our nature. I will endeavor to review the whole system, of which the present distress is a part, and of which it is a result; I will endeavor to seek out whence it has originated, and how it may be changed; I will endeavor to trace some of its causes, and to indicate some of its remedies. I must, of course, confine myself to a few striking points, not alone by the limits of our time, but by the requirements of the occasion. The occasion is one, that will not tolerate much that admits greatly of dispute; it is one that requires all the conciliation which truth can sanction. It will therefore be my desire, in analyzing causes, and in specifying remedies, to take as broad and common ground as, with my opinions, it is possible for me to take. It will be also my desire to give no candid or just man offence; and though such a man may dispute my positions, I trust that he will have no complaint to make against my spirit, or against my temper.

The causes of Irish distress many find wholly in the character of the people. On this topic, we cannot afford to enlarge; and that it may not stand in our way as we proceed, we will grant, for the sake of argument, that the character of the people is as idle and as reckless as these philosophers describe it, and still it will be seen that, to ascribe the state of Ireland to this cause alone, or to this cause mainly, is not only partial, but false; at variance alike with any comprehensive grasp of sound logic or personal observation. The cause of any particular suffering in Ireland is seldom local or temporary, seldom to be found within itself or near it. The causes even of the present destitution are not all immediate; they are not all in the failure of the potato crop, not all in the character of those who plant the potato and live on it. The potato, it is true, is a precarious vegetable, and the people of Ireland, who have fed upon it for generations, are not in all things the wisest and most provident of nations; but in any sound state of things, it would not, surely, be within the limits of any contingency, that millions should wither into the dust, which had failed to afford nourishment to a fragile root. Such afflictions as Ireland is now enduring, terrible as they are, are not singular in her experience. They have been but too often her misfortune; and though, to our view, they are strange, they are, in her story, sufficiently familiar. But these afflictions come not from the skies above or the earth beneath; and, therefore, we shall not ascend to the heavens, nor go down to the deep, to seek their causes. Most of them are within the range of very ordinary inquiry, and they are both intelligible and explainable. I shall speak on causes of two kinds; one historical, and one social.

And, first, of the historical. Ireland has long been a country of agitation. The elements of discord were sown early in her history; and throughout her course, they have been nourished, and not eradicated. At first, divided into small principalities, like all countries so circumstanced, strife was constantly taking place among them, either for dominion or defence. It did not happen to Ireland as to England, that these separate states had been subdued into unity by a native prince, before the intrusion of a foreign ruler. It did not happen to Ireland as to England, that the foreign ruler took up his residence in it, identified his dignity with it, and that his children became natives of the soil. England, previous to the invasion of William the Conqueror, was a united empire, and therefore, though at the battle of Hastings, the

occupant of the throne was changed, the integrity of the
nation remained. Ireland was made up of divided and conflicting states, when the myrmidons of Henry the Second
arrived upon its shores; and even after these had gained
settlements in the country, there was no adhesive principles
among the natives. Had Ireland been consolidated, she
could not have been conquered; or, being conquered, she
would, like England, have absorbed the conquerors. The
spirit of English nationality was never stronger than it was
in the princes of the Norman line; and they asserted it with
a haughtiness, oftentimes with an injustice, that rendered
them formidable to every neighboring state. They were
the most inordinately jealous of any internal interference
with the concern of their kingdom, either of a secular or a
spiritual character; for generations they guarded England
with even a ferocious pride, but, also, with a commendable
zeal, they reared up her native institutions, and brought out
her latent energies.

But the stranger came to Ireland, and a stranger he still
remained. English dominion commenced in Ireland in a
spirit of conquest, and it continued in a spirit of exclusion.
National animosity thus perpetuated, sustained the spirit of
war, and war raged on with a fierceness which time did
nothing to mitigate. The native chieftains, when not in
conflict among themselves, united against the common foe;
and the end of every new struggle was increased oppression
to the people. Covetousness was added to the other baser
passions; and rapacity inflamed the anarchy in which it
hoped for gain. Defeated rebellion brought confiscation;
insurrection was, therefore, the harvest of adventurers; soldiers of fortune, or rather soldiers for fortune, gathered
like wolves to the battle. They were ready to glory in the
strife and to profit by it; they enjoyed the soil of the wretches
whom they slaughtered, and the work seemed as great a

pleasure as the recompense. Exhausted, however, in robbing the aborigines, they sought new excitement in despoiling one another; and, tired of fighting for plunder, they began at last to fight for precedence. So it continued to the period of Elizabeth, and though that brought a change, it did not bring improvement; for to the conflict of race was now added the conflict of religion.

This age of Elizabeth, which was to Europe the dawn of many hopes—this age of Elizabeth, which was so adorned and so enriched with all that makes an age transcendent —this age of Elizabeth was only for Ireland a heavy and a starless night. The government of Elizabeth, which had so much glory for England, gave no promise to Ireland. Under the sway of Elizabeth, Ireland lay in tempest and in waste. Oppression, that makes wise men mad, will provoke even despair to resistance, and resistance was obstinate and frequent in Ireland to the rulers whom Elizabeth set above them. Resistance was put down by methods the most inhuman; the crops were destroyed, dwelling-houses burned, the population indiscriminately massacred, famine the most terrible ensued, and hunger withered those whom the sword had spared. The people were slaughtered, but not subdued; the soil was not enriched, but ravaged ; no arts arose; no principles of wealth or liberty were developed ; life was unsafe; and property in the true sense was scarcely known. Even the stony heart of Elizabeth at length was touched ; humanity, for once, shot a pang to her breast. " Alas, alas ! " she cried ; "I fear lest it be objected to us, as it was to Tiberius, concerning the Dalmatian commotions—you, you it is who are to blame, who have committed your flock, not to shepherds, but to wolves." And to wolves, they were still committed. Such was the rigor of the ordinary government, that a deputy of the most ordinary kindness, gained the worship of the unhappy Irish, and became hateful to the jealous queen ;

so that the gratitude of the people ruined, at the same time, their benefactors and themselves. And yet, this age of Elizabeth was a glorious age. Every where, but Ireland, it was filled with power and with promise. From the death of Mary to that of James the First, was a period such as comes but seldom, and when it comes, such as makes an era. A mighty life was palpitating among the nations; the head of civilized humanity was filled with many speculations, and the heart was beating with marvellous fancies and magnanimous passion. Genius and glory had burst as a flood of light upon the world. The feudal system was passing away. The arm of its oppression had been broken, but its high-bred courtesy yet remained; its violence was repressed, but its heroic spirit had not been quenched. The courage of the savage warrior had given way before the chivalry of the humaner soldier. The dominion of superstition, too, had been broken, but a rigid utilitarianism had not yet taken place. The spectres of night had vanished, but dreams of the wonderful and the lovely still hovered around imagination. The earth was not bare, nor the heavens empty. The merchant and the money-changer began to rule the city; but Queen Mab was not yet dethroned. She had yet her fairy empire in the green-wood shade; she had yet her dancing in the moonlit glen. The practical had not yet banished the romantic, and the soul had her philosophy, as well as the senses. Columbus had opened new worlds, and the old world hailed him as the Moses of the seas. Dreams of sunny regions; of Edens in the deserts; of El Doradoes in the treadless hills, wafted longing fancies from olden homes, and thoughts flew fast and far on the crest of the wave and the wing of the wind. Learning started from leaden sleep to earnest life. Philosophy poured forth her eloquent wisdom; and the thoughtful listened with enraptured ear   Poetry was filling the earth with her music;

and Fiction was delighting mankind with rare enchantment; and Religion was busying all brains with her solemn and profound discoursing. Bacon was sounding the depths of human intellect, and calling from their silence the energies of endless progression. Shakespeare was shaping, to enduring beauty, those wondrous creations which embody the universal life of man. Cervantes, the glorious Spaniard, in soul a brother to the glorious Briton, had sent forth among men's fancies, Don Quixotte and Sancha Panza ; the high-dreaming knight, and the low-thinking squire ; the grave in company with the grotesque, a goodly image of humanity for everlasting laughter and everlasting love. Luther had arisen, awful and gigantic, half the earth his platform, and millions of excited men his audience. Liberty had began to know her rights, and was gathering courage to maintain them. Traditional claims had already lost in the contest against natural justice. Priests and princes had ceased to be gods, and the people were fast rising to be men. Commerce had enlarged her boundaries ; wealth had increased its enterprise ; independence had grown with industry. The course of freedom went nobly onward. Britain had humbled Spain ; and Holland, after one of the most heroic struggles in the history of patriotism, had cast off the Spanish yoke. While Europe was thus rejoicing in spreading grandeur, the fairest island on its western border, with every means of prosperity and glory, lay like a ruin at moonlight, where pirates had assembled to divide their plunder in blasphemy and in blood.

James of Scotland, the successor of his mother's slayer, treated unfortunate Ireland with no gentler policy. Without accusation of sedition or rebellion, he alienated six counties from their owners, and colonized them with his countrymen. The outcasts wandered on their own soil, as strangers and as vagabonds. Fearful deeds were done in revenge and retribution during the terrible insurrection of 1641, which occurred in the reign of this man's son. Deadly passions mingled together in the strife, as elements in the hurricane; and the blood of Reformer and the blood of Romanist, swelled the common torrent. England, too, became convulsed with trouble. Charles endeavored to ingratiate the Irish, and to a considerable extent he succeeded. But, their assistance availed the unhappy monarch nothing; and ere his blood was well nigh clotted on the block, they had Cromwell of the iron hand, dealing death upon themselves.

It is not my province, here, even if my power answered to the task, to draw a complete moral portrait of Cromwell. I am simply to speak of him in relation to Ireland; and, in that relation, he was a steel-hearted exterminator. I have no inclination to deny him grandeur, and if I had, the general verdict would stand independently of my inclination. Whether the moralist approve, or whether he condemn, the world always enthrones will, and power, and success; and that which it enthrones, it worships. How much in Cromwell was the honesty of a patriot, how much was the policy of a designer; how much was purity, how much was ambition, which so predominated, the evil or the good, as to constitute his character; this will probably be decided in opposite directions by opposite parties to the end of history. Whatever be the decision on the man, measured as a whole, the facts of his career in Ireland show him to have been most cruel and most sanguinary.

Nor are these facts inconsistent with our general idea of the dictator's character. A dark compound of the daring soldier and the religious zealot, uniting in one spirit the austerest attributes of each, stern in purpose, and rapid in execution, he was the man for a mission of destruction. The Irish, on many accounts, were peculiarly hateful to him. They were the adherents of defeated royalty. They were not simply prelatists, which were in itself offensive; but they were papists, and that was hideous iniquity. They were not only aliens, they were worse than aliens; they were outcasts, the doomed of prophecy, the sealed of Antichrist. They were the modern Canaanites, and he was the modern Joshua, the anointed of the Lord, to deal judgment on the reprobate; and judgment he dealt with vengeance, with vengeance that knew no touch of mercy. His track in Ireland may be followed over ruins which yet seem fresh. We can trace him as we do a ravenous animal, by the blotches where he lay to rest, or by the bloody fragments where he tore his prey. The Irish peasantry still speak of this man with those vivid impressions, which, of all passions, terror alone can leave. They allude to him in the living phraseology, which only that can prompt which moves us nearly, and, therefore, moves us strongly; they allude to him, not as if he were a shadow in the dimness of two centuries, but as if he were an agent of recent days. Stop, as you pass a laborer on the roadside in Ireland; ask him to tell you of the ruin before you on the hill. You will hear him describe it in language far more poetical and far more picturesque than I can copy, but somewhat in manner such as this: "Och, sure, that's the castle o' the Cogans, that Cromwell, the blackguard, took away from them. But maybe they did'nt fight, while fightin' was in them, the poor fellows; barrin' there's no strivin' agin the devil, the Lord presarve us, and everybody knows that Cromwell, bad win to him, was hand and glove wid the ould boy; musha, faix he was, as sure as there's fish in the say, or pigs in Connaught. There's the hill where the wagabond planted his cannon. There's the farm which the Blaneys got for sellin' the Pass, the white-livered thraitors; there's the brache which he made in the walls, where brave Square Cogan—a bed in heaven to his soul—was killed, wid his six fine darlant sons, as strappin' boys as you'd meet in a long summer's day. Och, wirra, wirra, struh ; bud Cogan was a man it would do your heart good to see ; my vardi av, it wouldn't keep the frosht out of your stomach the blackest day in winther ; full and plinty were in his house, and the poor never went impty from his door ; as I heard my grandmother say, that heard it from her grandmother, that, be the same token, was Cogan's cousin. Och, bud, with fair fighting, Cogan didn't fear the face of man, and, sure enough, when Cromwell commanded him to surrender, he tould infarnal coppernose, he'd ate his boots first ; throth he would, and his stockings after, av there was the laste use in it ; bud the man's not born'd of woman, that can stand against a whelp of hell ; and, av ould Nick iver had a son, my word for it bud his name was Oliver."

The cause of the Stuart, that family so faithless to their friends, and so fatal to themselves, next made Ireland the battle-ground of faction. Again her green hills were sown with blood ; again her pleasant valleys were scorched with famine. The infatuated Catholics joined that wretched imbecile, James the Second, while the Protestants, with a wiser policy, gathered to the standard of William the Dutchman, the son-in-law of James, and his opponent. The fortunes of James received their first blow at the siege of Derry in the north ; were staggered at the battle of the Boyne, midway in the kingdom ; and were fatally decided at the taking of Limerick in the south. The fall of Limerick closed the war. James had fled ; and William remained the victor. Limerick did not go out of the contest ignominiously. Even the women threw themselves into the breach, and for that time saved the city ; nor did the city, itself, surrender, but on terms which comprehended the whole of Ireland. Limerick capitulated on the part of all the Irish Catholics. The capitulation was but signed, when a large French fleet appeared in the river, with extensive supplies and numerous reinforcements. But with the good faith of honorable men, fifteen thousand laid down their arms, and were true to their engagements. The terms of this treaty were fair and advantageous. They secured to the Catholics the rights of property, of liberty, and of conscience, and all things seemed to augur well for peace, for unity, and for happiness.

Had the victors been merciful with power, and generous with success, had they been just, nay, had they been wisely politic, Ireland might have been tranquillized, and her prosperity might have commenced. But it was an age of faction, and faction was true to its vilest instincts. The legislation that followed this event, was intensely exclusive, and it was exclusively Protestant. The whole power of the country was in the hands of a Protestant aristocracy. The first action, then, of the Parliament in Ireland, after the reduction of Limerick, was to annul its treaty, a treaty as solemn as any that history records; a treaty made in the face of armies, and which pledged the faith of nations. And, not only that, but it was followed by a code of laws, which would have been a shame upon the reign of Nero; a code of laws which made, at one time, the Catholic religion a capital offence; and which, when greatly mitigated, denied to Catholics the means of education, the claims of property, and the rights of citizens. Legislation like this was, of course, disastrous. Strange, indeed, if it were not. If it were not, history were a lie, and all experience a dream; if it were not, human nature were, itself, a confounding delusion. It was disastrous to the Protestant religion, which it pretended to support; it was disastrous to the interests of England, which it promised to maintain; it was disastrous, also, to the unhappy people, whose energies it crushed; but, that the law of compensation should not utterly fail—that some evidence should be given to earth, that even on earth crime does not go unpunished—it was disastrous to its enactors.

Man can never separate himself from his fellows. He can never make their evil his good. The darkness which he draws upon his country, will overshadow his own home ; and the misery which he prepares for his neighbor, will be misery for himself. So it was with the authors of these evil laws ; so it ever must be, while moral right binds actions to appropriate consequences, while a God of eternal justice governs the world by principles which are as immutable as they are holy. The possessions which rapine had acquired, and which wrong controlled, did not give such return as the covetous heart desired. By confiscation, by penalties, by all modes of harsh restriction, the kingdom was drained of its native intelligence and native strength. Wealth of sentiment, wealth of capital, wealth of skill, wealth of industry, wealth of muscle, were driven from the country, or paralyzed within it. The high chivalry which generous treatment would have retained, directed foreign courts, commanded foreign armies ; while a hardy yeomanry that indulgence could have made loyal forever, carried bravery to the ranks of England's enemies, and labor to their markets.

And, observe with what a solemn retribution the consequences return upon the class who enacted or favored this kind of legislation. · The laws against Catholics pressed upon the whole tenantry of Ireland, for the whole tenantry of Ireland were, and are Catholic. The laws, therefore, against the Catholics, were so many enactments against the interests of the landlords themselves ; were, in fact, so many tariffs against their wealth. Uncertainty of title disturbed industry; the soil withered under imperfect cultivation; absenteeism of proprietors left the laborers without protection, and the owners without profit. Only meagre harvests were gathered from exhausted fields. Trade had no scope in impoverished cities ; the peasantry were starving, and the gentry were poor. This gentry, poor, but luxurious, lived upon estates

that were miserably deteriorated, as if they were in pristine
freshness ; and doing nothing to enrich the soil, they would
have from it the utmost rents ; and thence they became
indebted, and thence they became embarrassed.   To dig
they were not able, but to beg they were not ashamed.
They begged pensions, places, sinecures ; and no work was
so unjust or mean, which they were not willing to do for
government, if government was liberal enough in patronage.
Gaming, gormandizing, profanity, licentiousness, became
aristocratic distinctions.   Honor there was to kill, but not
honesty to pay ; and the man who shot his friend for an
inadvertent word, could bear, if anything was to be gained by
it, the reiterated insolence of a viceroy's menial.   The wages
being ready, here was the hireling ; and the slave, in his
turn, became the tyrant.   The self-respect which he lost as a
time-server, he sought, after the manner of all low natures,
to regain as an oppressor ; and the hardship of the forlorn
serf paid for the mortification of the suppliant official.
These men who, in element and charitable duties, might
have been as gods, enjoying and dispensing blessings, taking
the evil way of persecution, found their due reward in being
despised by those whom they served, and in being detested
by those whom they governed.

If any one shall think this tone exaggerated, then I ask
him to look at the Memoirs of Sir Jonah Barrington, in
which he may study, at his leisure, the manners of the Irish
gentlemen in the last century ; the picture, too, is painted
by one of themselves ; by one who shared all their partial-
ities for combat and for claret, for pensions and for place.

Events rapidly proceeded to bring relief to Ireland, and
partially to bring freedom.   Cornwallis was captured at
Yorktown, and America sprung into her glory from a province to a nation.   The volunteers arose in Ireland, and forty
thousand, with arms in their hands, demanded independ-

ence. Henry Grattan gave their passions sublime expression. Corruption was startled from the apathy of indulgence, and the guilty were struck with fear as with the voice of a prophet. Grattan called Ireland up from the dust of most servile degradation. He put brave words into her mouth, and a new hope into her heart; and although upon his own lips the words afterwards sunk into complaint, and the hope withered to despondency, he was not the less heroic on that account. Speaking at one time of Ireland, he asserts that she is a nation. Speaking of her again, he says, "I sat by her cradle, I followed her hearse;" but always he was her champion, and he was her friend. Lowly as she was when he entered upon life, he determined that she should not so remain. He caused her to arise, august and majestic, before her tyrants, bound as she was with their sackcloth. He called on her to assume her might, and taught her the strength that yet slumbered in her breast. He was the fearless accuser of her enemies. He dragged the villains into open light, that trampled on her rights, and that battened on her miseries. He loved her with an enthusiasm that only death could quench. She was the passion of his soul, the devotion of his life. Mighty in his eloquence, he was yet mightier in his patriotism.

The effects of his eloquence are left in the history of his country; and in me it would be vain, as it would be impertinent, to describe, in my feeble words, the power of such speech as his—speech that made the proudest quail—speech that shivered and prostrated the most able and the most iniquitous faction, which personal selfishness and political corruption ever banded together in gainful wickedness. Rapid, intense, scornful, indignant, his spirit was formed for contest. Fiery in passion, and brilliant in intellect, his antithetic language shot forth as lightning, as beautiful and as fatal. Of stern and stoic grandeur, he was the Reformer who was wanted among evil, exalted, and educated men. He was not of the gladsome fancy, which gathers flowers and weaves a garland; he was of the impetuous temper which rises upon the storm, and plays among the clouds. With individuals, he may not always have been in the right, and with his country he was never in the wrong.

The French Revolution came, then, to rock political Europe with its tremendous earthquake. Hoary dynasties rocked on their foundations. Decrepid legitimacy trembled and looked aghast. The terrible insurrection of 1798 brought fresh desolation to Ireland. Some interludes of jail and gibbet being gone through, an afterpiece was added to this horrible drama in 1830, signalized by the death of Lord Kilwarden, and by the execution of the noble-hearted Emmett. You all know the story of his heroism and his love; you know how he fell in the prime of a most manly nature; you know how a true and beautiful spirit laid her broken heart upon his grave. Your own Washington Irving has told you this in words of rainbow light; your own Irving, whose liberal genius loves the good of every land; and when he gives their annals, none can add beauty to the record. You have the ashes of an exiled Emmett among you; shrouded on the soil of liberty, he lies in sacred sleep. You gave him in life a freeman's home; in death you have given him a patriot's grave.

Among the mighty spirits which have been lights to Ireland, I will mention one who, in this sad period, was preeminent. I allude to Curran, the glory of the Irish bar. Most exalted in his oratory, and most generous in his use of it, he was ever what the true man would wish to be, if his power enabled him—the defender of liberty, the champion of the wronged. With a moral intellect of the widest grasp, he had an imagination of subtle delicacy and of gorgeous wealth; and this intellect, impulsive with a superhuman fervor, and this imagination, lyrical as the very soul of poetry, became, in their union, an enthusiasm that dared the loftiest heights and gained them. But, though soaring, it was not solitary. If it mounted upward to the skies, it was borne thither on the aspirations of all generous interests. It carried others to its own proud climbings ; and they, for the moment, transported from the lower earth, burned with its electric fire, and became godlike in its communicated lustre. How various is the eloquence in which that opulent spirit found expression. It is wit,. ready and exhaustless ; piercing as the pointed steel, or lambent as a ray of light ; now playful as a gleeful child, and then mischievous as a merry fiend. It is humor, in all queer analogies, in all shapes of oddity, in all lights and hues of fantasy. It is sarcasm, which lashes its victim to despair. It is pathos, which wrings the heart ; which touches it in every nerve where agony is borne ; which searches it in every fold where the smallest drop of grief can lie concealed. It is denunciation. And here he is greatest of all. How does he exhibit the wrong-doer! How does he show the transgressor his ways! How does he display the tortures of an accusing conscience, the sickness of a guilty soul, the apathy of habit, the damnation of remorse!

And no matter who the wrong-doer is, let him tremble if Curran is to paint his deeds. Proud he may be in titles, boundless in wealth, hardened in the bronze of fashion ; if he is human, the orator's words shall transfix him ; wherever feeling has a sense, a barb shall rankle ; and for the time, at least he shall stand before the world, naked, bleeding, shivering, and despised—to his species a thing of scorn, and to himself a thing of shame. Office shall no more protect him than rank. Is he a judge, who sullies the purity of the bench with the malice of a partisan? His ermine shall not guard him from the advocate's indignation ; and the tribunal which he disgraces shall, in its very loftiness, but make his ignominy the more conspicuous. Neither shall a villain find a shield in the baseness of his work or the obscurity of his condition. Is he a spy, whom government pays for perjury, the hireling violator of human faith and human nature—a wretch that panders for the gallows, and steeps his feet in widows' and in orphans' tears? Cased and coated as his heart may be in adamant, callous as may be his brutish face, stolid as may be his demon-soul, Curran could cleave the armor of his wickedness, and shake his miscreant spirit with fear, when it had lost even the memory of a virtue.

It is not, however, the power of Curran's eloquence, but the purpose of it, which has relation to this lecture. It was for the weak against the strong. Curran lived in times which tried men's souls, and many souls there were which did not stand the trial. Some, with coward fear, sank before the storm of power; and others, with selfish pliancy, dissolved in the sunshine of patronage. But Curran was brave as he was incorruptible. In 1798, he labored with a martyr's patience, and with a hero's courage. He pleaded under the shadow of the scaffold. He defended one client over the dead body of another; and while the victim is expiring on the gallows, for whom yesterday he struggled, with no hope to cheer his labor, he struggles as manfully to-day for one who will be the victim of to-morrow. He was upright, when honor was rebellion; he was true, when integrity was treason; he stood by the accused and the doomed, when to pity was to participate; and he was loyal to liberty, when even to name her was almost to die.

The year 1829 saw the Catholic emancipated, and now he stands with other British subjects, in equality of privilege and equality of grievance. The later history of Ireland has had three grand epochs, and in each has had a man fashioned for the time. In 1781, the Parliament of Ireland contended for independence ; then there arose the majestic spirit of immortal Grattan ; all that was claimed, he asserted, and all that he asserted, he achieved. In 1798, the liberty of the citizens was set at nought ; the impetuous voice of Curran arose above the storm, and if it was not able to quell injustice, it bore witness to the right. In 1829, six millions were emancipated, and with that sublime event the name of O'Connell is forever associated. But, not with that year or that event alone, the name of O'Connell is connected with the indefatigable struggle of half a century ; it is not only sacred in the liberty of his country, but in the liberty of man ; and the fame of it will become wider and brighter, as freedom covers the earth, and a slave is not known in the world.

The historical aspect of our country presents us with nothing but disunion and mismanagement ; and the social to which we must now briefly refer, presents us with nothing better. We observe in the structure of Irish society, not merely that the elements of it are fragmentary, but antagonistic. There is, for instance, little of a native aristocracy ; and there is no country on the earth which so respects and reverences its mighty names. The old families, Celtic and Saxon, were successively stripped of their estates. It was asserted by Chancellor Fitzgibbon that the island had changed owners three times in a century. The aristocracy in Ireland have, therefore, remained away from the people. Their existence is entirely a separate one ; their education is distinct ; their feelings are antinational ; their sympathies are foreign ; they are aliens after two centuries of possession. No people are more easily governed than the Irish through their imagination and affections. Appeal successfully to these faculties, and you may rule them as you please. If you would have power with the English, appeal to their interest ; show to them that you can lessen their taxes, and that you can increase their loaf. If you would gain power with the Irish, appeal to their sentiments; show them that you would bring back to Ireland, the glory that has departed; that you would re-string their national Harp, and re-kindle her national oratory; that you would re-build the Halls of Tara, and flood them with the music of her bards; that you would re-open the doors of her senate, and fill its courts with the eloquence of her statesmen.

But, to understand a people, you must live with them; nay, you must have within you the life of their life; and without this understanding of a people, you will vainly try to work on their sentiments. You can work on their sentiments only by sympathy. You must freely appreciate their virtues; you must have that also in you, which can penetrate the spirit even of their vices. Herein was the power of O'Connell. It was not all in the genius of the man; nor was it all in the wrongs of the government. Much of the secret lay in the profound insight which he ever had of the character of the people; the complete identification of his nature with theirs. His words were resistless, for they were the echoes of the hearts around him, and with the beatings of these hearts, his own heart kept time. The Irish aristocrat has no such unity with the people; nay, he has scarcely an external acquaintance with them. He has not the affection of a native, and he wants the impartiality of a stranger. His life is a sort of penance for his birth. He would not be an Irishman, and he cannot be an Englishman. He looks splenetically across the channel, and mourns that his trooper-ancestor gave him any thing in Ireland but its acres. He then turns a sullen gaze upon the soil on which he has had the misfortune to be born, and which has had the still greater misfortune to bear him. He is to his tenantry not so much a protector as a superior; a claimant rather than a patron; an exactor more than an improver; always a receiver, and seldom a bestower.

This opposition of interior feeling between the higher and lower classes in Ireland, is lamentably exemplified by a corresponding contrast of external circumstances. Irish society is a living antithesis, of which the peer and the peasant are no fanciful extremes. The peasant shows what privations life can endure; the peer, with what indulgence it can become a burden. The peasant works, but does not eat; the peer eats, but does not work. The food of the peasant is, also, the food of the brutes; that of the peer were a banquet for the gods. The peasant sows, and reaps, and gathers into barns, and carries the crop to market, and carries nothing home; the peer sows not, reaps not, gathers not into barns, carries not the crop to market, and has all the gain without even the trouble of carrying it home. It makes some difference to the peer whether his territory is fertile or barren; for he has what ever it produces; it makes none to the peasant, for small crop or abundant, his lot is still the same, to toil and to starve. The manor houses of the Irish gentry are situated in the midst of extensive domains, surrounded by lofty walls, and guarded by surly gate-keepers. The finest of these places are often girded by deserts of the most squalid misery. The owners are in them on rare occasions, and then, it is to revel in the midst of want.

Suppose yourself a guest on one of these occasions. Look around you on the scene! The princely park without, and the ornamented halls within; slope, woodland, garden, hill, dale, and river, glowing in the outward prospect; the inward view, that of a kingly residence furnished for every refined desire; adorned with mirrors, statues, pictures, replenished with whatever can delight the fancy or feast the senses. Think, then, of a tenant peasantry, physically more deplorable than the serfs of Turkey; and when you have thus thought, look calmly on the assembly before you. Here, gathered at joyous night, is a throng of the noble and the fair; men of gallant bearing, and women of surpassing beauty. Lights stream over decorations which almost transcend what Eastern story feigned of Eastern magic; music floats upon the perfumed air, and grace rules the mazes of the dance. When you recollect the haggard country through which you passed, to arrive at such a mansion; when you recollect the hovels that afflicted you on the way, the sad faces that stared you as you went along, that constantly subdued your reveries to grief; when you recollect the fever and the hunger, that, as you traveled by then, appalled your very soul; all that you see in this abode of grandeur appears unnatural; it seems a brilliant, and yet an agonizing vision; an illusion by some evil genius, powerful to delight, terrible to destroy. You cannot reconcile it with your ordinary associations—with your sentiments of moral harmony; it is incongruous; a rejoicing in an hospital, a feast in a famine-ship, a dance in a charnel-house, a bridal in a sepulchre; your heart becomes convulsed, your head giddy, your imagination confused and sick. You look upon a social class that bewilders you, and you turn from the whole with loathing and disgust.

The social system in Ireland is disjointed and defective. The great proprietors are absentees, and the small ones are impoverished. Another decisive evil in the social state of Ireland is, the want of due gradation. Where there is not general equality, there ought to be successive ranks. But society in Ireland exists only in extremes. The two main divisions of it are the owners of the soil, and its occupiers; and between these there seems a gulf, which one

cannot pass to companion with the other. To fill up
this wide interval, there is wanted an active and enter-
prising middle class. Except in the learned professions,
social eminence in Ireland belongs only to the ownership of land. Money in Ireland has not accumulated into
capital; industry has not risen to ambition; and, thence,
while in England men climb from labor to aristocracy, in
Ireland men descend from aristocracy to labor.

But the most grievous need of Ireland is the want of
variety in occupation. Externally, Ireland is finely situated for commerce; internally, she is admirably constituted for manufactures. Commerce and manufactures would
not only train the people to skill and independence, but
relieve the soil from the pressure of an excessive population. The soil is the only source of life, and out of this
fact come many evils; one of the worst is that of extreme
competition. Every vacant spot becomes an object of
deadly strife. It is generally given to that person who
offers the highest price and shouts the loudest promise.
He soon finds out in his despair that he has undertaken
too much. The landlord has spent no capital on it; the
tenant has none to spend; and of the produce which is
torn from its savage nakedness, the bulk goes to the
absent proprietor and to the Established Church. The soil
deteriorates; the landlord will not lower his demands;
the tenant cannot pay them, and he is ejected. The landlord gives his place to another, and the ruined tenant
knows not where to find a shelter. Though law has driven
him out from his familiar hearth, nature compels him
to return. He will prowl around the miserable abode that
gave his poverty a refuge—the hut that gave his little ones
a home—the roof that shielded the mother of his children.
He cannot reason; his blood rushes back to its fountains;
his whole nature is excited; his brain is convulsed in de-

lirium ; he is mad in his houseless distraction ; and in his madness, he slays, perhaps, his blameless successor. His former landlord is, possibly, a magistrate. This magistrate hands him to the constable ; the constable delivers him to the judge ; after due forms of trial, the judge consigns him to the executioner ; and the executioner closes the tragedy. This is but one of a hundred, that vary little in plot or incident. The scaffold is the stage, with which, as yet, Ireland has been the best acquainted ; and on that she has witnessed many a terrible drama—black, silent, bloody, and monstrous !

Who does not see in these circumstances, rudely as I have described them, the sources of enormous evils ? Passions, the deepest and most lasting, were kindled and kept burning by crushing men upon their own soil—by irritating them in those sentiments that all. but the basest hold in reverence. Education was not only withheld, but punished ; trade was not advanced, but restricted ; home industry was suppressed, and foreign commerce was forbidden ; and yet, men are now wondering that this work of folly and of guilt should still be felt. Why, it is not greatly over half a century since any change for the better even began. But the effects of such a work does not pass away in fifty years.

What other effects than those which we have seen could be expected ? Discontent, that outlives the provocation ; anger, that survives the wrong ; disorganization, that follows servitude and misrule ; ignorance, deep and widespread, that bad legislation had long compelled, and that the best cannot hastily remove ; idleness, that law made a habit or a necessity ; poverty, coming out of idleness ; crime and misery, issuing from both—a complication of entangled difficulties that shakes the hope of the philanthropist, and that baffles the wisdom of the statesman.

But the evils indicate their own remedies; and it is encouraging to see, in the progress of recent events, that
national instincts are taking the direction that will gradually ameliorate national calamities. The Irish people must
be respected; and they must be practically respected; they
must have their due share in the legislation of the empire,
and they must be fully represented, according to their
numbers, their power, and their interests. There must
grow up in Ireland, too, a social unity. Men of the same
atmosphere must learn to love, and not to hate each other;
they must join heart and hand, to promote the good of
their common country; they must have hope for what is to
come; they must have pardon for what is past. The law
of tenure must be changed; the tenant must be protected.
The landlord shall not be denied his rights; but he must
be made to feel his duties. If he will not be true to his
obligations, like all criminals, he ought to meet with punishment; and the punishment he could most be made to feel,
would be punishment on his purse. This, when written,
was prophesy; much of it is now history; and the landlords
have so contrived matters as to prepare the punishment
for themselves. Relieve the land of the horrible pressure
that is on it; call in the amount of stalwart muscle that
withers away in idleness to healthy manufactures; let the
young men and maidens that wander over earth for leave
to toil have but that liberty given them upon their own
green island, and I shall challenge the world to show
a happier or a handsomer race—men more generous, or
women more lovely.

Oh that all classes and all creeds would unite in a broad
and generous sentiment of nationality; not a nationality
of vanity and prejudice, but a nationality of brotherhood
and peace. This would be for Ireland the day of her
regeneration. To the eye, she is fair, indeed, among the

nations ; but to the heart, her beauty has been covered with sadness. Her fields are luxuriant, and her hills are green ; yet the lot of her children has been in tears and blood. History, whose work at best is but melancholy, has written her story in despair. Hunger has lingered in her valleys ; sickness in her dwellings ; sin and madness in her secret places. Nature has given her a great largeness of bounty. Cattle cover her plains ; the horn of plenty has been emptied on her vales ; but sorrow and a curse have rained a blight on all. The airs of heaven blow upon her freshly ; but they swell no sails, except those which are to bear her children into exile. The glorious sea girds her about ; but it washes the shores of solitary harbors, and dashes an unloaded wave upon a virgin sand. A race of no mean capacities have lived in huts unworthy of the savage, and upon food almost too wretched for the brutes.

Ought it to be thus ? Is this the design of nature ? Is this the order of Providence ? Is this a fatal and perpetual necessity ? No, no, it is against the design of nature ; it reverses the order of Providence ; and the only necessity that belongs to it, is that which springs from misrule, mismanagement, and disunion. Let there be but a united people, and it cannot be longer thus ; let divisions be abolished by a holy love of country, combined interests and combined activity will issue in general prosperity ; let party names be lost in Irishman, and Irishman be a word for patriot ; then, the sun of a new era will bathe with glory "the emerald set in the midst of the sea ;" then will the land of a common birth be the land of a common heart ; and then,

> " Howe'er crowns and coronets be rent,
>   A virtuous populace will rise the while,
>   And stand, a wall of fire around their much-loved isle."

The course of these observations had led us along painful topics, but we will not leave them in despondency. If days which are gone have left but painful memories, days that are to come may cheer us with bright and gracious hopes. If a soil the most fertile has borne but a starving peasantry; if noble rivers have flowed unburdened to the sea; if capacious harbors have been ruffled by no freighted keels; if mines of wealth have slumbered untouched in the sleeping earth; still, I do not despair for my country. The soil is there yet in its beauty, and its children may yet live upon its fullness; the rivers are yet majestic, and will not always be a solitude; the broad and sheltered bay that now mirrors but the mountains and the heavens, may yet reflect the snowy drapery of many a gallant ship; and the hills on which now the ragged and dejected shepherd wanders, may yet yield up their treasures to the light. Nature is not dead; nature is not dead in the works of creation or in the soul of man; nature is not dead, but ever in its generous beauty covers and supports us. No foolish passions can dry up the kindly heart of earth, or consume the fatness of the clouds, or shut out the glory of the skies. Nature yet survives—survives in her limitless bounty—survives in her eternal youth; and the people, though impoverished, are not destroyed. No wrongs have been able to crush them; no wars to render them inhuman. From every savage influence they have come forth—not indeed uninjured, but yet not deeply degraded, nor ruthlessly depraved. From the worst experience in the history of nations they have saved elements of excellence that may be shaped into the noblest civilization. From a long and dreary night of bondage they have escaped with the vivid intellect, the cheerful temper, the affectionate spirit, the earnest, the hopeful enthusiasm that springs elastic from every sorrow.

The hour now seems dark in Ireland, but the light is not quenched ; it is only for a season obscured. The cloud is thick and broad ; it rests heavily over the shivering millions ; it is most dreary, and it seems filled with threaten-ings ; but the moveless sun is shining tranquilly above it in the benignant and the everlasting heavens. The cloud may break in tempest ; but stillness and beauty will come when the hurricane has spent its strength and the storm has passed away. But no tempest will, possibly, come at all. The cloud may dissolve in rain ; it may give freshness where it had only given gloom, and cool the ardor of the beams which it had excluded. Dark skies bring lightning ; lightning brings the shower ; then comes the sunshine on the grass, and all the fields are sparkling with glory and with gems.

Let me so think of the moral atmosphere that now hangs around and over Ireland. It is not to continue. God is in his universe, and guides the nations in their way. We will hold to our goodly trust ; and in the strength of that earnest trust we will firmly believe that He has rich bless-ings yet in store for Ireland. Where often we can see nothing but evil, our gracious Father is preparing good ; and we will so believe it now for sad, afflicted, mourning Ireland. Oh land of my heart, of my fathers, and my birth! I will ever keep it in my thoughts that God is looking down upon you with pity and with grace, and that He will call you up more brightly from your calamity. The times, indeed, seem bad, but suffering will leave its blessing. Plenty will come again ; and humility, and gratitude, and mercy, and penitent and softened hearts will come along with it. Peace will be established ; confidence will come with peace ; capital will follow confidence ; employment will increase with capi-tal ; education will be desired ; knowledge will be diffused ; and virtue will grow with knowledge. Yet, even if these things should not soon be ; if all that is now anticipated should long be hope deferred, and many a heart should sicken in waiting for relief ; yet I will not despond, I will not despond for Ireland ; I will not despond for humanity; I will entertain no doubt in the agency which guides the world, and no mistrust in the destiny whereunto the world moves.

IRELAND AND THE IRISH,

IN 1848.

THE three journals named below are in opposition to the British government in Ireland, but with different degrees of antagonism. *The Tablet* is a paper in the interest of the Roman Catholic Church, and, though English in its spirit and editorship, it sympathizes with the struggles going forward in Ireland. It denounces the Union, it pleads for Repeal; but it does not commit itself to any danger of legal prosecution.

The Nation is a journal pledged violently to more than Repeal—peaceably if possible, forcibly if it must be. It contains much spirited writing, and reports of speeches, that defy the legal authorities, and despises all compromise. This is the organ of "Young Ireland," and of a portion of the physical-force party. Still, though it hints at republicanism, it does not openly avow it. It professes loyalty to the imperial crown, but disowns the right of the imperial legislature to make laws for Ireland. The real purport of its views is, not simply repeal of the Union, but the absolute nullity of the Union. Meagher is its leading genius.

The Nation was either not strong enough for Mitchel, or Mitchel was too strong for *The Nation*, and so he set up *The United Irishman*. *The United Irishman* carries the doctrine of resistance out in its most logical consistency and to its utmost consequences. It spits upon Repeal, it cries for independence ; it calls not only for a national parliament, but for national sovereignty. It laughs at the "golden link of the crown," and holds no terms with O'Connell, to whom this phrase, we believe, is attributed. It scouts Victoria, and mocks Conciliation Hall with as much scorn as it does Conciliation. It demands a republic at any cost; and with fierce earnestness it preaches the gospel of the pike. It tells the starving masses of Ireland that they cannot be worse off, and that, with courageous hearts and a strong right hand, they have the power to be better off. It goes even beyond a mere republic. It attacks the present laws and distribution of property, reprobates political economy and its theories, and insists on a reorganization. The editor, John Mitchel, is the son of a Unitarian minister, esteemed by all men who knew him while he lived. He closed a good life, and a long and useful ministry, a few years ago, in the town of Newry, in the North of Ireland. His son, John Mitchel, is undoubtedly a young man of fine talents, ready to do, and dare, and die ; and, if we can judge, prepared for either fortune—for victory or death, the tribune or the scaffold. His eloquence is brief, bold, fiery, and condensed. If Meagher be the Cicero of the Confederates, Mitchel is the Demosthenes of the Democrats. The *Tablet* calls him "the Irish Danton," and so far as strong and burning words, that neither modify nor compromise, are concerned, the designation is not unsuitable ; yet those who know him speak of him as singularly gentle in personal temper.

It is not our design to enter into either the politics or the purposes of these journals ; but they suggest some remarks on the present condition of Ireland, physical and social.

"Ireland" and "Irish" seem very simple terms, yet do they stand for very complicated things. Ireland, to an American imagination, consists of space extremely limited ;

yet, from its earliest history, that space has been most minutely divided. It would not, in mere space, form a leading State of this Union, yet it was once an empire, comprising kingdoms, princedoms, chieftainries. These kingdoms, princedoms, chieftainries had their respective customs, laws, prejudices, with the feuds and factions that spring from such a constitution. Even now Ireland has her provinces, counties, baronies, in the civil arrangement, with archdioceses, dioceses, parishes, in the ecclesiastical. The English invaders found Ireland a country of manifold partitions, with a people as subdivided as its surface.

"Irish" is a word of most composite signification also. We wonder at the ignorance of writers on this country in their strictures on American character. But surely the ignorance of our own writers on the character of other nations is scarcely less, and much less excusable. We wonder that authors of any intelligence should confound, under one general idea, the reckless men of the West with the orderly men of the East; the ardent men of the South with the cool men of the North; the men who hold slaves, with peculiar training as well as peculiar institutions, with other men who have no such training and no such institutions. Yet we are ourselves in much grosser error in our popular conception of the Irish. We have, in general, no notion of them but as exiles and drudges. "Irish" means with us a class of human beings whose women do our house work, and whose men dig our railroads.

Judging merely by the senses, we are not much to blame, for these are the relations in which, from infancy, we are accustomed to know them. We have indeed heard of Burke, and Grattan, and Curran, with many other great names besides; we have a sort of persuasion that these were Irishmen; but when we try practically to consider them as the compatriots of a mud-covered laborer in the bed of a canal, the contrast is too violent, and by no force of imagination can we bring such extremes together. We, as a people, are intolerant of ragged garments and empty paunches. We would replace the rags by decent raiment, and we would fill the paunches with wholesome food; but we have only small respect for those who come to us in tatters, and who rush to us from famine. We are a people who have had no experience in physical tribulations ; and we do not understand the virtues or the vices which such tribulation can produce. We do not know the fearful selfishness which exceeding want may generate; but neither do we know the blessed charities which it may exhibit, the holy self-denial which it may manifest. As a consequence, the ill-clad and destitute Irishman is repulsive to our habits and to our tastes. We confound ill-clothing and destitution with ignorance and vice, for thus they are associated among ourselves ; and that fancy is a rare one which can emancipate itself from the power of habit and the impressions of experience. The crowds that cross the Atlantic to seek a refuge here are, in general, a ragged contrast to our own well-covered masses ; and, thus rude in external appearance, many find it hard to reach the kindred and immortal humanity which is so coarsely tabernacled. Many of us only look on the outside; we do not enter into the soul. We observe the crushed animal, but we hold no converse with the hidden spirit; we have abundance of pity, but we fail in reverence.

It is a foolish thing to judge of a building by a brick; but the folly is yet greater not to examine even the brick. Irish society is but very partially represented by the portions of it that we have the opportunity of seeing. The structure of Irish society has been very variously and gradually built up, and by materials from a great many quarries. First, there was the old Celtic race ; then the

Milesian; then the Danes; then the Anglo-Normans and Anglo-Saxons; then the Scottish colonists sent by the first James; then the troopers of Cromwell and the boors of the third William. Now each of these successive invasions deposited a new element of discord, and stratum was laid upon stratum of rebellion and confiscation. Out of rebellion and confiscation have proceeded perpetual strife and hatred. But among the worst results, we must regard that condition of things as the most unfortunate which transferred the whole soil of the nation to the hands of strangers, and which placed over the people an alien and unsympathizing aristocracy. We have some observations to make on this condition of things as we proceed. The English in the beginning found the Irish broken up among themselves into conflicting factions. This, too, was unhappy. Had it been otherwise—had the Irish been one—had they been concentrated into a national integrity, as the Saxons were when William the Conqueror gained the battle of Hastings, then either the invaded would have repelled the invader, or one would have absorbed or exterminated the other. Neither of these results followed; and the strange paradox is accordingly exhibited in the universe, of a progressive physical amalgamation of the bone and sinew of Ireland with the bone and sinew of Britain, carrying along with it an unceasing, an undying hatred of its government. It is therefore very absurd to speak of the Irish as if they were a single, simple, primitive, unmixed race. The very contrary is the fact. Perhaps there is not a country on the whole earth so limited in its dimensions, so complicated in its population; and this, not only in the elements that still continue separate, but also in those that have mingled and coalesced.

It has been common to ascribe the agitations and disorders which so frequently convulse Ireland to the impa-

tient and turbulent passion of the Celt, to his inherent love
of battle and disturbance, to his unruly and rebellious disposition. No position was ever more false than this; not
only is it without proof, but against proof. The Celts are
not especial rebels; and, indeed, they never have been.
The districts in Ireland most troublesome to Britain have
always been those which the British colonized; and thus it
has been from the days of Strongbow to those of Mitchel.
The region in which Cromwell found his hardest task, and
that in which he left the most atrocious memory, was that
which had its population from English blood. If England
has done Ireland wrong, Providence has brought a chastis-
ing retribution on her, by means of her own children. The
sins of English fathers are not merely visited on their
children, but through their children the visitation comes.
The most sanguinary page of Cromwell's campaign in Ireland, is that which opens at Drogheda and concludes in
Wexford. Likewise in 1798, the counties which earliest
entered the conflict, and which longest sustained it, were
those wherein the descendants of the British chiefly resided.
Wexford fought with desperation, and fought to the last;
and Vinegar Hill, with its broken windmill, remains to this
hour a memento of courage and a monument of despair.

Let us now take a rapid survey of the two broad divisions
of Irish society. We begin with the aristocracy. And by the
aristocracy we mean, principally, the owners of the soil; we
mean, in general, the landlords and their immediate kindred.
Most of those who have fortunes sufficiently large live in
England, or on the Continent, deserting at the same time
their country and their duties. The greater number have
inherited their estates by conquest or confiscation; and
they have never become native to the land that gives them
luxury, but that denies life to the wretched men who till
it. Accident has made them Irish, and their life is a long

regret for being so. They scourge the unhappy nation in which they have had the misfortune to be born, and which has had the still greater misfortune to bear them. The members of this class, who have to stay at home because they are not rich enough to go abroad, constitute the local magistrates, and fill most of the influential local offices. A large majority of the class is utterly bankrupt—insolvent over and over. Most of these men have but the name of property ; for what are called their estates lie under piles of mortgages and incumbrances. Debt has been heaped upon debt, by each generation in its turn, so that it would be as puzzling to a lawyer to discover the original possession, as it would be to a geologist to describe the primitive condition of this planet. Entails, and other artificial contrivances, have long kept estates in families, and held them from the last action of the law on the part of creditors. But even if they could be sold, they would afford only a miserable percentage on the sums for which they have been, time after time, pawned. There is a story of an Irishman who traveled over England with a pig of peculiar sagacity and buoyancy. The pig was lean, lank, and rough ; but she had the vigor of a race-horse, and the elasticity of a greyhound. Walls she despised, and gates could not confine her. Her master, each morning, was a little space on his road, when she was after him, and each morning they began a new day most lovingly together. Availing himself of the animal's excellent qualities, the fellow sold her at every stage of his journey, being certain, at each successive sale, that he would have her to sell again. The pig which was thus so often sold was, probably, not honestly come by at first. This elastic animal is no bad representative of landed property in Ireland ; we leave it to the imagination of our readers to find out the analogy and to apply it.

Nature has its laws in society, as irrefragable as those it

has in matter. Not in one case more than in the other can there be any permanent violation of them. Soon or late, they vindicate themselves. A state of things like that which we have just described cannot last. It must die of its own corruptions, or it must explode by the force of a pressure that has reached the limit of enduring capacity. The ancestors of Irish landlords bequeathed them broad domains, but with them they bequeathed titles to them that were written and sealed with blood, guarded by a system of legislation that was shocking to humanity. They bequeathed memories of rankling irritation, which the descendants of the injurers were as unable to forget as the descendants of the injured; which the descendants of the injurers were more unwilling to forgive. Wealth that is acquired by violence is seldom spent with wisdom. Economy is as much the offspring of virtue as of labor. We manage that, and that alone, well, which we gain, not simply by toil, but by honest toil. Let no body of men imagine that they can grow rich by conquest. It is not merely a crime to assume such a position, it is a folly, a delusion—it is a blunder. The most dearly purchased treasure is that which is acquired by the sword. The highest price for land or gold is blood. Every nation which has gained either on such conditions, has perished by them; and it deserved to perish. The ancestors of the Irish aristocracy, from the Catholic Normans to the Puritan Cromwellians, thus obtained their property; they left it to their children, adding to it the penal legacy of prodigal extravagance and profligate habits.

Our description is general. We know that among the gentry of Ireland there are many and noble exceptions; and being exceptions, they have our greater admiration. The most common virtues become sublime, when the opposite vices are all but universal. When neglect and oppression of the poor spread over a land, the spots on which they receive some degree of care and kindness appear as little Edens; but they are Edens in a desert. We speak of the Irish gentry as a class; and as a class neither their origin nor training—neither their temper nor circumstances, fit them to conciliate, to foster, or to improve the masses that surround them. They never had power over the hearts of the people; and that power of coercion which they once possessed, they have not ceased to love, though they have for ever lost it. We mean, especially, their monopoly of political influence. Their power as proprietors they yet hold and love; they do not fail to use it either, and to use it as badly as ever. Becoming, as we have seen, deeper in debt with each generation—one anticipating the income of the other—their tastes and desires have, in the same order, been growing more costly. They may have become more refined, but they also have become more expensive. The deadly competition for land in Ireland enables them to raise rents to the highest sum that human labor can produce, and to press down living to the lowest condition that human nature can endure. The tenant is cast upon the ragged soil, to tear from its bosom payment for his master, and starvation for himself. In the latter he always succeeds; and when he fails in the former, the master, by means of arrears, holds in his hands the power to expel him. The owner spends no capital on the soil; he builds no houses or offices; he furnishes no implements; he pursues no experiments in agriculture; he does not instruct the tenant, either by theory or example; and when some year worse than others leaves the tenant at his mercy, the mercy that many a landlord shows is to turn him off, with neither allowance nor compensation for such improvements as he has struggled in his poverty to make.

We fancy some of our readers complaining about the everlasting historical references, to account for the state of

Ireland. Why, we conceive them saying, why this reiteration of matters that are gone to the grave of centuries, to explain what our eyes see and our ears hear? But they are not gone to the grave of centuries; they were but sown in the living soil of centuries, and now they are ripened into a heavy harvest of a most black and bitter crop. We cannot understand present events without understanding their historical connection, and least of all can we understand those of Ireland; and to us, especially, young among the nations, the example of our elders is important. As it is, the lesson that history teaches does not seem entirely needless to us. Recent as is our independent existence, we have gone far in the pathway of the Old World, and, instead of looking to it as a beacon, we seem rather to follow it as a star. It is more our model than our warning; we study the lesson the wrong way; and it is well if we do not in that wrong way outrun the instruction. We, too, have our oppressions and our injustice. Under the very shadow of our Capitol, while the welkin rings with gratulations which are to stir with joy the heart of France, a mob gathers to crush free thought—thought dedicated to the widest liberty and to the highest humanity; nay, at the very time that shouts of execration were sent across the broad Atlantic to blast a fallen monarch in his exile, tyrants with hearts harder than the hearts of tigers were tearing off their human brothers and sisters from the region of their native affections, consigning them to a slavery, compared with which their former slavery seemed freedom—dead to their agony of spirit, chaining them with iron that did not gall half so terribly as the iron that had entered into their soul; and all because, prompted by instincts which God and nature had implanted, they sought that freedom for which God and nature had designed them. What a mockery is this! What right have such men to hoot at Louis Philippe, contrasted with whom Louis Philippe is an angel of light? What title have such men to vociferate acclamations for liberty? Liberty is but insulted by their praise. We, too, seem in a fair way to enthrone the soldier, and to idolize the sword; to give strength the place of virtue, and victory the place of right. But let us not be deceived. God is no more mocked by nations with impunity than by individuals; and nations, as well as individuals, will reap according to what they sow. We may despise the lesson of history, but we cannot reverse it laws; and this law is made evident in the records of all ages. Wrong and right make no account of time; they are certain and eternal: their consequences may not be instantly seen, but they are not lost; nay, they do not even linger.

There is but one step from the aristocracy to the peasantry in Ireland, and that step is over a fearful precipice into an abyss of indescribable, of unimaginable desolation. There are but few intermediate grades to break the view, or to soften the contrast; it is a yawning gulf, exposed in all its horrors, from which the gazer shrinks back affrighted, with a reeling head and with quivering nerves. Yet must we, however loath, ask our readers to lean with us for a moment over it.

The physical state of the Irish peasantry did not, in past times, seem capable of being lower than it was. Even then it was the lowest which any region of the civilized world could present. Their dwellings were hovels; their clothing, rags; and their food, an almost unseasoned root. But all this was paradise to what their state has been since—to what it is now. The very root which was so despised, we have come to regard almost with reverence; and when we see how, by the withering of this single root, hundreds of thousands of human beings withered along with it, we can understand how the heathen Egyptians bowed down to leeks in worship. The grave of the potato-seed was the grave of men, women, and children ; but the potato died knowing not its own existence, while the men, women, and children that perished with it expired in ghastly and consuming torture, with blank despair of this inhospitable world, yet, thank God! not untrustful of a better. Far off though it was, we heard the low moaning of that despair, for at the extremities of earth the heart of man can feel the pantings of another heart that suffers, and, even where it cannot give relief, it fails not to give pity.

Who can faintly picture what even one family must have endured in such circumstances? Think of them turning their weary eyes around on the arid fields, and up to the sky, that seemed to grow sickly to them from hour to hour; awaking in the morning, without a morsel to greet them watching through the day, counting minute after minute, awaiting the possible relief that never came, or that came too late ; clasping each other on the filthy straw, or bare cold floor, through the miserable night ; sleeping to dream of feasting, awaking to die of famine. And yet we have not reached the worst part of the case. The most fatal pain lies here, not in the appetites, but in the affections. Look at the emaciated father, who comes in after vain search all day for food, and has nothing to offer his wife and little ones but a meal of unwholesome herbs, picked out of the ditches ; look at him when he can find even these no longer, when competition has consumed them. Has it entered into the heart to conceive of his affliction? Yet is that of the wife and mother even greater, who beholds the manly form bent and wasted of him that had been once her strength and her guide ; who beholds her chickens clustering about her, opening their craving mouths for food, and drooping as they get none. This picture is pale to what the reality must have been ; and of such realities there was no small

number. It is to be feared that they have not yet passed ;
nay, it is to be feared that some are now passing.

The Irish peasant in former days had a hut, such as it
was ; but in these days his master hunts him out of it, as if
he were a rat, and the land refuses him a hole for shelter.
The workhouse is full ; the jail would be relief, and he
breaks the law for refuge in a prison ; but by and by crime
itself will be as fruitless as charity, and the prisons will not
bear the throngs that seek them. In former days the Irish
peasant sat down to his potatoes, and while they laughed in
his face, his partner and his offspring laughed around him.
His cabin was of mud, covered with sods or straw ; but it
gave him a home, and, in general, love and peace abode in it.
Nor was hospitality absent. No poor-laws existed, yet were
beggars fed; no workhouses were in being, yet were beggars
lodged ; the pauper had his seat at the peasant's meal, he
had his covering under the peasant's roof.

If his condition even then was physically still below that
of the Russian serf or the negro slave, what shall we say of
his present condition ? The Russian is a filthy creature in
all his habits ; but his filth coexists with comfort and abundance. His filth is of his own creation, and he remains
filthy because he chooses to do so. His dwelling is rude,
but it is warm ; his food is coarse, but it is plentiful. He
is in no fear that any landlord will turn him out, for he has
the right to continue where he toils, and to die where he
was born. If he must serve the emperor when the emperor commands, he knows what his lot is, and he does
not complain of it. In general, he glories in it ; for to
be changed from being a serf into a soldier, is to rise in
his own esteem. Without overlooking the degradation of
humanity, and the sorrow which slavery inflicts upon the
negro, in the mere matter of bodily well-being, there is no
comparison between his state and that of the Irish peasant

It is the interest of his master that he shall have at least so much care as shall render him a saleable article or a profitable laborer. His master is induced to give him a healthy youth, and he is bound to provide for him in age ; it is his interest even that he shall enjoy mental quiet and contentment, for the more cheerful he is, the more useful. No doubt he is often subjected to cruelty ; but even to the slave Christianity is a protection, for it infuses a sentiment into the moral heart, and creates a power of social opinion, which is stronger than law—stronger than tyranny; and these, if they do not break the yoke, alleviate bondage. Unlike the Russian serf, the Irish peasant's home is uncertain, and it is his master's desire not to keep him, but to cast him off ; and while all the power is on one side, there is no acknowledged claim on the other. Unlike the negro slave, the Irish peasant has no hold on the interests of his lord, as he certainly has no hold on his affections. He has no public opinion, in the class to which his lord belongs, to shield him from oppression, and the sympathy which he has among his own is such as tempts him often to revenge himself by methods always to be lamented. He may stand in manhood or sink in age, there is none but God on whom he can cast the burden of his care ; for among men, those who feel for him and with him are as helpless as himself.

We have already stated a sad case, but we know from every week's report, that, at present, other terrible elements are at work. The potato withered last year ; this year the pike is forged and whetted. Fierce and dark passions are boiling in the breasts of men, and threaten to burst out in the tempest of civil, bloody strife, with all its hatreds and terrors. Despair has ceased to be quiescent ; it has started up in wildness from its lair, and shakes its Gorgon locks in deadly anger ; it has ceased to wail, it thunders ; and if it does not strike, it grasps its weapon.

It were vain to enter specially into causes which have produced effects, such as these we have been describing. Whatever causes we might assign, remote or proximate, there is still an actuality before us of a most appalling character—a whole people starving amidst fertility, and arising in madness to look for hope in the face of death. Before this spectacle, abstract questions lose all their interest; our gaze is fascinated by the misery which is before us, which stares on us with horrid eye, and from which we cannot turn away, though we look on it with trembling. The plain, open wretchedness is there; but it so appalls us, that we are unable to inquire or to discuss how it came to be there; and the babble of discussion on hypotheses to account for hunger and revolt, by men who feed amply and feed at ease, is as offensive to our taste as the affliction itself is painful to our feelings. Whatever series of causes has issued in the effects which we contemplate, we see evidently and with alarm that it cannot stop, that it is not exhausted in these effects. We hope and trust that all these irritating elements may be lost in peaceful amelioration.

The British power has many and grave crimes to answer for; but we should lament with no common lamentation the wound that civilization must receive, not merely in the disruption of the British empire, but in any severe shock to it. The shower of lava that buries a single city, the earthquake that shakes one to pieces, history notes down in words of pathos and sadness that move the heart for ever. But the disorder which should tear to atoms laws, letters, culture, customs—which should crumble to dust beautiful structures of public and private taste—which should reduce to chaos arts of fancy and utility—all of which it has taken centuries to rear—would be a calamity to be compared, not with a shower of lava, a torrent, a hurricane, an earthquake, but with a deluge which should come down from the black wrath of heaven, and bury in its flood, not millions only but the works of millions also for a thousand years. Yet we feel that in the British islands affairs cannot continue as they are. In no part of them are the people contented in Ireland they are mad. They are in the extremity of wretchedness ; it is no wonder they should be in the extremity of desperation. The Irish people are starving, and yet the Irish soil is not barren. With all the ill treatment which it has to bear, it yet continues rich ; the clouds pour down fatness, and the earth gives forth abundance, yet multitudes do not so much live as wither. The soil is vital, while the people die.

It seems a mystery to the inhabitants of this country how thousands should expire of hunger at a time when provisions were sent away from every port ; and why, while the war-ship went in with charity, the merchant-ship should go out for gain, both freighted with the staff of life. The mystery is easily explained. The manufacture and the commerce of Ireland consist generally in the production of food and its exportation. The manufacturers are the tillers of the soil, who give in their labor all the capital, and pay high rents besides for that on which they toil. The landlords are the owners of the soil, who expend no capital, and who take even more than the profit. The land cannot support these two classes as they are at present related. The landlord must have state and luxury, not expending time, or labor, or money, though the tenant, spending time, and labor, and money, has not subsistence. The best of the produce, animal and vegetable, is exported to meet the landlord's demands ; the worst is retained to supply the cultivator's wants. The cultivator must pay or quit. He sells his wheat, his oats, his stock, to pay; he reserves the potato, on which to exist. The potato fails ; the cultivator becomes a pauper or a corpse. But all are not thus at once;

and so, while wheat is going out from Cork from some to pay the landlord, maize is coming in for alms to others, who have already paid him. A man will feed his pig with potatoes, but he may never feed himself with pig. The man feeds the pig but to sell it, and he sells it to pay one who had never had trouble in rearing it. Rent not only takes the surplus production of the tiller's labor, but constantly anticipates even more than the whole. It may, then, easily be seen how the mass of a plentiful general productiveness may be going out from a country, while the mass of its producers are running to the workhouse or famishing in their cabins.

We write practically and prosaically. We should more delight ourselves, in writing on Ireland, to write poetically· for Ireland has much, indeed, to stir the spirit of poetry Ireland is a land of poetry. The power of the Past there, over every imagination, renders it a land of romance. The past is yet an actuality in Ireland ; in all the other parts of the British islands it is a song. The tragedy of Flodden Field moves a Scotchman's feelings, but it does not disturb his business ; the battle of Bannockburn calls up his enthusiasm, but, though it keeps him late at the bottle, it never keeps him late from the counting-house. The imprisonment of the poet-king Jamie softens his affections, but it leaves his judgment perfectly clear on bills of exchange and the price of stocks. Even the battle of Culloden is gone long ago to the calm impartiality of things that were. The Welshmen take English money without remorse, and say not a word about the assassin, King Edward, and the murder of their bards. Even the English themselves have but faint remembrance of the heptarchy, the revolt of the barons, the wars of the roses, the death of the first Charles, and the abdication of the second James. But events do not pass so rapidly in Ireland. Ireland is a country of tradition, of meditation, and of great idealism. It has much of the Eastern feeling of passion added to fancy, with continuity of habit, as in the East, connected with both passion and fancy. Monuments of war, princedom, and religion cover the surface of the land. The meanest man lingers under the shadow of piles which tell him that his fathers were not slaves. He toils in the field or he walks on the highways with structures before him that have stood the storms of time, through which the wind echoes with the voice of centuries, and that voice is to his heart the voice of soldiers, of scholars, and of saints. We would pen no chilling word respecting the impulse of nationality that now seems astir in Ireland. We honor every where the spirit of nationality. We honor the glorious heroism which, for an idea and a conviction, if it cannot do, can always dare and die.

Much there is in Ireland that we most dearly love. We love its music, sweet and sad, and low and lonely; it comes with a pathos, a melancholy, a melody, on the pulses of the heart, that no other music breathes, and while it grieves, it soothes. It seems to flow with long complaint over the course of ages, or to grasp with broken sobs through the ruins and fragments of historic thought. We are glad with the humor of Ireland, so buoyant and yet so tender; quaint with smiles, quivering with sentiment, pursing up the lips while it bedews the eyelids. We admire the bravery of Ireland, which may have been broken, but never has been bent—which has often been unfortunate, but which never has been craven. We have much affection for the Irish character. We give unfeigned praise to that purity of feeling which surrounds Irish women in the humblest class, and amidst the coarsest occupations, with an atmosphere of sanctity. We acknowledge with heartfelt satisfaction that kindred love in the Irish poor, that no distance can weaken, and that no time can chill. We feel satisfied with our humanity, when we see the lowly servant-girl calling for her wages, or drawing on the savings' bank for funds, to take tears from the eyes of a widowed mother in Connaught, or fears from the soul of an aged father in Munster. We behold a radiance of grandeur around the head of the Irish laborer, as he bounds, three thousand miles away, at the sound of Repeal, at the name of O'Connell; and yet more as his hand shakes, as he takes a letter from the post-office, which, rude as it may be in superscription, is a messenger from the cot in which his childhood lay—is an angel from the fields, the hills, the streams, the mountains, and the moors wherein his boyhood sported. We remember with many memories of delight, too, the beauties of Ireland's scenery. We recollect the fields that are ever green; the hills that bloom to the summit; the streamlets that in sweetness seem to sing her legends; the valleys where the fairies play; the voices among her glens, that sound from her winds as with the spirits of her bards; the shadows of her ruins at moonlight, that in pale and melancholy splendor appear like the ghosts of her ancient heroes. We would, could we choose our theme, rather linger on the beautiful songs of Moore than on the prosecutions of Meagher or of Mitchel; and if in this paper we have dwelt more upon the physical and social wants of Ireland than on her higher and more ideal qualities, it is because the immediate pressure of present events has left us neither soul nor strength to do otherwise.

But what is to come out of this pressure? We ask the question with fear and doubt. Is Ireland to come in conflict with England? We cannot always trust rumor, but rumor is at present dark and ominous. The event may not come; but the very sound of it is fearful. War, in any way, is a monstrous calamity; but civil war is a calamity that transcends imagination. War between England and

Ireland would be a civil war—there is no disguising it—and a civil war of the worst description. We ask not which party would be right, but still we reiterate that this would be among the greatest of calamities. We do not inquire what title England has to govern Ireland, but we do ask what means Ireland has to combat England.

We think that in revolutions, as in all human movements, there are certain ethical conditions, as well as prudential ones, which true men and wise will always respect. War has its morals as well as peace. Moreover, as war is of all controversies the most afflicting, and it is that which most involves innocent persons who have had no part in bringing it about, who yet may suffer the worst of its consequences, it should be the last, as it should be the most solemn, of human resolves. And if war is not to be sustained by civilized measures—if there is no guaranty that humanity even in its last strife shall be respected, to originate it is to assume a terrible responsibility. If citizen is to butcher citizen—if the revolters are to exterminate the loyal, and the loyal to show no mercy to the revolters—if one has no power to compel the other even to military moderation, alas, alas for him who sets on the strife! Revolution may be an accident; but if it be a calculation, it should be a very sober calculation; at best, it should be a very sad one. The simple fact, that a man thinks little of his own life, gives him no title to our respect; for the lowest of the human family have been found in this predicament. We have seen culprits at the bar stand up to receive the sentence of death, and even among the basest we have noticed those who listened to the sentence perfectly calm, and the most unmoved. When the lives of others are concerned, the man who cares nothing for his own often the longest hesitates. With the most determined conviction of the right, it is the thing most sorrowful beneath the stars to have brothers of the same soil making a red sea with the life-streams of each other's hearts, in which, with curses and detestation, both sink in despair together.

Then, in cases that involve vast consequences both to masses and to individuals, the prudential does, in the highest sense, become ethical; so that what is extremely danger-ous is extremely wrong. What are the means and resources of war, at present, in the war-party of Ireland against England? This is not an unwise question, for He who was best and wisest has said, "What king, going to make war against another king, sitteth not down first and consulteth whether he be able with ten thousand to meet him that cometh against him with twenty thousand?" They who would by force deliberately revolutionize, must, if true, thoroughly ponder this question, and in the great court of conscience they must not only ponder, but decide. A physical struggle with England, as a mere physical struggle, would to a thoughtful man just now present a serious case within this court, and outside of it the consequences would be most solemn. England is at peace. England is, on the whole, prudent as to her colonies and her foreign relations. England has fleets and armies compactly organized and thoroughly disciplined. England impels all the organic machinery of the law and of power. Within Ireland she has a numerous party, and the most consummate statesman-ship, which would oppose Irish nationality; the most veteran soldiership, which would fight against Irish inde-pendence, would be of Irish production. The composite nature of the British empire, which might appear to be a weakness, is in reality a principle of strength. And this, by a revolutionary thinker, should be considered in relation to the *materiel* of the British army.

There is no army in the world in which the soldier is so separated from the citizen as in the British. There is no

army in the world, which, from its compounded character,
the government can better wield. A man from the North
of Scotland may stand in the ranks beside a man from the
South of England; both may be opposed to an Irish insurgent—be cordially willing to shoot him, and, if cause
demand, to shoot each other. The army is so mixed, from
localities, religions, prejudices, that it has no unity of
spiritual sentiment or of social purpose; it fears not to
rush against the deadliest resistance, but it would not dare
to disobey the most faintly-whispered command. England
can use this gigantic instrument. It is for those who would
lead Ireland into a war, to think what Ireland can bring
against it. England has a tremendous artillery, both on the
land and on the sea. Nor is her strength in force alone.
She has on her side the fears of the timid, and the hopes
of the aspiring; the distinction that allures the ambitious,
and the riches that bribe the sordid.

If, however, there be ethical and prudential considerations
to be taken into view on the side of resistance, there are
those of infinitely more solemn obligation on the side of
authority. On the moral side of the question, it is for
rulers to inquire whether the madness and misery of the
people are not traceable to the neglect and misusage of the
people. It is for rulers to ask themselves whether the
millions have had justice done even to their bodies. Have
men had leave to toil, and when they have had that melancholy leave, have they had by it the means to live? In
what way have the vanity or indulgences of the few interfered with the industry and comforts of the many? And
when the many, at last, make their sufferings felt, is complaint to be silenced by force? If, in the end, the blood
of thousands flow, upon whose head must that blood be
charged? The conduct of members in the British House
of Commons, on the evening of the day of the Chartist

meeting, strikes us with a painful surprise. Bodies of gaunt men gathered within view of the metropolis—a cloud of silent but of potent passions, that hovered on its margin with dread foreboding. The metropolis itself was one vast garrison. Men were silent, women feared; and neither breathed freely till the assurance came, with night, that danger had disappeared. On the other side of the Channel, resistance was openly and fearlessly preached, and it was not alone preached, but prepared for. On that solemn night—a night one might suppose in which the most reckless would be serious, when, if men stood in England on solid ground, the rest of Europe was heaving with a moral earthquake—on that night, the assembled Commons of the British empire met the complaints of infuriated masses with peals of contemptuous laughter. This was assuredly as far from the grave decency which they owed to the occasion, as it was from the dignity of senators and the wisdom of statesmen. When heathen Nineveh was threatened, her rulers decreed penance in sackcloth and ashes; when Christian London was threatened, her legislators laughed. Such laughter sounds more like the rebound of cowardice freed from danger, than the levity of tranquil courage; the laughter, not of self-possession, but of trepidation. If thoughtless, it was folly, and if intentional, it was worse. Are property, privilege, and power to have all attention and respect, while want and labor are for mockery and scorn? Such conduct implies neither magnanimity nor good sense.

It is for rulers to ask themselves whether the millions have had justice done to their minds. Ireland has had for centuries a Church of monstrous inutility and enormous wealth forced on her, against her creed and her consent, with revenues that would have instructed all her people, and done much to feed her poor. England lavishes funds with imperial prodigality over the whole earth, as well as within her own borders, but is penurious with miser meanness in the support of popular instruction. The cost of Prince Albert's stables would educate a province. The cost of the Queen's nursery would educate a kingdom. How are incongruities like this—and this is but one of a legion—to be endured in the nineteenth century, when the human mind has awakened to its rights and to its power—when human energies assume a might with which they never acted before ? The most ragged Chartist is a man, as well as the best clad lord ; and take the clothes away, God and nature have not placed any immeasurable distance between them, after all. Of the two, the Chartist may be the better man, and the Chartist is beginning to feel this. If the Chartist owes submission to the laws of his country, his country owes obligations to him ; and all moralists concede that there is a boundary beyond which submission ceases to be a virtue. It is the duty of wise and good rulers never to let that boundary be reached. If authority demands obedience, authority should be so used that the obedience may be willing as well as rational. This is not only true humanity; it is good policy.

Thus expediency teaches the same lesson to rulers as morality. The victory over the Chartists, notwithstanding the boastings of the middle classes and the nobles, was a doleful victory. If it showed the strength of government, it equally displayed its danger. Masses made the commencement of a demonstration, which may be only the beginning of an end. The Chartists were dispersed ; but was Chartism annihilated ? Were the grievances extinguished out of the depths of which Chartism cries with its loud and strong appeal of agony ? It may, for the time, retreat to its cellar-and-garret concealment ; moody and wordless, it may sit brooding on its wrongs, but, passive though it seems, it is but preparing for other efforts of greater vigor and of calmer decision. In the tactics of society, as well as in the tactics of war, it may be a fatal error to mistake retirement for defeat, or the possession of the field for victory. For the present, Chartism may be discouraged in England, insurrection may be put down in Ireland; but English Chartism and Irish insurrection, come out from sources which no outward force can reach. The agency that can reach the fountains from which they spring, that can purify or change the direction of the streams, must be inward, radical, and moral. The pikemen of Ireland, it is true, might be hewn to pieces; but when bodies lay stiff upon the ground, and gibbets tainted the air—when native blood darkened the stream and sullied the field, nothing would result from triumph but fresh calamities and increase of enmity. Even as to physical security, the strongest government is liable to err. Rulers may think themselves safe within their battlements of bayonets, but their thoughts may be delusive. Desperation may achieve what no discipline could attempt; enthusiasm may be more than a match for skill; passion may shatter calculation; and against the uproused fury of excited millions, garrisons, artillery, the most solid columns of soldiery, might prove as feeble as an Indian's tent upon the prairie in the midst of a hurricane. The risk of collision is great on both sides; but rulers have their share in it as well as the people. How great that is, recent events, the money-lenders of Europe, vagrant ministers, and kings out of place, can plainly tell. It is better to conciliate than to provoke; and surely that old saw, "Prevention is easier than cure," is a precept as worthy of observance by doctors of the body politic, as by doctors of the body corporal. What would seem grace at one time, becomes unworthy of acceptance at another; and to know that point at which concession should anticipate compulsion, implies a degree of administrative sagacity, and

of legislative foresight, which it is rarely given to politicians
or to ministers to possess.

The politician is among the most common and the most
vulgar of characters ; the statesman, among the highest
and the most infrequent. England, and other countries
which we shall not name, may start a politician from every
hedge ; but it requires a generation to supply a statesman.
There is a time when concession may be grace ; let that
time pass, and the very offer becomes insult. It is then too
late. "Too late" is a phrase, in its ordinary use, of harrow-
ing significance. When love becomes despised, vows are
then too late. When friendship, known often to be vio-
lated, implores reconciliation from betrayed friendship, dis-
trust has entered, and the prayer is too late. When disease
has fixed its seat in central vitality, and the neglected
physician is called to remove it, he looks only on the eye,
he touches only the pulse, and he says, it is too late. That
"too late" is despair to those who hear it ; but the fact is
certain then, and they cannot remove it with many tears—
no, if their tears should make a deluge. "Too late" is the
burden of all the tragedies of individual and of private life,
and just now it is the burden of desolated thrones. The
individual heart that breaks in its remorse, groans out, "It
is too late ;" and so does many a royal one exclaim, that
withers in its exile. "Come, let us sit upon the ground,"
says one of Shakespeare's characters to another, "and tell
strange stories of the deaths of kings." The phrase, to suit
our present age, should be, "Come, let us sit upon the
ground, and tell strange stories of the flight of kings."
England's sovereign may feel secure amidst the crash of
dynasties ; but those who would keep her safe, must not despise the warning that booms around them. If her throne
would be secure, it must be founded in righteousness ; and
if her sceptre would be honored, it must be a sceptre of

peace. Her throne must not have beneath it the fear of any, but the love of all; and her sceptre must be a wand that waves not amidst complaints, but amidst blessings. England may seem strong, Ireland may seem weak, but there is no strength except in justice; and if Ireland, in this, has the advantage of England, she is stronger, though Ireland were small as the Duchy of Baden, and England were large as the empire of China.

After all, we are moralists, not politicians, and we cannot forget our vocation. We may be accused of repetition, but we shall not risk the charge of unfaithfulness. England has been deeply guilty towards Ireland, and Ireland has now become her punishment. England, within late years, may have had kinder intentions towards Ireland than the England of former ages; but, notwithstanding her kind intentions, the Ireland which she so long ill-treated has become her perplexity and her penalty. The Ireland which, by neglect, by partial or adverse legislation, she has impoverished or kept in poverty, deluges her cities, swamps her labor-market, paralyzes her industrial energies, reduces the wages of her people, and continues to pull them down rapidly to Irish hunger, Irish nakedness, and Irish despair. Wrong is indissolubly bound to retribution. This we have before expressed, but it can hardly be too often reasserted. Nations, as well as individuals, may want that large foresight which sees afar into the future, and which perceives, in all circumstances, that it is not merely the dictate of virtue, but the wisdom of calculation, to deal justly, to do right. They may be blinded by the present passion or the present gain, but the law works on, though they do not, or cannot, or will not see it, until the crash of its power awakens them to doom. Late repentance is better than perpetual sin, but sin plants seeds of evil which produce their envenomed crop, despite the most penitent remorse. That justice alone is safety, and that unrighteousness is sure destruction, is written on every page of life, on every page of history. It is a lesson which all that run may read, and yet it is a lesson which is as universally neglected as it is universally admitted.

Physically, socially, morally, the present state of Ireland is most gloomy and most disastrous. Hunger and hatred go hand in hand; hunger yearning for the potato, while hatred prepares the pike. The cloud of agitation gathers, and seems every hour to grow darker. The bursting of the cloud threatens to be near; but as yet, there appear among the people no man who could "ride upon the whirlwind, and direct the storm." The people are not only divided into manifold and inveterate parties, but parties are again divided among themselves. Young men harangue the people against the troops, and these troops preserve their lives from the passions of the people. What mind has yet shown itself so calm in thought, so comprehensive in reflection, so decisive in action, that it could reconcile all the contradictions of popular Ireland, and bring them united and compacted against the disciplined and regulated force of England? Fervor there is in abundance; enthusiasm, passion, ready utterance, and daring speech, the most impulsive eloquence. We doubt, indeed, whether in Ireland, in the grandest day of her oratorical renown, there ever shot forth a crop of finer words than comes out now from the soil of her young and impassioned genius. But though a great man said that "words are things," the agents who have created greatest things, were men of fewest words. Washington could not have made an oration to save his life, and Jefferson, who wrote the Declaration of Independence, had but small power of thinking on his feet. We do not underrate the influence of grand and impassioned speech; we hold that utterance is a sublime faculty—that it can set the brain on fire, and the heart in flame ; but to guide a nation, when that nation has reached its climax of excitement, the finest utterance will be feeble. It was Moses who led the hosts of Israel out from Egypt, and to the borders of the promised land, yet Moses was poor of speech ; Aaron, who was eloquent, was but the mouth of Moses, and Aaron was always only secondary. At the present hour we behold on the popular side of Ireland, no commanding mind—no mind of large capacity for counsel —no mind of varied resources for command. There is no great mind on the other side either ; but the other side controls all the machinery of government, and has all the prestige of power.

We sympathize with the sufferings of Ireland, and we lament her evils ; we look with a painful interest upon her present crisis ; but at this distance, were it even within the province of our journal, it would be idle in us to speculate on remedies. Whether a repeal of the Union would remove the grievances of which Ireland complains, it is not for us to say; it is clear, however, that the enactment of the Union did not prevent them. When the Union was first mooted in the British Parliament, Pitt presented the measure in a speech of remarkable compass and power. Imposing as a rhetorician, quick as a debater, and possessing a fluency wonderfully correct, Pitt was seldom grandly eloquent, but in this speech he became so. In picturing the future which was to open upon Ireland under the sunshine of an imperial parliament, he rose to a kind of millennial grandeur. Sectarian strifes were to be allayed ; political divisions would be assuaged ; capital would flow into the country; industry would be encouraged ; commerce would advance ; tranquillity and comfort would abound. Large promises were given, and bright prophecies uttered ; but where are the fruits of the promises, and where are the things foretold in the prophecies? After half a century, there is not one spct in Ireland which answers to the anticipations of Pitt. The Union was no measure of the people ; it was a contrivance of intriguing ministers, effected by acting on the base motives of men, who grasped at the bribe and gave up their country.

Had the Union been honest—had it it been the fair choice of the whole people, and on terms approved by their wisest counsellors—had it been cordial and reciprocal, it is not for us to conclude, from what we now see, what might have been. Had imperial legislation given emancipation at once to the Catholics, and given it generously and graciously—had it relieved the country from the Church establishment, and left the care of each form of religion to those who professed it—had it introduced a bounteous system of national education—had it treated the sacred feelings of the larger division of Irishmen with kindness and respect—had it done justice to popular sentiment in the distribution of politica. offices—had it separated the administration of law from the spirit of faction, by showing the misguided that the balance of justice never swerved except on the side of mercy—had the Union been a bond of friendship and an interchange of benefits—it would have been a reality. But none of these things took place, and, as it was, it was not a union, but a cheat.

The delay to grant Catholic emancipation doomed the people of Ireland to thirty years of struggle, and the manner in which it came at last tended rather to irritate than to pacify. The long struggle educated them in the consciousness of their strength, taught them how to use it, and emboldened them for continued resistance. The galling vexation of tithes and church-rates was long sustained, and that huge anomaly, that monstrous blunder of folly and injustice, still remains—a Protestant Church supported by a Catholic people ; the Church the richest in the world, and the people the poorest.

The Union has assuredly not produced social order. If it has, where are we to look for it? Shall we seek it in Conciliation Hall, or in that of the Confederates? Shall we hear its voice in the modulated complaint of John O'Connell, or in the fierce defiance of Smith O'Brien ; in the florid imagination of Meagher, or the concentrated passion of Mitchel? Shall we turn for its pleasant sounds to the anvil on which the pike is shaped? There is the "Song of the Bell," and the "Forging of the Anchor;" shall we dedicate a lyric to the social order of Ireland in the "Song of the Pike?" Shall we take, as evidence of its existence, the congregations of moody peasants that a word can bring together, and that a motion can excite? Or shall we prefer to see it in fortifications, where death lies in wait for thousands, should these thousands show signs of fight? The truth is, the whole condition of Ireland is disjointed, and whether Repeal could remedy it or not, we do not aver, but, as we have observed, the Union has, at least, not averted this monstrous, this appalling wretchedness. The wealthy and the poor are in no true relations to each other. Their relations are those of coercion on the one side, and sullen discontent on the other ; a discontent that seems growing to the boldness of an open resistance. Complainings are in the streets ; disease is in the hovel and the cellar ; the dying go where the weary are at rest, and the surviving stay behind, not knowing how to live. Cities have become garrisons ; palaces are turned into barracks ; the land is bare of bread ; it is filled with soldiers. Come the tourist into Ireland, whence he may—from France, England, Germany, Russia, Asia, or America, from any region of civilized man between Cape Horn and Gibraltar, from the Ganges to the Tiber—the wonder is alike in each,

the testimony as uniform, the expression of it as unvarying
in phrase, as the sources from which it is derived are
diverse and independent—each finds in Ireland a singu-
larity of wretchedness, an originality of misery, which out-
runs not only his experience, but his fancy. "Well," said
Colonel Napier, while describing the state of Europe at the
commencement of the Peninsular War—"of Ireland it is
unnecessary to speak; her wrongs and her misery, peculiar
and unparalleled, are too well known and too little regarded
to call for any remark." The author who wrote these words
is at present commanding, we believe, in Ireland. What
would he say of Ireland, if he should undertake to write
another book?

These agitations in Ireland arise from no superficial
causes. It is short-sighted and vain to ascribe them to
temporary influences, or to the agency of individuals. As
well might the fever which burns through the body of a
patient be ascribed to the quickness of the pulse, which is
the concomitant, but not the cause, of the disease. No man,
no class of men, no combination of talents, no force of
genius, no subtlety of scheming, can widely agitate or long
control millions of people who are governed well and feel
that they are. No such power can disturb a nation permanently, when the masses of it are content; and they will
be content, when they know by experience that in its prosperity they have their due share, and in its adversity no
more. The potency, therefore, which leaders have over
multitudes, they gain not all from character, not all from
mental superiority; they gain it from the uneasy elements
which the multitudes themselves contain. Though the Irish
leaders, therefore, were as bad as their opponents paint
them, the question as to the real condition of the country
would remain the same; that is a settled fact, untouched
entirely either by the eulogium or the abuse of this man or

the other. These agitations cannot be subdued by force, for though they may disappear for a period, it is only to come up again with maturer strength. They arise from radical causes, and they will cease only with radical changes. Whether by an imperial or domestic legislature, Ireland must be governed by her consent, not by coercion—by the power of opinion, and not by the edge of the sword. She must no longer be a military province. She cannot continue to be as she has been and as she is. The time has come for her to insist on a higher place in the empire—in the world—and not insist in vain. That she ought to have it is the decision of that sentiment of justice, which acts strongly, and more strongly with every successive change, in the conscience of all Christendom.

In the opening part of this article we suggested a lesson of warning to be learned from the present state of Europe. In this closing part of it, we would suggest a lesson of encouragement. The youngest and the oldest of us have heard little from the political writers of Europe but prophecies on the instability of our government, or on the certainty of its failure. We were either so wise or so rash as to take no alarm from these prophecies. That we were right to feel at peace, most of them will now admit. These forebodings were written under the shadows of thrones that have tumbled to pieces about the writers' ears, and the thrones, which were to stand securely on their simple and sound foundation, while our clumsy and unwieldy confederacy was to go to pieces, went in fragments to the earth before the ink was dry upon the printer's paper ; yet probably our institutions may be firm, when dynastics that mocked us shall be forgotten.

Our government, it was said, was but an experiment ; it proves now not an experiment, but experience—an experience from which men of ancient States are able to learn.

We have our mobs, and mobs often of the worst kind ; but they quickly dissolve, and leave no more impression on the solidity of our social structure than a snow-shower does upon the granite of Monadnock. We have evils among us, we confess, that cry to heaven ; we have abuses of which we may well be ashamed ; we have sins that call for deep repentance ; yet, not indulging in any idle trust, but active with individual effort, we may hope that Providence will in time cause much that we lament—that the good and true everywhere lament—to be seen and known in our country no more for ever. We may have unworthy men in the administration of our affairs, and unworthy motives may often dictate our measures. In this we are not singular among nations ; but we are thus far singular among nations, that the substantial rights of the people cannot be essentially injured even by the bad purposes of scheming politicians, nor the framework of the government overturned. We preserve unity with a diversity of independent States, and with a widening and complicated suffrage. With the greatest latitude of individual action and individual opinion, the administration of affairs is conducted, upon the whole, with order and tranquillity. We have, as have other countries, crimes against life and property; but, except in some wild regions, life and property are as safe here as anywhere upon earth.

One fatal mistake the rulers in Europe committed, from which we were free. They supposed they kept power from the people because they kept the franchise from them. But the people have power all the same, whether they possess the franchise or not; and the people will use it too. The question which seems to agitate the mind is, In what way will they use it best? By irregular demonstrations and by external pressure, or by orderly arrangement and organic representation? Each man here acts through his vote, and, as all the people have votes, there is not even the possibility of an external pressure. It is by this external pressure, by this irregular agency of the unfranchised mass, that revolutions are effected ; and no nation thus circumstanced is secure from revolution otherwise than by force. But force has greatly lost its power, and will soon cease to be a protection. If men are not fit for the franchise, then it is the duty of the government to qualify them. The duty in our country is so to educate men that they may use intelligently the votes they hold of right ; the duty of other countries is so to educate men that they may be prepared to use the votes which, if not given by reform, they will take by revolution.

The agitations which at present excite all Europe are of solemn import. They indicate a progressive development of great ideas—a progressive recognition of grand principles. The soul of humanity has been at work in them, and that is a power which no armies can conquer. From the soul, society has its existence and has its glory. Give the soul freedom, and there is life ; straiten it, wrong it, and you prepare destruction. It has a might which can sweep away the strongest ramparts, which can silence the loudest cannon, which can blunt the sharpest spears. The point of the bayonet, it was once thought, could quiet all popular remonstrance ; but the bayonet has ceased to be invincible. Sentiments have become stronger than weapons. Society begins more and more to feel its humanity. A revelation has come to multitudes that they are men, and it is this faith which works in them with most wondrous efficacy. It is in the strength of this that they burst their chains asunder, and dash their fetters at their keepers. Beneath the outward events of the world—the battles of parties, the schemings of factions, the plottings of intriguers, the elevation of peoples, and the fall of kings, the doings of the active, and the theories of the speculative—the Providence of God is operating in the depths of humanity, invigorating its capacities, guiding its destiny, and preparing it to vindicate everywhere the Divine likeness in which it was originally created.

DANIEL O'CONNELL.

[In the course of this lecture on Daniel O'Connell, I propose to trace the leading incidents of his life—to consider him as a man of public action, as a man also of public speech, and, lastly, to attempt an estimate of his mind and character.]

DANIEL O'CONNELL was born on the 6th of August, 1775, in Cahir-civeen, in the County of Kerry. He was of an old family which claimed to be of royal descent. When thirteen years of age, he was sent to a classical school in Redington, near the Cove of Cork, kept by the Rev. Mr. Harrington. This is said to have been the first school publicly opened after the repeal of those laws which made it penal for Roman Catholics to educate their children. With youth, fresh from the mountains—with a mind trained in healthful simplicity—with an imagination which had received its first impressions from the cloud-capped headlands of Kerry, and from the billowy and boundless Atlantic —with a memory stored from the treasury of Celtic legend, from the wild and passionate complaints of song and story—he entered the College of St. Omers, a seminary for Catholic instruction. After a short interval at Douai, he came back to St. Omers, and was thence excluded by the French Revolution, and escaped to England. The profession of the law was opened to the Roman Catholics in

1793: O'Connell studied for it, and in 1798 he was called to the Irish bar. He was among the first of his Church to avail himself of this relaxation of the penal code. He entered the political arena at the same time, and immediately became, as he afterwards continued to be, the champion of Irish nationality. He made his first public speech in 1800— a speech which at once gave notice that a great orator and a great man had been born into the world. Shortly after, in 1802, he married his cousin, Mary O'Connell, with whom, as he declared, he had thirty years of as pure happiness as it is given to man to enjoy on earth. Thus blessed at the entrance of household life, he began at once a course of prosperous activity. He had not long to wait and bitterly to fear, as many a young man of worth and genius has, in the first struggles of his profession; to have the hope of love deferred until the heart is sick or withered; or to risk the martyrdom of domestic penury—in which sympathy itself becomes a knife in the hand of Indigence, whetted on affection, to cut the flesh that is nearest to the heart—in which the puzzled brain is often called on to do its best, when malicious Fortune has done her worst. O'Connell had no such trials. Practice came to him early, and to the last it continued to increase. "The first year I was at the bar," said he to Mr. Daunt, "I made £58; the second, about £150; the third, £200; the fourth, about 300 guineas. I then advanced rapidly, and the last year of my practice I got £9,000, although I lost one term." But the great work of O'Connell's life was to labor for the political emancipation of the Catholics. "For more than twenty years," he says to the Earl of Shrewsbury, "before the passing of the Catholic Emancipation Bill, the burden of the cause was thrown on me. I had to arrange the meetings, to prepare the resolutions, to furnish replies to correspondence, to examine the case of each person complaining of practical grievances, to rouse the torpid, to animate the lukewarm, to control the violent and inflammatory, to avoid the shoals and breakers of the law, to guard against multiplied treachery, and at all times to oppose, at every peril, the powerful and multitudinous enemies of the cause." Such was the work which O'Connell had for a quarter of a century to do, and to do it gratuitously: for it was not until he entered Parliament that popular provision was made to supply him with an income. That the position had even personal danger, was proved by the duel which D'Esterre, a member of the Dublin Corporation, forced on O'Connell in 1815, evidently from political rancor. D'Esterre was noted as a marksman· but at the first shot, O'Connell killed him; an event which, though driven to it by the tyranny of society, he never ceased to repent of and to regret.

The organization which O'Connell worked successively changed its name, but never changed its nature. In 1804, it was the Catholic Board; in 1808, the Catholic Committee; in 1823, the Catholic Association. When the organization was forbidden under one name, it merely assumed another; did not die, but only lived a stronger life. Such it was by the power of O'Connell; and the power of O'Connell consisted in the might and force which enabled him to grasp the genius of the People within the embrace of his sympathies, his passions, and his intellect. So it was that the association, thus inspired, grew into its greatness, and gathered to its strength, until, from a few individuals in an obscure room, it consisted of millions—became not only commensurate with the island, but spread its influence throughout the world. Another spirit was, however, in this organization, who, though subordinate in it to the genius of O'Connell, should not be left unnoticed. I allude to Richard Lalor Sheil. Very different from O'Connell Sheil was in many particulars—not the least in social and political tendencies. O'Connell sympathized generally with the radical democracy; Sheil with the moderate and literary whigs. While the laws excluded both from Parliament, both battled on the same arena. When that exclusion ceased, their different tastes prompted divergent courses. But however Sheil differed from O'Connell in opinions and disposition, he stood beside him in eloquence and genius. Sheil had a mind of the finest nature and of the richest cultivation; a vigorous intellect, and an exuberant fancy. His speaking was a condensation of thought and passion—in brilliant, elaborate, and often antithetical expression. He happily united precision and embellishment, and his ideas in being adorned became not only attractive, but distinct. Images were as easy to him as words, and his figures were as correct as they were abundant. With a faculty peculiarly dramatic, he gave vivid illusion to scenes and characters with which he filled the imaginations of his hearers. He compressed into a passage the materials of a tragedy, and moved, as he pleased, to terror and to pity. He was not the less the master of invective and of sarcasm. He was, in prose, almost as effective a satarist as Pope was in verse — as scathing and as lacerating. He clothed burlesque in as mocking a gravity; was as bitter in his irony, as polished in his wit, as elegant in his banter, and sometimes as unmerciful in his ridicule. In the battle for Catholic emancipation, this splendid and impassioned orator was heard everywhere in Ireland shrieking forth the wrongs of his people. That shrill voice of his cried aloud and spared not. It stirred his brethren to indignation and to action; it pierced into their souls, and awakened to torture the sense of their degradation. It was heard in metropolis and village; on the mountain and in the market-place. It rang out from sea to sea, and was chorused by the shouts of sympathetic multitudes. O'Connell was the legislator and the doer, but in the agency of speech Sheil was indefatigable, and had no superior.

In 1828 O'Connell was elected for Clare. But he could not take the oaths which lay between him and his seat. In 1829 these oaths were removed, and O'Connell was again triumphantly returned for Clare. From that time till his death, he continued to be, for one place or another, a member in every Parliament. He used, indeed, to call himself the member for all Ireland; and, in some sense, such he was. In 1842 he opened his agitation for repeal of the union. Upon the prosecution of Government, at the instigation of Sir Robert Peel, he was convicted of sedition, sentenced to be imprisoned for a year, and to pay a fine of £2,000. On appeal to the House of Lords, the judgment was reversed; O'Connell and his fellow-prisoners, after three months confinement, were released. In the course of the discussion in the Upper House, Lord Denman spoke the memorable words, "that prosecutions so conducted would render trial by jury a mockery, a delusion, and a snare." O'Connell was released; but imprisonment had left its ineradicable mark upon his spirit. It did not injure his body, but it entered into his soul. It proved him vulnerable; and when a man is thought invulnerable, a wound in the heel is as fatal as the splitting of the head. His person till then was as the person of a tribune, which no man must rudely touch and live. The spell was broken; he felt it was, and he began to droop. The majesty that doth hedge a king had been attacked; though not despoiled, it had yet been profanely treated. He could no longer reign: his battles had not henceforth the prestige of victory or of hope. The hard but exhilarating contest in which his life had passed must succumb to prosy forms; the wild eloquence that shouted in its free power over the surging seas of multitudes must sink to cautious tameness in the presence of a government reporter; must give account of itself at the bidding of Tory judges. The charm was dissolved, and with it the glory of unquestioned dominion. Division, disunion, and feud began to rage around his throne. The impatience of younger enthusiasm spurned his veteran policy resistance to his long-honored authority completed the dismemberment of his kingdom, and broke to pieces the unity of his might. He sickened. He went to the Continent in 1847—not so much with the hope of restoration, as on a religious pilgrimage; and he died at Genoa on May the 15th of that year. His heart, according to his desire, was embalmed and borne to Rome; his body was carried back and buried in his native Ireland. The name of Peel also was soon added to the death-list. In the blaze of his fame and wealth, the horse which he rode threw him and crushed him into fragments. While nations waited on his word— while artists hung upon his smile—while there were yet bright around him glory and genius, and literature and luxury, the kindred that loved, and the millions that applauded—in a moment, in the twinkling of an eye, he was a bruised and a lifeless thing. O'Connell and Peel fought each other throughout their lives; both went almost together out of earth. Mighty men were both in their day; but in the presence of death, the mightiest are nothing, and we feel that, as the French preacher said over the corpse of Louis XIV., " God alone is great."

II. In proceeding to consider O'Connell as a man of public action, I observe a relation between the leading events of his life, to changes in the laws which concerned Roman Catholics, that has, I think, more than the interest of a merely curious coincidence. O'Connell was born in a period when some among the harshest of the penal laws had been modified and softened. The cruel portion of the code had been generally abolished, but the humiliating portiou of it was still in force. The birth of O'Connell had preceded by a few months the declaration of American independence. There was need of soldiers; there was corresponding need to conciliate the Irish, and the laws were accordingly ameliorated—so far, at least, that, by the time O'Connell was thirteen, a Roman Catholic might go publicly to school. But university education was still denied him, and for this he was obliged to go abroad. In the mean time the French Revolution broke out; and then again a need for advanced conciliation of the Irish. Roman Catholics obtained the elective franchise, and were admitted to the legal profession. O'Connell became a lawyer. Still his religion would have excluded him from the bench—from every governmental office at the bar—from all honorary distinctions; he could never hope to change his stuff gown for a silk one; he must bend himself to hard work; he must be content with fame—and fees. At last, a Roman Catholic could enter Parliament. We notice, in tracing this course, that from entrance on life till entrance on its decline, the successive changes of the law just enabled O'Connell to take one step at a time to the completeness of emancipated citizenship. He was among the earliest in the first public school open to Catholics; he was among the earliest of Catholics called to the bar ; and ere the bolts had been yet drawn, he was already waiting at the door of Parliament. This succession of experiences could not have been in vain for O'Connell. Such experiences must have had passionate meanings for him; they must have entered into the very spirit of his life, and, from one stage to another, they must have trained him for his work, and trained him *in* it. He was born in the right hour; and he was the right man. A generation earlier, his life would have been too soon ; with all his native vigor—with all his indignant ambition— with all his innate force of genius, the laws would have been

too strong for him, and his would have been an unheard-of
grave in the cemetery of a foreign convent, or in a churchyard among the Kerry mountains. Born under those laws,
O'Connell lived to see the last of them; but even then, it
was at the cost of a struggle—long, constant, and obstinate.
In this struggle O'Connell spent the vigor of his life. But
what were these laws of which we hear so much, and
without reference to which the social characteristics of
modern Ireland can neither be explained nor understood? I offer a very condensed abstract of their leading
provisions. A Roman Catholic could not inherit real
estate; he could not purchase it; it could not be purchased or held in trust for him; and the estate that he
would have by entail went to the next Protestant heir, as if
the Roman Catholic were dead. A Roman Catholic could
not have a lease for more than thirty-one years, and if
the profits of such lease exceeded more than one-third of
the rent, any Protestant who could prove the fact took
possession of the property. A Catholic wife, on turning
Protestant, was allowed an increased jointure. A Roman
Catholic father could not be guardian to his own child
under a penalty £500; and a Roman Catholic minor, who
avowed himself a Protestant, was immediately delivered to
a Protestant guardian. If one child abjured the Roman
Catholic religion, though he were the youngest, he inherited
the whole estate, and even his father had no legal claim on
it for support. No Roman Catholic could marry a Protestant, and it was a capital crime for a priest to celebrate
such marriage. Indeed, the fact of merely being a priest
subjected a man to transportation for life, and, in case of
return, to death. For a Roman Catholic to teach a school
was felony; to aid in sending another abroad to be educated
in the Roman Catholic religion, subjected the parties to a
fine, disabled them from being executors or administrators,

from taking any legacy or gift, from holding any office, from suing in law or equity, to a forfeiture of all their chattels, and of all their real estate for life. No Roman Catholic was eligible to any civil or military office, to sit in Parliament, or to vote at elections. If Protestants lost property in war by the privateers of a Catholic power, Catholics alone were to make it good. That these laws should not be evaded by mere passiveness, *not* to attend the Established Church— not, in fact, to be actively Protestant—exposed the individual to odious privations and to exorbitant fines.

Those laws were all enacted *in* Ireland, and *by* legislators who claimed to be Irishmen. They were the code of an Irish, and not of an English Parliament; and they have evidently in them a spirit of vindictive and of local hatred. They go beyond all the severities and restraints which a governing minority, in fear and self-defence, impose on a subjected population. "If," says Arthur Young, "such a system as would crush the minds of a conquered people into slavish submission was ever necessary, it must have been under that new and in many respects weak establishment, when the late conflict might have been an apparent justification; but why such a system should be embraced six or seven years after the death of King William, is not so easy to be accounted for." The reasons for these laws lie more deeply than Arthur Young examined, and for their object they were not so senseless as he considered them. There was more in them than even the zeal of religious persecution, and more than the immediate passion of military success; there was a profound energy of angry vengeance—an evident desire to show contempt, as well as to inflict pain. From the time of Queen Elizabeth, the laws were harsh; but still, the Catholics of Ireland had wealth, and no small share of power. Even after Cromwell, the Catholics had something to lose, both in property and

social eminence. It was not until after the siege of Limer
ick, and even the death of William, that the laws against
the Catholics of Ireland assumed their utmost fierceness.
There was not merely the ordinary bitterness of domestic
strife, civil and religious, to make them so, but there came
among the soldiers of William—many of whom shared in
the spoils of confiscation—the French Huguenot, furious at
the revocation of the Edict of Nantz; the Dutch Calvinist,
always in power, cruel, and from his memories of Spain,
steeped in hereditary aversion to Catholics; other adventurers, who were merely unprincipled hirelings of the
sword; all these united, put their evil dispositions into
statutes, and gave to their worst passions the authority of
laws. But there was more than passion in these laws;
there was purpose—compact, settled, systematic purpose—
that purpose was, either to abolish the Roman Catholic
religion in Ireland, or to reduce the Roman Catholics
themselves to absolute serfdom. The laws failed, from the
outset, in the case of religion; but with regard to the other
alternative, they came near to being successful. They were
admirably contrived to work out a people's degradation;
for, in the first place, they tended effectually to make them
poor, and as effectually, in the second, to make them
ignorant. Rendered landless not only as to proprietorship,
but even as to secure tenancy; shut out directly from many
mechanical trades; shut out from the guilds and corporations, with which were connected all the gainful and influential modes of industry; ineligible to every office and
profession that could excite or keep alive ambition, law
to the utmost of its power made poverty the inevitable
condition of Roman Catholics—universal, perpetual, igno-
minious poverty. There was no possibility allowed by law
for the poor Catholic to rise; and the rich Catholic,
excluded from all honorable activity, deprived of the means

of increasing, of securing, of transmitting, almost of using his wealth, must either quit the country, or sink down, as many of the aristocratic Catholics did, into common serfdom. Still a man may be poor in worldly substance, and yet be rich in the spirit of his mind. Leave a man art and letters, he still has imperishable treasures. He has the sense of his human dignity left, and this can support him against many a painful humiliation. Thus the Jews sustained themselves through long ages of oppression ; they had their language and their literature ; much as they were wronged, I do not remember that, by the code of any nation, they could be hanged for teaching or learning Hebrew, for expounding the Prophecies, or for chanting the Psalms. They had still the refuge, not only of their faith, but of their intellect. Take from a man the culture of the intellect, then you make him poor indeed. Impoverish a man, you certainly do him evil ; but close to him the avenues of thought and knowledge, you blind him to the light of light—you attack him in his life of life. Whom do Christian writers rate as the deadliest persecutor of all the Roman emperors? The mild and cultivated Julian. Yet Julian put no Christian to the cross—gave no Christian to the beasts; he merely forbade Christians to learn, and shut them out from the schools. Even Gibbon, his eulogist, shows that no more fatal injury could have been imagined or contrived. But Julian soon died, and his purpose died with him. The laws in Ireland, which improved on Julian's malice, remained, and for more than two generations were not inoperative. The letter of these laws, it may be said, was not in force ; it was not because it could not; but their spirit was not inactive or without result. It kept the people from wealth ; it kept the people from education ; it kept the people from the means of education ; it broke their spirit ; bowed them down into submission, and went far to extinguish in them for ever the life of independent manhood. This is the truth, and there is nothing to be gained in denying or concealing it. Read the pamphlets and speeches of those times, and you cannot but feel to what social degradation the Catholics of Ireland were reduced. Swift, in his political and polemical writings, always refers to the condition of the Catholic Irish as that of the lowest and the most hopeless submission. And this was such as Swift approved ; such as from principle and inclination, he would counsel, confirm, and perpetuate. For the physical destitution which he beheld around him, he had a sort of savage pity; he would willingly have relieved the distressed, and he was zealous for the general prosperity of the country; but if a proposal were possible, in his day, to extend civic freedom to the Catholics of Ireland, or even religious toleration, Swift would have been the first to denounce it with all the fierceness of his temper, and with all the vigor of his genius. What Macaulay says is, therefore, to the letter true : "The domination of the colonists was absolute. The native population was tranquil with the ghastly tranquillity of exhaustion and despair." "Scattered," as he again observes, "all over Europe were to be found brave Irish generals, dexterous Irish diplomatists, Irish counts, Irish barons, Irish knights of St. Lewis, of St. Leopold, of the White Eagle, and of the Golden Fleece, who, if they had remained in the house of bondage, could not have been ensigns in a marching regiment, or freemen of petty corporations. These men, the natural chiefs of their race, having been withdrawn, what remained was utterly and helplessly passive. A rising of the Irishry against the Englishry was no more to be dreaded than a rising of women and children against the men." Lord Macaulay is often figurative and florid ; but in these statements he is exactly literal and simple. Catholics were slightly regarded in the discussions of the Irish Parliament; and whenever a Catholic ven·tured to put his grievances into printed appeal or explanation, his manner was cautiously moderate—almost, indeed, shrinkingly timid. So late as 1781, when the heroic Henry Grattan arose and shook the nation with his eloquence, his power was not by means of Catholics, but by means of liberal Protestants; his agitation in favor of Catholics was not as their representative, but as their advocate; and the brief parliamentary independence which Grattan conquered was through the short-lived passion of a merely Protestant nationality. Even Lord Charlemont, so much loved and lauded, refused his consent to let Catholics have the elective franchise; and to the last hour of his life he was opposed to Catholic emancipation. The Catholic commonalty was inert; and Wolfe Tone alleges, in his Memoirs, that "the Catholic aristocracy was not only quiescent, but subservient." "Such an effect," he remarks, "had the operation of the penal laws on the Catholics of Ireland—as proud a race as any in all Europe." Arthur Young's testimony is to the same effect. The edition of his Travels in Ireland to which I refer, is a Dublin one, printed in 1780. Physically, indeed, the people were not so badly off, as frequently they have been since; they had then a humble plenty, which in later years they had often sorrowful occasion to regret; but socially, their state in some respects was worse than serfdom.

Such had been the Ireland which was just receding behind O'Connell's youth. The Ireland was not quite so dark on which his working manhood entered, but still it called for a giant's toil. O'Connell had not merely to arouse a people—he had, first of all, to create a people. Having created a people, he had to shape its instincts—to direct and rule them. Hannibal is esteemed the greatest of generals, not because he gained victories, but because he made an army. O'Connell, for the same reason, must be considered among the first of legislators—not because he won triumphs, but because he made a people. The people, whom he called up almost from death, he had not only to work *on*, but to work *by;* first, he worked *by* them to overcome the apathy of Catholic aristocracy; and, secondly, he worked *by* them to overcome the combined forces of anti-Catholic resistance. In teaching the people to know their own power, and to show it, he presented motives of action to the interest, the ambition, and the genius of those who were on their side; in the degree that he thus united minds and masses—in the degree that he added all moral and social energies to the influence of numbers, he made opposition formidable to the prudence, the policy, and the fears of those who were against them.

O'Connell seemed singularly fitted to his mission and his time. The Rebellion of 1798 was scarcely quelled, when he appeared. The heaving swell was yet rocking society, and the blood-red clouds had not passed from the moral atmosphere. Tears were yet falling from unsleeping eyes, and the desolate yet mourned with a grief that would not be comforted. The convulsion of the French Revolution was still agitating Europe, and not with the less force because all its elements had converged their power within the personality of Napoleon's stupendous mind. The cannons of Napoleon boomed through the sky from the Danube to the Nile; and mingled with the din of conquest were the shouts of peoples and the crash of thrones. War on the sea was not less fierce than war on the land. Britain was sweeping the ocean with her fleets; Nelson was tiring fame with the rapid succession of his victories, until, at last, his career was closed in the ecstasy of battle. While these terrible men shone amidst the gloomy majesty of war, O'Connell, too, had visions of renown, but they arose from the anticipated achievements of humanity and peace.   A crisis had come in the history of his country, and he was the man to meet it.   He was the only man.   Curran, as an advocate, had bravely done his melancholy duty, and there was no more that he could do.   Grattan, as a senator, was not silent, but he was disheartened.   But had both been in their prime of genius and of hope, neither of them had fitness for the mission of O'Connell.   The millions for whom the battle was fought were Roman Catholics; it was therefore meet that the leader who commanded should be one of themselves; and O'Connell was the greatest Roman Catholic genius who had yet arisen in Ireland since the Siege of Limerick.   But O'Connell was not only a great Catholic, he was a great man—great in all the qualities which his situation demanded.   A man of reflection, yet of decision; of boldness, but of prudence; ever fertile in resources, ever master of his faculties, the hour and the difficulty found him at no time unprepared.   His words were daggers, yet not libels; and while passion burned in his heart, caution kept watch upon his lips.   He instructed the Irish masses to exhibit strength without using it; to nullify bad laws without transgressing them; and to gather the fruits of conquest without the risks of war.   O'Connell, like Carnot, organized victory; Carnot's was the organization of force, and O'Connell's was the organization of opinion.   The labor which O'Connell went through was gigantic.   That which O'Connell *did* has been underrated, because of *that* which he did *not*.   But if we contrast the political condition of Ireland as O'Connell found it, with the political condition of Ireland as he left it, we shall see how grand and successful he was in his political agitation. He found an oligarchy that seemed unapproachable in the height of its ascendancy, impregnable in the strength of its position; he fronted its arrogance, defied its power, pulled down its pride, swept away its privileges, and ground its monopoly into atoms. He found the Catholic peasantry serfs, he made them free; he found the middle-class timid and dependant, he stirred them into courage—he raised them into citizens; he found the Catholic aristocracy time-servers or idlers, and he shamed them into dignity. Every Catholic, high or humble, had been made an alien on his own native Ireland; O'Connell restored him to his place in the commonwealth; and if he did not arouse, or care to arouse, the spirit of national independence, he did very effectually that of personal and political independence. After a long sleep of submission, he called up millions to the desire for freedom. Surely this, for one man, was a great work. And yet O'Connell did not die in time. Men there are in history who, dying at a certain time, would leave on us the impression of immeasurable genius, but who, by surviving the turn of their fortunes, lose by comparison with themselves—for with themselves we still compare them; and while we diminish our estimate, we seem to forget how great they must be, since we think never of comparing them with others. For this reason, Charles XII., of Sweden, should never have survived Pultowa; Napoleon should have died soon after Austerlitz; O'Connell should have died after he had gained Catholic Emancipation, and made his first and best speeches in the House of Commons. If he had thus and then died, his genius as a popular leader must have been a theme of wonder even to opponents, and the manner of dealing with his memory would have been that of admiration, and not that of criticism. As it is, the world shows hardly another man who has singly done so much as O'Connell, and by merely moral and intellectual means.

III. To estimate O'Connell as a speaker, would in itself alone require a lecture; and here it must be attempted

in a fragment.   Such a lecture would have three natural
divisions: O'Connell as a lawyer, as a legislator, and as a
popular tribune; or O'Connell as speech revealed him at
the bar, in Parliament, and in the open assembly of the
people.   On the first two positions, I must be brief; but
this is of less account since it is in the third O'Connell had
superlative and characteristic distinction.

That O'Connell was able at the bar we might safely infer.
We know that he was industrious, studious, and ambitious;
that he had much knowledge of men, as they live in the
world; that he had instinctive talent in the acquirement of
this knowledge — talent improved by practice and opportunity; that he had an athletic understanding, much sensibility, imagination, and great force of passion ; that he
had caution, coolness, and extraordinary powers of labor
and endurance; that he entered the profession of a barrister
with the education of a scholar; and that, along with all, he
had the genius which spontaneously brings thought, feeling,
and word into the unity and music of expression, which we
call eloquence.   Such qualifications meeting in one person,
would have made him a good general lawyer, would have
made him also a successful advocate; and such qualifications
did meet in O'Connell.   We are not, however, left to inference; we have the evidence of fact.   The best opinion we can
give of a lawyer is to employ him.   Orangemen constantly
employed O'Connell; and they were his political, if not his
personal enemies.   O'Connell, as an advocate, was often
called on to defend journals which the most opposed him.
"Oh! a broguish Irish fellow, who would listen to him?"
said an English snob once, in conversation with Sir Robert
Peel.   "If I wanted," replied Sir Robert, "an eloquent
advocate, I would readily give up all the other orators of
whom we have been speaking, provided I had with me this
same broguish Irish fellow."   O'Connell was universally

recognized as the leading advocate, and the best general lawyer of his time. He was especially great in all jury cases. He had a singular power of making juries averse to himself personally, and politically favorable to his case and to his client. He seemed even to have some art by which he turned that aversion to account, and made it subservient to the purpose of his argument. He did often, no doubt, insinuate scruples in the minds of conscientious jurors politically opposed to him, which made them fear, particularly when conviction was capital, to give a verdict of "guilty," lest it might be the foregone conclusion of prejudice, and not the solemn decision of justice. But most singular of all, O'Connell could not only conceal his opinion of the jurors, but make them suppose it the contrary of what it was. I once heard him before a Cork jury defending men tried for seditious conspiracy. The jury were strong Tory Protestants—the prisoners strong anti-Tory Catholics. As I knew the jury, I had small hope for the prisoners. But as O'Connell advanced in a most ingenious, conciliating, and pathetic speech, I fancied myself in error both as to the character of the jurors and the fate of the arraigned. The jurors, as I thought, were not the men I took them for—men who would find a fragment of treason in the paring of a Papist's nail, and the essence of disloyalty in every hair of O'Connell's wig; they were evidently moved; "tears were in their eyes; all their visage wanned;" I set them down as just, generous, impartial men; and I entirely believed that so did O'Connell. After a short charge and brief absence, they came back with a verdict of "guilty." O'Connell turned towards them with a look of such mock reverence, and such real derision, as it is impossible to describe, and said, "Gentlemen, it is just what I expected from you." In dealing with witnesses, O'Connell was equally a master. In general he was cautious, civil, even polite but in cross-examination of an informer, whom he was sure of breaking down, there was an exhibition of the comic and the terrible. It was a sort of tiger-play, in which a murderous perjurer seemed the object of deadly sport. O'Connell looked amiable; the informer looked angry. O'Connell pulled at his wig and smiled; the informer trembled. O'Connell became droll; the informer in the mean time turned around, as if he were seeking for escape. With O'Connell there was meaning in every gesture—there was purpose in every motion—there was fatal calculation in every question. The people laughed, but the laughter was fitful and spasmodic. There was interest too awful for mirth dependent on the issue; and when, at last, O'Connell gave the blow, which he delayed only in order to strike with certainty—the blow which smote to death the prosecuting testimony—a burst of relief came from the audience, and the cheer that disturbed the forms of the court was the instinct of joy at the saving of innocent lives. I was witness of such a struggle between O'Connell and an informer, and the shout which hailed the lawyer's triumph was such as bursts from the pent-up feelings of a crowd that watches a strong swimmer, buffeting with stormy waves to rescue a fellow-creature from their depths, when he has bounded on dry land with his human brother living in his grasp.

No one, however, denied that O'Connell was a great advocate; neither did any deny that he spoke with wonderful effect to a multitude; but many insisted that he would miserably fail in Parliament. Very great lawyers, very great demagogues, even very great men, have failed in Parliament. O'Connell did *not* fail there; nay, *there* were some of his most distinguished triumphs. He was not, as his opponents prophesied he would be, alarmed or overmatched; on the contrary, he at once took a commanding position in the House, opened there for himself a new sphere of fame,

and was listened to as much for the delight which he gave
by his genius as for the influence which accompanied his
vote. Still, O'Connell has been equaled or excelled at the
bar and in Parliament; in the popular assembly, he has not,
in modern times, been approached. Now, when I say this,
I do not mean that O'Connell had merely the rude and
ready talent which many seem to think is all that is neces·
sary to gain over multitudes — the victories of speech.
O'Connell was not rude; and rudeness in itself is never
power. O'Connell never wrote a speech, and he did not
often make a set oration. His speaking, compared with
such formal efforts, was as a grand sweep of country is to a
little bit of well-trimmed flower-garden. The method of
O'Connell was that of nature, yet not entirely without art—
an art that was all his own—not of models, books, or rules.
Directly or remotely, he made everything he said subser·
vient to his design ; and while to the stop-watch critic he
might seem the least an orator, he was best securing the
success of oratory. O'Connell gave himself most to multitudes, because it was by their means he could best obtain
his object; and always for an object O'Connell spoke—never
for the sake of oratory or for its praise. For such he cared
but little. Like every man of practical and massive genius,
his mind was intent upon an end; and to that his speech
was merely incidental. He was no mere rhetorician; he
was a leader, he was a ruler, and language was only an
instrumentality to his power. If he was ready, it was with
the readiness which intellectual vigilance and constant
industry bestow. His industry he never relaxed. Study
was an essential part of his industry—a part which no fame
or power caused him to neglect. When others were yet
dancing into daylight, he was to be found of wintry morn-
ings in his library—not merely preparing for the battles of
the day, but for the battles of the age. The fruit of such

application was not only various and solid acquirements, professional and general, but also confidence in himself, a secure versatility, and a fearless aptitude. O'Connell was not superficial. He spoke much frequently, and on a great variety of subjects; but he never spoke at random; he never depended on his reputation; he never taxed indulgent partiality; he never went beyond his distinct ideas. He always left the impression that he had mastered the matter which he handled, and had more and better things to say. The mental elasticity which has not been trained into culture, is mere flippancy; the boldness which has not security in knowledge, is but reckless impudence, an uncertain guesswork, or a desperate leaping into darkness. So it never was with O'Connell. From childhood, he was assiduous in the discipline of his faculties. Separately and in combination, he nurtured the strength of each and all. He learned to master and direct this strength at will; to be prepared for every emergency; to leave nothing to chance, and to venture nothing upon risk. He was intellectually constant in observance and acquirement. The demands of his position were ever present to his attention, and, from sustained exercise, his mind had formed the habit of being at the same time active and meditative. There need but the contact and the impulse to elicit from such a mind the flash that dazzles and the bolt that kills. This is no sudden accident, no surprise of happy chance, but the natural effect of cultivated power. And this power, too, was, in O'Connell, a cultivated personality. O'Connell, the man, was in all that he spoke. His knowledge mingled with his nature, and made part of it. All that he got from reading—all that he learned from men—all that he was by nationality, passion, prejudice, or circumstance, entered into the living identity out of which he spoke.

O'Connell was in every way made for a great tribune.

Of commanding height and solid breadth of body—with elevated head, open face, clear, piercing eye, a full, sweet voice, imperturbable cheerfulness, ready wit, vernacular expression, and earnest address—in thought, forcible and direct—in passion, kindly or angry, as the case might be—in impulse ever-varying, from the whisper of emotion to the tempest of excitement, from the hush of prayer to the rage of indignation—O'Connell, as he willed, ruled a popular assembly. He put positions into broad, brief, and homely statements ; he clinched them with pertinent instances, and then he let them take their chance. He dealt much in aphorism, proverb, anecdote. He ever and ever changed his topic and his manner ; and joke, story, insinuation, sarcasm, pathos, merriment, a lofty burst of passion, a bold personality, indignant patriotism, or subdued, conciliating persuasion, came in quick succession—so that all within hearing of his rich, strong, musical voice, became unconcious of fatigue, and wished only the enchantment to continue. He was never boisterous, was not often even vehement; and though he could, and frequently did, rise to transcendentally figurative and impassioned speech, his general matter consisted in simple and earnest argument, in vigorous and homely sense.

It is true that the popular assemblies which O'Connell was accustomed to address were Irish, and that Irish multitudes are susceptible and impassioned is also true. O'Connell had naturally his first school among such multitudes, and a most excellent school it was. No other multitudes can be so electrified by flashes of emotion, or can be so aroused by the expression of a sentiment. They are quick to every allusion of tenderness ; and to wit, humor, and melancholy, they are alive in every fibre. Irish assemblies are not critical, but sympathetic. Eloquence is the child of confidence ; and therefore it is that eloquence springs up in

Irish assemblies as a native instinct. O'Connell in all such assemblies was an incarnation of the Irish soul. His genius was the genius of the nation, and faithfully it gave expression to the native mind of Ireland. One moment in jest and banter, sparkling like the streamlets in Irish glens; in another, like a tempest amidst Irish mountains; now soft as a song to the Irish harp; deep as the wind upon an Irish heath; again mournful as waves around the Irish shores. The people felt their being in the personality of O'Connell; the sorrow of the past and its anger; the love of their country and its afflictions. They felt this in words plain to their intellect, in a poetry bold as their hopes, and in a prophecy as wild as their enthusiasm.

Yet O'Connell's sway as an orator was not limited to an Irish multitude. I heard him in Scotland, when his triumph was as complete as it could have been in Ireland, and more splendid in its circumstances. He stood on Calton Hill, which overlooks the City of Edinburgh. The sky was clear and blue, and a mellowed sunlight spread afar and along upon flood and mountain. Some tens of thousands ranged themselves on the side of the hill, and gazed upon the stalwart man from Ireland. The city lay below them—the city of palaces—the city of romance and story—the city of Mary, of Knox, of Scott—the city of heroic memories and of resplendent genius. The panoramic vision stretched into the infinite, through glory and loveliness; and the eye strayed over frith, and lake, and brae, and highland, until the heart was dazzled and drunk with beauty. To this sublime scenery O'Connell pointed, and opened with an earnest eulogium upon Scotland The Palace of Holyrood was beneath. He called up the shade of Bruce, and quoted Burns. He glorified the beauty of Scottish women, and the bravery of Scottish men. He said to the women that he would tell their sisters beyond the Channel that the daughters of Scotland could feel for the woes of Ireland. He dwelt with enthusiasm on the independence which Scotland had always maintained—giving sovereigns, but receiving none, and allowing no foreign king to keep his foot upon her heathered hills. He spoke of the Covenanters, whose dust made the soil which held it consecrated ground. He did homage to the sanctity of conscience for which these heroic men had fought, prayed, and died. He then turned with an eloquent despondency to Ireland. He pictured the long, the hard, the desolate sway of the oppressor—the humiliation which for centuries had crushed his countrymen, who, never willing to be slaves, had always vainly struggled to be free. He enlarged on the charms of his native land and her miseries—on the loss of her Parliament—the waste of her energies—the decline of her nationality, and the sinking of her heart and hope. Then he gradually arose to more cheerful strains, and closed in the rapture of jubilant and exultant prophecy. After three hours he was silent ; then the collected enthusiasm of that sublime mass burst into one loud shout ; it rent the skies with its boomings, and rolled in long-sounding echoes through the rocks and hills.

IV. I had hoped that, when I came to speak of O'Connell in relation to character, I should be able to do so with fullness of illustration ; but some disjointed hints are all that time will now permit. O'Connell, like every man of powerful activity, was strikingly individual. He was entirely himself, and it was evident that he had the strongest sense of self. A certain *O'Connellism* was noticeable in the very curls of his wig, in the cut of his cap, in the disposal of his cloak, in the whole air of his person—in every movement, in every gesture. The emanation of a strong interior personality gave character to his face, his body, and his motions. We may be told in general terms, that he was tall, large, bulky ; that he had stout limbs and broad shoulders ; that his face was fresh and comely; that his brow was ample ; that his eye was gray, quick, and piercing ; that in his look and walk there was a combination of plebeian force and kingly freedom ; but until we have infused the whole with what I have called *O'Connellism*, we have no image even of the outward man. We must see in the big body the struggling soul of a great agitator. The face that seems placid at a distance, reveals, as we look more closely, thoughts of discontent, which only lean men are said to have. Sternness, even melancholy, is seen in those features wherein we had fancied only smiles ; and in that gray eye, which, to the passing look, seems to sparkle with merriment and mischief, are observable, to a more careful gaze, depths that reach down to passions into which had come the anger and the grief of centuries.

O'Connell was no less national than individual. Perhaps we might more correctly say that nationality was incorporated, identified with his individual consciousness. To think, speak, act, was to him to live in the life of Ireland. Therein he "must either live or have no life." There can be no doubt that O'Connell loved Ireland, and that in all his measures he contemplated her interest and her glory. If he accepted in his later years a munificent income, he gave up a large one in giving up his practice. The revenue which he received was gratefully contributed. O'Connell spent it generously ; hoarded nothing ; died poor, and to his family left little but his fame. Some have had doubts of his faith in Repeal : those who were nearest to him had no such doubts. His most intimate companions assert that he not only regarded the return of the Irish Parliament as practicable, but as certain—not only as certain, but as near.

All individualism and nationality, to be otherwise than cynical or bigoted, must belong to a character of cordial humanity—must be alive to its affections, its charities, and its rights. As to the affections of humanity, no one can accuse O'Connell as having been wanting in them. Some of O'Connell's allusions to his family in his public speeches might have exposed him to jocular criticism, if it were not for the *love* in them that immediately won men's better feelings, and those gleams of domestic sunshine which often threw a gracious illumination over the arid spaces of political discussion. The friends who were the most with O'Connell, and who knew the most of him, were the most attached to him. O'Connell had that tendency to sing which belongs to kindly natures and to genial tempers. He was constantly breaking out into snatches of ancient song—sometimes from an English ballad, sometimes from a Latin hymn. He delighted in hearing and telling old stories. He had that love for children which is ever an instinct of tender and of noble hearts. He had, too, that generous reverence for woman which brave and honorable men always feel; and passages are in his speeches so inspired with this sentiment as to rise to the poetry of eloquence. He was hospitable; and in the harmony of his household festivities, he was glad to forget the contests of the world. I will not dare to say so much for the spirit of O'Connell's public speeches as I have said for that of his private intercourse. Yet even here we must not judge too sternly. O'Connell's position was between extremes. He was a man the most applauded, and a man the most decried—a man in all Christendom the most loved and the most hated; and if he was, as he himself said, "the best abused man in Europe," it must also be admitted that he was the best abuser. But, with few exceptions, there was nothing sardonic or satanic in the political combats of O'Connell. Even his abuse had a sort of buoyant exaggeration that made it almost kindly. Besides, in these combats, O'Connell was too sure of victory to be malicious. He had an intellectual enjoyment, a happy self-satisfaction, which always kept his spirit in them free from rancor. One night, as Lord Lyndhurst was in the full career of an eloquent tirade against O'Connell, O'Connell himself entered the House of Lords. The noble orator was climbing to the pinnacle of a climax, and reached it by applying to the Liberator the famous apostrophe of Cicero to Catiline. "What do you think of that?" said a friend to O'Connell. "Oh, simply as it should be," replied O'Connell; "I have just come from the Freemason's Tavern, where I have been abusing him. It is only tit for tat, and turn about is fair play." Most of O'Connell's attacks were in this spirit of reciprocity; and though he did sometimes apply an epithet or phrase which burned ineffaceably into his opponent's memory, and which, when dead, might be found stamped upon his heart, as Mary of England said that "Calais" would be on hers, it was seldom that such invectives much more than repaid their provocation. O'Connell was never implacable, and it was easy at any time to soften or conciliate him. No one was ever more fiercely, or more ably, or more successfully O'Connell's antagonist than Lord Stanley, aftewards Lord Derby. On one occasion, when O'Connell had spoken in his usual strain on the wrongs to Ireland, Lord Stanley asserted that he was as much a friend to Ireland as was O'Connell. "If that be so," replied O'Connell, "you can be no enemy of mine. Let our hearts shake hands."

As to O'Connell's sense of human charities and rights, we have every proof which testimony can offer that he was merciful, tolerant, liberal; that, morally, socially, and politically, he held in deepest reverence the claims of man. He was in the van of every movement that favored liberty, or that aimed at the elevation of unfavored multitudes. He was opposed to capital punishment; he disliked war. He showed a want of political foresight when he supposed, as he did late in life, that moral force would take the place of war. But this says nothing against his moral feeling. He detested war—not from want of courage or want of manliness, but from the force of a sympathetic imagination, which conceived vividly of war, of its atrocities and miseries. He never could overleap these to the something beyond on which most minds find rest. He had by the necessity of his temperament to pass through the vision of carnage and death, and long before he got near to the other side, he sickened, staggered, and retreated. I need not say that he was an enemy to slavery, and that for the zeal with which he denounced it, he was in turn, throughout America, denounced. But all that O'Connell said and did in this cause, he said and did in pure and most disinterested principle. He in no narrow struggle for his own creed, forgot his kind ; and his greatest exultation was, that every success in contest for the right, in favor of any class or people, was still a victory gained in the grand battle of universal emancipation. He insisted always that man has rights inseparable from his nature—rights which lie at the foundation of morals and society—rights which cannot be bought, which cannot be sold, and which imply as the essential of rational and immortal manhood—that the individuality of the human person can by no law be human property. This logic of spirit, of mind, of life, of equity, and of nature, which justified his own claims, he argued, would justify every man in asserting the rights of his humanity. The logic which he maintained for himself, he applied to all; for he believed that all had in the God-given soul the same divine and eternal title to the liberties and dignities of intelligent existence that he had. In this conviction he lived and labored ; it was his earliest—it was his latest ; he fought its good fight to the last, and even unto death he kept its faith.

JOHN PHILPOT CURRAN.

I PROPOSE to speak to you on the life, character, and genius of a great man—I mean JOHN PHILPOT CURRAN.

I begin with some hurried allusions to the leading events of Curran's biography.

John Philpot Curran was born in 1750, on the 24th day of July, in New Market, a small town in the County of Cork, Ireland. He was the son of James Curran, seneschal of the manor, a minor sort of local magistrate. His mother's maiden name was Sarah Philpot. This name enters into Curran's baptismal designation, and has become immortal in his fame. Curran ascribed to his mother his inheritance of intellect, and to his father that of a small person and of homely features. But his father was a man of respectable education, and but for *that*, Curran's inheritance of natural gifts, whencesoever it came, might have been to little purpose. Of inborn genius, and the son of a man well cultivated, it was in the order and the destiny of character that he should aspire.

Aided by the Rev. Nathaniel Boyse, the Protestant clergyman of the place, he was prepared for college. He entered the Dublin University as a sizar. He had a good classical education, and he was fond of classics to the end of his life. In due time he went through his law studies in London. Though subjected to severe scarcity of funds, he bore his privations with cheerfulness and gayety. Frugal and laborious, the pleasures and pomp of a great metropolis excited in him neither envy nor despondency; and he closed his sojourn in it without having contracted either debts or vices. Curran married in 1774, and was called to the bar in 1775. His practice became rapidly eminent and lucrative. But his practice in Chancery was impeded early by the judge, his political opponent, the Lord Chancellor Fitzgibbon, Earl of Clare. Curran estimated his aggregate loss at £30,000. On grounds political, professional, or personal, Curran fought four duels. First, with the Hon. Mr. St. Leger, brother to Lord Doneraile ; second, with John Fitzgibbon, the Attorney-General for Ireland ; third, with Major Hobart, the Irish Secretary of State ; fourth, with a lawyer named Egan. Egan and Curran had been friends. The duel arose out of a casual dispute, and is only memorable as giving occasion to Curran for one of his witty sallies. Egan, a man of huge bulk, complained of the disproportionate risk between himself and his antagonist. "Have my size," said Curran, "chalked upon yours, and let every shot outside it go for nothing." This was in Ireland the era of the pistol.

Curran in 1797 closed his parliamentary career, and was approaching the culmination of his forensic grandeur. Curran's eloquence in Parliament has not been ranked with his eloquence in the courts of law. I have no time to examine the grounds of the comparison, or the truth of the decision. It is enough to say that Curran's character and genius are seen as distinctly in Parliament as in the courts. We see in it, on all occasions, the spirit of manliness, wisdom, and justice broadly and vigorously exhibited. Great as has since been the advance of enlargement and of enlightenment in the application of political principles to the government of society, it has not yet gone beyond the truths which, amidst the clash of factions and in the worst of times, Curran urged, defended, and reiterated. Whatever the most fervent oratory could do, he did, in warning, entreaty, threatening, and argument. All in vain. The prophet's words were true, but none would believe their report. Ere long the prophecies became facts, in blood, in crime; and of all tragedies in history, the record of these facts in the struggle of 1798 is one of the most terrible. The scorned forebodings of the patriotic and the wise, as well as the prudence of their liberal exhortations, were soon terribly proved sound by the calamities which followed in the deadly battle-field, in the crowded dungeons, in the loaded gibbets, in the despairing wretchedness, and in the pitiless atrocities with which the neglect of advice and argument covered the afflicted kingdom.

Curran had severe personal and domestic sorrows. The abortive attempt at insurrection in 1803, and the murder of his friend, Lord Kilwarden, were heavy blows against his peace. A heavier blow still was the concealed attachment of his daughter for Robert Emmett, and the tragic close of Emmett's life; but the heaviest blow of all was the desertion of his wife with a profligate clergyman named Sandys, after she and her husband had lived for a quarter of a century together. She afterwards repented, and was supported by Curran's bounty.

In the short-lived Whig ministry of 1806, Curran was made a Chancery judge, as Master of the Rolls—an appointment which was to him more a grief than a glory, and one for which neither his natural genius nor his professional experience gave him fitness. The last public speech which he ever made was in 1812, as a candidate for the representation of Newry in the imperial Parliament. He was defeated—and after that, listening multitudes heard his electric voice no more. Three or four years before his death, Curran resigned his judicial office; and on the 14th of October, 1817, he died at Brompton, near London, being above sixty-seven years of age. In 1837 his remains were removed to Glasnevin, in the suburbs of Dublin, and there they rest in his loved and native soil. Choicer ashes than Curran's, Irish earth does not contain ; and the fire of more impassioned eloquence than his, never inspired human clay.

Like Robert Burns, Curran loved popular sports, and was nurtured amidst popular traditions.

Curran identified himself in feeling, interests, and objects with the Irish people ; but he was peculiarly attached to the humbler classes. He understood the Irish people in their virtues and their vices, in their sufferings, and in their wrongs. He was their true friend, and if, at times, he justly blamed, on all right occasions he as generously praised. They in return loved him ; they loved him with an affection of admiration and enthusiasm which was no base idolatry, but a noble worship. Curran was conscious of this popular love to him ; but being conscious also that he deserved it, he had nothing in him of the demagogue. His intercourse with the people was marked by cordiality and dignity, and his demeanor was as simple as his spirit was sincere. His personal manners were unpresuming and unpretending. He was courteous, with that genuine courtesy which is easy, unobtrusive, informal, and that loses the sense of self in sympathy with others. Much as he talked, he was never his own subject, as most talkers are. In this he was the contrast of Erskine, his most celebrated forensic contemporary. On a certain occasion he administered to this vain and great orator a severe rebuke. "Come, come," said Erskine once to Curran, "was not Grattan intimidated at the idea of a first appearance before the British Parliament?" "Indeed, my Lord," answered Curran, "I do not think he was, nor do I think he had any reason to be. When he succeeded so splendidly with so eloquent and so discriminating a body as the Irish House of Commons, he need not have apprehended much from any foreign criticism." "Well, but, Curran, did he not confess he was afraid?" insisted Erskine—"did you not hear him say so?" "Indeed, my good Lord, I never did. Mr. Grattan is a very modest man—he never speaks of himself."

Curran was the delight of a wide social circle, with which he always maintained kindly relations. He was ardent in his profession and in politics, but in neither was he vindictive. At his own table he was generous; at the tables of other men he was genial; always, he was humorous—rarely, intemperate; and to the very last, while his mind could govern his words, his sayings had the stamp of power. Even when mental gloom had shut out for ever the light of happiness, and mortal disease took away all hope of health, the special originality of his wit and humor did not forsake him. Even in the breaking up of nature, there was still his genius, in its extraordinary combination of the serious and the gay, of the brilliant and thoughtful soul; it was still there, in its wonderful union of idealism and oddity, of irony and sympathy—of the mirth which is bred in the heart of melancholy, and of the fancy which relieves despondency by laughter. Throughout life, Curran's conversation seems to have given to all that heard it the pleasure of constant enchantment and surprise. A sense of wonder and delight appears to excite all who allude to it.

In obedience to what lecture-hearers expect, I present two or three sayings of Curran's out of numbers which tradition insists on calling examples of his wit and humor. But I do this almost under protest, for the wit and humor of Curran so interveined his mental life, that they cannot be illustrated by posthumous dissection, or exhibited in bit-and-bit specimens. I may properly—as an Irishman, privileged to blunder—begin by showing Curran's humor in a saying which was not Curran's. It was that of his colored servant, who refused to live with him any longer. Curran wondered why he desired to go, and entreated him to stay. "No, massa," said he, "I cannot live longer with you; I am losing my health; you make me laugh too much." Curran was told that a lawyer, who was dirty in his person and sparing of his money, had set out from Dublin to Cork, with one shirt and one guinea. "Yes," said Curran, "and he will change neither of them till he returns." This saying is the carcasm of good humor. Sometimes his sayings are whimsical and droll. To this effect was his contest with a Cork fish-woman. She was gaining such advantage on him, that he was for retreat. But retreat, as Curran observes, was to be achieved with dignity. "So, drawing myself disdainfully up," he goes on, "I said—Madam, I scorn all further discourse with such an individual." "*Individual!* you wagabone!" she exclaimed, "I'm no more an individual than your mother was."

At times his drollery is touched with pathos, and merges into poetry. One morning, near to Curran's death, the doctor observed to him that he coughed with more difficulty than he had on the preceding evening. "That is very surprising," said Curran, "for I have been practising all night." In a less dangerous position, when Curran feared he had a premonition of palsy, the physician assured him there was no danger of the kind. "Then," said Curran, "I am to consider what has lately happened was a runaway knock, and not a notice to quit."

To come back once more to the grotesque. The wig of a stupid barrister was awry. Curran smiled. "Do you see anything ridiculous in my wig?" said the barrister. "No," replied Curran, "nothing but the head." A pretentious witness feigned ignorance of Irish, and spoke in English badly. "I see, Sir, how it is," said Curran, "you are more

ashamed of knowing your own language than of not knowing any other." Many in spirit resemble this poltroon ;
they are ashamed of being Irish, and yet are often themselves the disgrace of Ireland.

I quote these sayings in obedience to popular desire, and
in reverence to traditional affection. But in the intellectual
estimate of them, I entirely agree with Thomas Davis.
"What avails it to us," he says, "to know the capital puns
which Curran made in college, or the smart epigrams he
said to Macklin? These things are the empty shells of his
deep-sea mind—idle things for idlers to classify. But for
men who, though in the ranks of life, are anxious to ordei
their minds by the standard of some commanding spirit—oi
for governing minds, who want to commune with his spirit
in brotherly sympathy and instruction—to such men the
puns are rubbish, and the jokes are chaff."

Curran had an unconquerable aversion to the labor of
writing. In the composition of his speeches, Curran
trusted only to meditation and memory. He tried at first
to write his speeches, but immediately gave up the attempt.
Writing was not to him an aid, but an embarrassment. He
much loved walking, and as he walked, he loved to think. In
these thoughtful walkings much he mused, and out of these
musings came many of the electric brilliancies of his speeches.
He loved music too; and having some skill on the violencello,
while he poured along the strings some love song, or war
song, or death song, he composed and elaborated his orations.
But though Curran did not write his speeches, he was no
merely extemporaneous speaker, as indeed no great speaker
can ever be. His preparation was one of careful and most
thorough labor. What he was to speak, he made ready to
his thought, that it might also be ready to his tongue ; and
this he did by toil, which it required the utmost ambition
and enthusiasm to undertake or to bear. Curran was a

man of genius, and because he was such, he was a man of labor. He neglected nothing which could perfect his gifts, but was honestly vigilant that, in all which work could do, his gifts should not be vulgarly or profanely spoken of. He trained an obstinate voice into musical obedience ; by the habit of nobly thinking, he gave glory to homely features; and nature blessed him with an eye that, large, grand, and deep, was as variable as the phases of the sky—living as the spirit mind—soft and tender to pity or console—gay and sportive to amuse or delight—earnest and solemn "to threaten or command.

I do not propose to give a critical review of Curran's speeches, but simply to estimate the spirit of his oratory. The measure of time proper to a lecture will not permit more, and if it would, more were hardly possible. We have no complete or correct report of Curran's speeches, but only hurried notes, which give us merely hints of what the speeches actually spoken must have been. The reports have preserved, indeed, the idiom of his manner, of his mind, but evidently they convey no adequate idea of his rich and rounded power.

I shall only glance at a few of the speeches which are most marked by Curran's manner, and characterized by his genius.

His speech in defence of Peter Finnerty, as the printer of what was deemed a libel on the Irish Government, is very able. It is powerful in logic, law, and passion—especially passion—the passion of angry despair, of patriotic sorrow ; calling into use all the sardonic or sportive fancy, all the faculties of ridicule, scorn, irony, and sarcasm which his wonderful talent had so sovereignly at command. This speech is one of the noblest defences that was ever made for the rights of the citizen and the liberty of the press.

The defence of Finney, prosecuted for high treason in

1798, has passages terrifically ironical in their dissection of the character of Jemmy O'Brien, the hireling spy and informer of the government. The speech for Oliver Bond is distinguished by gravity, reflectiveness, and melancholy—burning up, at times, into the flame of consuming energy. The speech against Major Sirr carries irony, ridicule, contempt, hatred, and scorn to the utmost limits of language. In the plea for Owen Kirwan, the advocate feels that he cannot save his client, and becomes despondently eloquent on the condition of his country. Curran's argument for Judge Johnson is tender, learned, classical, and is famous for a passage in which he alludes to a former friendship with Lord Avonmore, who presided on the trial—a passage which more than renewed their friendship; for the barrister and the magistrate had for some time been alienated.

The speech for Hamilton Rowan is grand and large. The speech for Henry Shears, and that for Lady Fitzgerald, are remarkable for pathos and moral beauty. The speech for Shears was made under the most dismal and discouraging circumstances. The trial began at nine o'clock in the morning, and fifteen hours of vigilance and hard work had been gone through when Curran was called on, after midnight, to begin his speech for the defence. He requested a short interval—no so much, he said, for repose as for recollection. The request was refused; and, in a condition of the last exhaustion, he commenced his terrific task. The speech against Headfort contains Curran's best excellencies, and all the elements of the highest forensic oratory. This was his last great effort at the bar. I have in this enumeration observed no strict chronological order.

I will occupy the remainder of the lecture in giving my general idea of Curran's eloquence. I am impressed deeply with its moral simplicity, and its moral elevation.

Curran found the data of his forensic or legislative rea-

soning in the common nature of man; and the knowledge
of that nature which genius, observation, and experience
gave him, became the substance of his logic. He appealed
directly to intuitive sentiment and thought—to humanity in
its everlasting principles of morality. Curran's power of
reaching the moral life of the inward man—that part of
human nature which is not dependent on customs or enactments, which is not local or temporary, but universal and
everlasting—is one of the most obvious qualities of his eloquence. Accordingly, Curran is constantly forsaking the
logic of law for the logic of life—piercing into hidden sources
of emotion, awakening slumbering compunctions, or recalling forgotten truths—giving fresh colors to the web of
faded associations—carrying his reasoning upward to the
highest appeal, or carrying it outward into broad and
ethical relations. This is what gives to his eloquence its
heartfelt impressiveness, its elevation, and its rectitude.
Curran, with all his subtlety of mind, with all his intellectual
ingenuity and inventiveness, is seldom sophistical. He
speaks from no cunningly-contrived device, or artificially-
arranged theory; he has indeed a very marked mannerism,
but he despised tricks of thought and tricks of tongue.
From such he was saved not merely by his genius, but
also by the momentous concerns which called forth his
most memorable speeches. These concerns were too
weighty to admit of quibbles, and if they did, quibbles
were beneath Curran. He tried to give to forensic discussion the grandeur of moral reason ; he tried often, like a
valiant prophet, to argue with the consciences of men,
whose passions, as he knew, had already condemned his
clients. He rose to the height of this great argument ; he
sustained it by philosophy and ethics ; he strengthened it
by the solemn fears of a judgment to come, and by the
mysteries of eternal retribution. An appeal to such ultimate

laws was in Curran an unostentatious sincerity ; it was the habit of his mind, and we feel the influence of it in all his eloquence. The great passages in this eloquence are great in the boldness of their moral grandeur.

What next impresses me in Curran's eloquence is its imaginativeness. It is not essential to an orator to have the constitution of a poet. Great orators have been who were not in the least poets. But though not essential, the poetic spirit, especially in union with impassioned imagination, grandly aids the orator. Such poetic spirit was Curran's, and such impassioned imagination. These qualities gave to his oratory its richness of beauty, its elevation, its music, and its magic ; above all, that electricity of idea and of thought which ever and ever darted through his speaking in flashes of inspiration. "The mind of the judge," said Curran, pleading against the authority of a cruel and obsolete statute—"the mind of the judge is the repository of the law that *does exist*, not of the law that *did* exist ; nor does the mercy and justice of our law recognize so disgraceful an office as that of a judge becoming a sort of administrator to a dead statute, and collecting the debts of blood that were due to it in its lifetime." But in the speech against the Marquis of Headfort for the seduction of Mrs. Massy, I find a still more impressive illustration—one in the highest degree pathetic and imaginative. He pleads for ample damages, and thus proceeds :—

"The learned counsel has told you that this unfortunate woman is not to be estimated at forty thousand pounds. Fatal and unquestionable is the truth of this assertion. Alas ! gentlemen, she is no longer worth anything. Faded, fallen, degraded, she is worth less than nothing. It is not her present value you are to weigh, but it is her value at the time when she sat basking in a husband's love, with the blessing of Heaven on her head, and its purity in her heart

—when she sat among her family and administered the morality of the parental board. Estimate that past value, compare it with its present deplorable diminution, and it may lead you to form some judgment of the injury, and the requisite extent of the compensation. And yet, as the advocate argues, the injury in such cases as this has no outward measure, and admits of no worldly compensation. In any other action, he says, it is easy to calculate. If a tradesman's arm is cut off, you can measure the loss which he has sustained ; but the wound of feelings and the agony of the heart cannot be judged by any standard with which I am acquainted. And you are unfairly dealt with when you are called on to appreciate the present suffering of the husband by the present guilt, delinquency, and degradation of his wife. As well might you, if called on to give compensation to a man for the murder of his dearest friend, find the measure of the injury by weighing the ashes of the dead. But it is not, gentlemen of the jury, by weighing the ashes of the dead that you would estimate the loss of the survivor." Here we have no piling of epithets, no multiplication of tropes, which many persons mistakingly- confound with the action of imagination; but we have that working of the spirit with the inward essences of thought and life, which is most truly the action of imagination. In a different manner, alluding to the Attorney-General, who accused a newspaper article, which he adjudged a libel, of being scurrilous and disrespectful. "He abuses it," says Curran, "for the foul and insolent familiarity of its address. I *do* clearly understand his idea. He considers the freedom of the press to be the license of offering, that paltry adulation which no man ought to stoop to utter or to hear. He supposes the freedom of the press ought to be like the freedom of a king's jester, who, instead of reproving the faults of which majesty ought to be ashamed, is base and

cunning enough, under the mask of servile and adulatory
censure, to stroke down and pamper those vices of which it
is foolish enough to be vain."

Curran's eloquence is full of allusions, epithets, turns of
expression, that show not only how rich his imagination
was, but also how original. Imaginativeness is particularly
striking in his descriptive passages. In these passages,
scenes, persons, objects seem to have an intensified reality.
The whole region of the ideal seems entirely at his command; and at his bidding the creations of thought become
things of life. He is never visionary, and never merges the
particular in the general. Vigorous and able speaking is
common and abundant. Men do not wonder at it. But
the speaking of Curran must have seemed to his hearers
almost a miracle—the instinctive, spontaneous, outpouring
of all that is extraordinary in passion, invention, image,
idea, thought, and word. A great speaker is one in a
thousand of good speakers; but to be eloquent is to be one
man in a thousand, even of great speakers. It is in this
sense that Curran was eloquent. The lawyer disappeared
in the man, and we lose sight of the advocate in the orator
and the poet. "I have met Curran at Holland House,"
wrote Byron. "His imagination is beyond human, and his
humor is perfect. I never met his equal." The poet-peer
improves even on this. "Curran," he exclaims—"Curran's
the man who struck me most. Such imagination! There
never was anything like it. He was wonderful even to me,
who had seen so many remarkable men of the time. The
riches of his Irish imagination were exhaustless. I have
heard that man speak more poetry than I have ever seen
written, though I saw him seldom, and but occasionally."

Curran's fancy was equal to his imagination, and fancy
was the chief ingredient of his wit. His humor was even
greater than his wit. But both wit and humor gave way

to sterner qualities in all his higher eloquence. Curran
was strong in the force of passion ; but the passion which
fired his eloquence was ever mighty and indignant against
cruelty and wrong. This it was which made him above
most orators a master of denunciation, of invective, and of
ridicule. For clemency and justice he was bold and brave ;
towards oppressors and tyrants he was scornful and fierce.
He despised baseness as he hated wrong. It is when this
godly anger and this human sympathy move him, that he
rises to those commanding passages of eloquence which are
the genuine utterances of his greater nature. The supreme
tasks of oratory which have made Curran historical, were
too gloomy for smiles—too replete with grief for laughter;
and Curran was not the man to trifle with such tasks. He
could not "bandy quirks, or think a deadly bloodshed but
a jest," while his client stood face to face with mortal doom
and that sympathetic humanity which gladdened the banquet could only be thoughtful and tragic in the ante-
chamber of the scaffold. In trials for high treason in his
day, the criminal court was just such an ante-chamber.
Not only the danger of his client, but the affliction of his
country compelled him to be solemn. And the man has not
breathed that ever loved his country more than Curran
loved Ireland. But Curran's love of country had its roots
in the love of humanity. His love of country went into the
love of kind, and transcended passion. It broke down the
limits of patriotic circumscription, and rose to the enthusiastic prophecy of liberty for man. Of such purport is the
celebrated passage in his speech for Hamilton Rowan, on
the genius of "Universal Emancipation."

To this result of universal emancipation all generous and
hopeful souls look forward—not in the spirit of British law,
as Curran says, but in the spirit of human right—not within the limits of the British earth, but within the wide

compass of the world. It is a progress which every advance in knowledge, in liberal-mindedness, and in goodness helps along. But this emancipation is not from one kind of bondage alone; for such would not be "universal," but very partial emancipation. There are many kinds of bondage: bondage of mind as well as bondage of body—slaveries of appetite and lust, of gain and greed, that blind reason and debase the heart. There are social slaveries—slaveries of class, of custom, of opinion, and, with them, corresponding sets of bigotries, in each of which we see reconciled the submission of servitude and the arrogance of despotism. That is an inadequate idea of slavery which gives it to us only in its extreme condition. Men enslave others, or wish to enslave them, in manifold forms; and they do so in the degree that they are themselves enslaved. When men begin to understand fully the best liberty, they desire that all should share it, and share it to the utmost. When the true spirit of liberty—that is, the spirit of humanity and of right, of equity and of charity—has power in the world, then, verily, it can be said of man, that "his soul walks abroad in her majesty, that his body swells beyond the measure of his chains, and that he stands redeemed, regenerated, and disenthralled by the irresistible genius of Universal Emancipation."

Curran has suffered the critical penalty which every brilliant and emotional man has to suffer. His force of thought is not recognized by reason of his force of passion, and the rectitude of his judgment is decried in the praise of his imagination. Many portions of Curran's speeches are as prosaic as the dullest formalist could desire; many portions would also please the greatest thinker in their plain sense, solid argument, and calm sobriety. Such portions are seldom, by his ordinary admirers, considered eloquent. To me they are often the most eloquent, because they are the most serious, the most simple, the most logical, and the most to the purpose. But a speaker must be judged not in the fragments, but in the wholeness of his power. More than almost any other speaker, Curran must be so judged, or the judgment will be inadequate or untrue. Curran has been no less depreciated as a lawyer than as a reasoner. He knew, it is probable, more law than a learned jurist would give him credit for, because such a man could have no respect for any attainments short of erudition. This, I suppose, Curran had not; and yet he had, I apprehend, sufficient legal knowledge to serve his need. The legal learning of Curran would be small in comparison with that of a Holt, an Eldon, a Marshall, a Story, or a Kent, and yet in the sphere of his practice be other than contemptible. Curran was, however, by nature an orator, and not his ignorance, so much as his instincts, unfitted him for technical arguments. But men may underrate Curran's logical or legal intellect, and yet be very unworthy to criticise it. There are men whom devotees may censure, that, behind their very defects, have religion enough to make an assembly of pietists. So there are men to whom pedants deny the credit of cogent thinking, that have more intellect in their little fingers than such pedants have in their souls and bodies. Curran, like every supreme speaker, was always more occupied with the spirit of reason than with the machineries of syllogism.

I cannot omit referring to the dramatic powers of Curran's eloquence. Every great orator has the art of the player, and something more. The player has the speech that he speaks set down for him; the orator not only speaks his speech, but makes it. But the player and the orator may assist each other. The orator may study the ideal of speech in the player; the player may study the actual of speech in the orator. Curran, I think, must have surpassed any man who ever rose to oratory in English, in melting the ideal and the actual into speech. Of all orators, Curran was one of the most earnest, and he was also one of the most dramatic. Having this genius from nature, destiny gave him a stage appropriate to its exercise. Criminal trials in Ireland have been usually dramatic. I speak of Ireland as it used to be. Especially in disturbed times, the national character shows itself to the extreme in all its peculiar qualities—in its picturesqueness, oddity, and originality—in its impassioned ardor—in its wealth of phrase, of pathos, and of humor. The most dramatic trials in Ireland have ever been those connected with agrarian, seditious, or revolutionary passions. The accused have risked their lives, but they have not, among the people, lost their character. The smallest theft would have covered them with disgrace ; but agrarian or political offences often raised them into popular dignity. At all events, they appear on trial entirely free from obloquy. An Irish court-house is then a theatre for drama more exciting than poet ever created—drama that is thoroughly human and profoundly real. Striking contrasts of life, of condition, even of history and of race, are there. In the mass, the audience are peasantry, clean and hardy. The prisoner at the bar is one of themselves. They feel *with* him, and they feel *for* him. No word or motion that concerns him escapes their attention. His relations and neighbors are usually close to him. Learned judges, robed and ermined, listen in all the gravity of silence to witness and to counsel. Irish judges were in past times, and of such times we speak, seldom allied to the prisoner either by the sympathy of creed, or by the kindred of race. The passions of common life are among the jury — sometimes with the prisoner, and sometimes against him. The attorney-general or the solicitor-general, soberly, solemnly, solidly, makes out his case, and brings

his argument to a conclusion as fatal as the certainty of
doom. The evidence of circumstances and of the prisoner's
accomplices sustains him. The defending advocate hopes
against hope, and struggles manfully when hope is over.
In this wrestling against despair for his client's life, the
advocate often becomes sublime, above aught that tragedy
can show. This frequently was the sublimity of Curran.
The verdict announces the catastrophe; then burst out the
groan, the wail, the irrepressible agony of desolated hearts.
But in ordinary trials of this kind there would be some
element of suspense, and always the possibility of a doubt.
The advocate or the audience would not be overpowered by
the dreadful gloom of a legal predestination. Some rays of
promise still glimmer through the darkness; and while this
is so, no Irish court-house will be void of humor. The
judges will smile—perhaps they may mildly jest; the lawyers will banter; the witnesses will beat counsel in retort
and joke; the jury will laugh outright; the audience will
share in the exhilaration. The matter, as a whole, is a
tragedy—but a tragedy of the Shakespearean kind, in which,
though death comes at the close, mirth and folly play their
parts along the way. But the treason-trials of 1798, in
which Curran was concerned, admitted of no such mixture.
The tragedy of those trials was purely Greek—a tragedy in
which death and doom rule from the beginning to the end.
Imagine a court-house after midnight dimly lighted. Two
brothers sit wearied in the dock. Stern and still the judges
sit wearied on the bench; they are faintly recognized by
their crimson robes and their solemn faces. The jury are
grouped away in shadow. Government swearers and orators have been for long and many hours doing their utmost.
The fate of the brothers is already sealed. Curran, woefully
worn out, is called on to defend them. He begs for time to
meditate and rest, but he begs in vain. Then, in that dreary

night, encompassed by all that was chill and cheerless, he speaks on for hours with grand and despairing eloquence. While he speaks, corpses of strangled clients for whom he lately pleaded are not yet cold ; and before the sun shall twice arise, the brothers will be corpses for whom now he pleads. Was not this tragedy? Ay, tragedy of a darker terror than Eschylus ever wrote ; and Curran was equal to it in all the fearfulness of its power.

An element in the eloquence of Curran to be specially noted is that of pathos. In pathos he was above most orators, in whatever sphere of speech, or in whatever line. This was partly owing to his temperament. He was constitutionally pensive. He was of a thoughtful imagination, much given to solitary musing. Like the Jacques of Shakespeare, "by often rumination, he was constantly wrapt in a most humorous sadness." Full as he was of mirth and fancy, he was yet more a man of meditation and sensibility. He loved the lonely walk, and he loved also to play old Irish airs on his violincello, while he brooded over those thoughts which were to become in speech the voice impassioned, sweet, and strong of a mighty pleader. And here I may also observe that Curran's pathos was in part owing to his country. In the twofold tendencies of the Irish to merriment and melancholy, Curran was a representative character. He could set the table in a roar, but he could also move a multitude to tears. It was not women only that heaved with convulsive sobs when he drew pictures of suffering and crime — bearded men grew faint, and even hackneyed officials showed symptoms of humanity.

Another incitement to the pathetic in the spirit and speaking of Curran came from the times in which he lived. These were momentous times, and to any man who was a conscientious agent in them, they were full of awful duty. But Curran worked in them with more than conscience, and he felt the crime and cruelty that darkened them with more than offended virtue—he felt them with the keenest grief and pain. The evil of the times pierced him to the soul, and made him passionately sad. His intellect and his heart were steeped in sorrow. He pleaded pathetically and passionately for his clients, but the great affliction was in the woes of his country. No one can read even the meagre reports which we have of Curran's speeches without feeling how profoundly his life was in the cause of Ireland, and how his heart was bowed down under the burden of her calamities. This interest in his country is the central inspiration of his eloquence, and in his day his country was clad in mourning.

Ever and ever the spirit of patriotic lamentation comes into utterance, and cannot be suppressed. These large feelings make Curran's pathos great. There is nothing more contemptible than maudlin or affected pathos—pathos which has not the truth of life or the grace of acting—pathos which is but a mockery of the stage, without its poetry or its art. Such was *not* the pathos of Curran's eloquence. His pathos was not simulated or professional; it was natural; it was in the man. It was no cheap moral or melodramatic ranting, at which silly people whimper; it was genuine, manly, muscular—always justified by cause and circumstance. It was the utterance of conviction; it was true to terrible realities; sometimes like a prophetic cry amidst a wilderness of graves—a wail over measureless calamities, and sometimes like a mournful psalm which might have been chanted by the rivers of Babylon. And this strain well suited Curran; for he was by natural constitution both melancholy and musical. He was the most lyrical of speakers. He was one of those whose thoughts make melody in conception, and which coming into words are born into song. All his faculties were musical: his intellect, his imagination, his emotions ; and these all having spontaneous union and utterance in his eloquence, made that eloquence the witchcraft and magic that it was. This made it different from all other eloquence—not in power, but in kind ; it was not so much an eloquence of logic as of enchantment—not so much like the sword of Goliah as like the harp of David.

What I last note in the eloquence of Curran is its courage. Danger is the test of manhood, whether in action or in words; and hardly a speech historically great has ever been spoken but at momentous hazard. This, here, I must simply assert. All who are conversant with the subject know that the assertion can be proved. No speaker ever had more courage than Curran, and no speaker ever more needed it. His courage was physical, mental, moral, political, constant, and consistent. Mortal combat was in the times of Curran frequently the cost of a word, and this cost, more than once, Curran was obliged to pay. At the very entrance of his active and professional life, he gave a magnanimous example of moral independence and physical intrepidity. An aged Catholic priest, Father Neale, in the discharge of his sacred duty, at the injunction of his bishop, excited the anger of a Protestant nobleman. The profligate aristocrat, Lord Donervaile, accompanied by his brother, Mr. St. Leger, rode to the old man's cottage, called him out from his devotions, and, at his own door, beat him almost to death. But such was the dominion of Protestant ascendency at the time, that lawyers refused to be concerned for a Catholic priest. Curran immediately undertook the case, and fearlessly and fiercely stigmatized the culprits. Considering the power which these culprits possessed, as Ireland was then ruled, the audacity of a young barrister in daring it was to some heroic, to others insolent, to all a novelty and a wonder. Curran gained a verdict against the nobleman, fought a duel with the nobleman's brother, whom, in the course of the trial, he had characterized as a ruffian and a coward. The venerable man whose wrongs he so eloquently exposed, in quitting this mortal life soon after, sent for the generous advocate, and gave him his dying benediction. But well might Jeffrey, while commenting in the Edinburgh Review on these events, express his astonishment that such things could ever have been. Demosthenes, it was said, ran away from battle. This was probably a calumny. But against Curran no such calumny was possible. Cicero has been accused not only of being a trimmer, but of being timid; and Mirabeau, it has been alleged, sold the popular cause for regal bribery. But Curran was as bold politically as he was personally, and he was as above interest as he was above fear. We cannot at this day estimate what Curran sacrificed to the popular cause, or how much risk he encountered for it. The part which Curran took in the rebellion-trials of 1798 has nothing in the whole history of defensive oratory with which we can compare it. Curran's position was a singular one, and the man was as singular as the position—as singular as either were the circumstances which created the position, and which glorified the man. A strange unity of national character prevailed then in Ireland amidst the most irreconcilable political hatreds. This very community of national genius, impassioned and intense, rendered contest all the fiercer, and made enmity all the darker. Power in its victory was cruel and unsparing; weakness in its defeat had nothing to plead, and nothing to hope. Humanity was asleep; conscience was blind; pity was deaf; but vengeance was all alive and all awake. Law was a dead letter; trial by jury was "a delusion, a mockery, and a snare." Any one who reads the records of those times will learn how universal was then in Ireland the reign of terror.

The Marquis of Cornwallis, Lord Lieutenant of Ireland, at the close of the insurrection, says that the executions by ordinary courts, or courts martial, were nothing compared with the butcheries and burnings committed by armed and licensed murderers, who were not less abhorrent to the high and humane among the rulers than they were monstrous and merciless to the people. In such a condition of things Curran had to stand nearly alone. He had to speak for the speechless, when words for the accused were almost accounted crimes; and he had to take the side of the doomed when the rancor of party spirit often confounded the advocate with the client.

Curran says, in 1794, while defending Dr. Drennan, to him a perfect stranger, prosecuted for a seditious libel—"I feel that if a barrister can act so mean and despicable a part as to decline, from personal apprehension, the defence of any man accused, he does not deserve to be heard in any court of justice." And in the same speech he says—"I have been parading through the capital, and I feel that the night of unenlightened wretchedness is fast approaching, when a man shall be judged before he is tried, when the advocate shall be libelled for discharging his duty to his client; that night of human nature, when a man shall be hunted down, not because he is a criminal, but because he is obnoxious." The last speech which Curran ever made in Parliament was in 1797. In this speech he also alludes to the risks which he had to meet in being true to the most sacred duty of his profession.

In most of the state trials the law and the evidence were fearfully against Curran; and if they were not, packed and prejudiced juries were sure to be. This last circumstance seems to have caused him the severest labor and the sorest distress. To watch his manner of dealing with such juries, to observe the versatility of motives and means by which he tries to obtain a fair consideration of his client's case, and to know that despair is at the bottom of it all, has an interest that is painfully and grandly tragic. Such a strife of genius against destiny and doom suggests to us the struggle of a noble gladiator with beasts in the Roman circus. The gladiator knows that the beasts will kill him, but none the less he maintains his manhood to the last. Curran, in the trials of 1798, encountered all sorts of dangers. He was hooted by the armed yeomanry; persecuted with anonymous letters; hated most heartily by officials and their slaves; he was hated with deadly hatred by the inhuman purchasers of lying oaths, by the perjured sellers of their brothers' lives—by men hungry and thirsty with a vindictiveness that the pangs of the scaffold could not satiate—by men made savage and cruel by their passions and their fears. With the local statutes against him, with the executive authority against him, with all the strength of an enraged, a sanguinary, and a powerful party against him, he did most heroically strive in his great vocation.

Curran's eloquence must not be criticised by men who live at ease. Work like his is not to be judged by men at home in the ordinary elegancies of professional routine. The man who can look critically at the eloquence of a speaker situated as Curran was, is a person who, as he could have no sympathy with the spirit of speech like Curran's, could have no true knowledge of its excellence. Such a man has no authority to an opinion on its defects. When occasions are fatal and big with destiny, we think little about artistic finish — we note not the artist, but the man; and not only imperfections of taste, but the glories of genius escape our attention in the hero who bravely dares such occasions, and is equal to them. Curran was not only equal to terrible occasions, but surpassed them.

The supreme eloquence of nations, when I think of it

historically, impresses me with more of sadness than of exultation. Supreme eloquence of this kind is ever in the highest degree impassioned and pathetic, and the passion and the pathos are born out of terrible strifes—out of the depths of moral and social agonies. Eloquence is then the voice of national or political tragedy; it is usually either the groan of expiring liberty or the cry of new-born revolution. It was near or at the close of an independent nationality that the Hebrew prophets arose, and shared with their brethren the captivity which they foresaw, but could not prevent. Never was eloquence grander or more patriotic than in the passionate sublimity of Isaiah, and the pathetic despondency of Jeremiah; and both prophets appeared amidst the calamities of their race. Demosthenes spoke his most electric speeches amidst the ruins of Grecian republics; and when he pronounced the funeral oration over those who fell at Chæronea, it may be truly said that he also pronounced the funeral oration of Grecian liberty. Cicero was the greatest orator of Rome, and he was the last. It was always when the crisis of public affairs in England became disturbed and dangerous that men were mightiest in speech. So likewise it was " the times which tried men's souls " in America that called forth the daring declamation of John Adams and Patrick Henry; and the times which have here again tried men's souls with a sterner ordeal, were preceded and accompanied by an intense and powerful rhetoric.

It was in the throes of revolutionary France that the terrible voice of Mirabeau was heard rolling above the tempest, and commanding it. And so, that of all the eloquence for which the English language has been the medium, none has been greater than that which shrieked and wailed amidst the gloom of Irish state prosecutions in 1798, or than thundered in the Irish Parliament during the struggle for its rights, and during the closing sessions of its short-lived independence. Occasions for the supreme eloquence of nations are rare ; so is the genius equal to them ; and this is good for the world. Such eloquence bursts out from the tempests of society. But the best interests of society grow strong in silence; they are nurtured by thought, education, piety, industry, and peace.

IRISH EMIGRATION.

There are naturalists who assert that, as the elephant is found in one climate and the bear in another, so are different races of men. Such races are indigenous to the soil, they say, and belong to it, as a palm-tree or an oak, a cabbage or a potato. But there are naturalists of quite as high authority who maintain that mankind consists of a single race, and must have proceeded from one pair of parents. As I am not scientific, and in these matters must rest on authority, I take the authority which is on the side of the moral feelings. That humanity has but one earthly parentage is an idea which carries with it the blessed sentiment of family and kindred—that brings along with it a sense of all the holy affections and duties which are instinctively associated with the idea. To that idea, therefore, will I hold; and the intuition of the soul, which reveals to me the universal brotherhood of man, I shall never give up for the conjectures of ethnology or the reasonings of comparative anatomy.

I do not, however, deny the existence of varieties among men. To do that would be to blind our intellects as well as our eyes. I take facts as I find them, and leave theories where they ought to be left, in the region of speculation. "When the wind is southerly, I know a hawk from a hernshaw"—but there is no reason why I should not also know it when the wind is northerly. Thus I can know a black man from a brown, and a brown one from a white ; and I can know all this without a theory. I shall accordingly judge each in what he shows himself to be ; even in doing that, I shall take more into account his opportunities than his climate or his color. With mere abstract capacity, I have no concern ; I have no measure for duration or possibility. History is young ; and if we had every fact in our memory that history could afford us, and could apply it with the rectitude of infallible science, we should still feel that our data were poor ; we should still feel, if we felt rightly, that we were inadequate to predicate concerning the early past of man of any type, or of his distant future. I cannot say to what man living I would give the primogeniture of the past, and there is no man from whom I would take the inheritance of the future. If the past is a claim for pride, no man can prove his title ; if the future is the right of hope, every man is born to it. Hope is the common property of life, and he who tells his brother to despair, utters an accursed speech. I would, if my words could reach or could encourage him, say to the lowest savage, "Grovel not ; be a man, and hope." He is, indeed, of a wretched and of a puny spirit who is content to fall back upon his race for assurance of respect, and who is not conscious that all which can most degrade him, and all which can most exalt, belongs to his individuality. He is of a menial soul who cannot respect himself until he find some one lower than himself to scorn ; but, indeed, he who scorns any man for his race, has none lower than himself to find. In practical life, take a man for what he is worth, and let his worth be the measure of the MAN. But my subject is "Irish Emigration."

It was in 1847 that I saw in its most impressive form the movement from Ireland which stirred the hearts of millions for voluntary expatriation. Had it not been so clear in the light of fact, it would have had an epic grandeur ; as it was, it had not a little of the solemn and the tragic. I do not attempt to give the philosophy of it. The fact itself was so terrible and so sublime, that it seemed to overpower the mind, and render it incapable of logic or analysis. A whole people was in motion—mighty as an ocean, and continuous as its waves. Compared with the crowds which were then steadily quitting Ireland for ever, the armies that all Europe furnished for the Crusades were trifling bands. The movement, too, was characterized by singular unity, persistency, and decision. Multitudes in spontaneous action were changing, finally, their nation and their homes. The young mother with her first-born was among them, and so was the grandmother ; the boy in the first decade of his life, and the patriarch verging towards his century. They hoped not to return. Those whom they left behind had their worst grief in being left, and their best consolation in the hope to follow. What is there in the world, what is there in history, upon which the mind can dwell so wonderingly and so sadly ? Those multitudes fled not before the sword ; there was no sound of arms in the land. They left it in silence ; their steps were not heard. They raised not their weepings ; they went down quietly into the holds of ships, and darkness and the noises of ocean were about them. Their exodus was not, like that of the Israelites, a flight from bondage; it was a departure by choice. It was not from a foreign soil ; it was from their native land ; and yet they loved their native land with all the force of passion. But in one sense they were very unlike the Israelites in quitting Egypt—they left no flesh-pots behind them to regret. Alas that it should be spoken ! —not in jest, but in gloomy truth—they had not even potatoes to lament. In lower value also than the Israelites, their rulers did not hinder, but hasten their departure, and there were some who seemed to boast of it as an advantage. Depopulation was the new idea of a political millennium, and space emptied of its native human bone and muscle, to be replaced by the beastly bone and muscle of sheep and oxen, was thought to be the clearing for a future Hibernian Eden. But when the terrible Crimean War came, with its tempests of blood and fire ; when the supreme struggle of the Indian Mutiny came, with its long-suspended agony of terror and despair—then it was understood that one brave human heart was worth a hecatomb of bullocks—the cattle upon a thousand hills were not then worth the soldierly soul of a peasant from Yorkshire, Lanarkshire, Galway, or Tipperary.

In the emigrating movement to which I have referred, physical privation was the sternest impulse—a privation aggravated to extremity by famine and evictions. To this I may add political despair. The aspirations which were awakened by O'Connell, and kept alive by his agitations, his promises, his prophecies, and his eloquence, opened to a people like the Irish, of quick imagination and passionate nationality, brilliant vistas of independence and of glory. But successive delays began to undermine faith, and repeated disappointments to wear out patience. Desire was strong as ever, but coming no nearer to fruition, it grew into despondency. Wish and belief ceased to correspond. Nationality was the strongest sentiment in the native ; and that great majority whom this heart animated, had no sympathy with British imperialism. Nay, they had a most decided repugnance to it. They had no pride in it ; it did not belong to them ; they did not live, they were only lost in it. Of its honors they had little ; of its glories they had none. Its fullest citizenship did not meet that aching which centuries of subjection could not stifle. That Ireland should be swallowed in the vastness of British imperial power, was worse even than servitude. A sway which had to be maintained by force implied a vigor in the governed which was feared; so that pains, and penalties, and coercion, hard as they were, were still evidence that nationality was not subdued, and the persistency which was still strong enough to provoke them, was also strong enough to endure them. There was in this endurance dignity, and any suffering had compensation, which proved that the nation was not extinguished. For national extinction, imperial freedom was no equivalent. If this freedom did not serve as a means to national restoration, it was esteemed of small value by the mass of the people. Nationality, not constitutionalism, was the idea which kindled popular enthusiasm. But nationality had been, even to the most sanguine, losing the show of probability. Years gathered on O'Connell—gloom gathered on the people. The imprisonment of the great tribune was a stroke of palsy to their expectations. There was then no likelihood that the Halls of Tara would ever be rebuilt; the harp of silent memories was not to be again re-strung, and give them sounds of renovated glory. "The songs of the olden time" were not to be hymns of victory to a new generation. From the dispiriting citizenship of British imperialism, not a few looked back with regret to the era of 1782, and even to the bad days beyond it. They were not, indeed, times to be commended; but there was life in them; there was hilarity in them; and above all, there was hope in them. Bigotry and faction, local tyranny and political corruption, abounded among the gentry; but numbers even of the vicious among them were kindly-hearted, and among the virtuous there were a few patriots, who would have redeemed the worst ages, and adorned the best. The peasants had no votes, but they had frolics; they were, indeed, degraded, but they were not outcasts. Dublin was confined, compact, and dirty. Its streets were not broad and lofty, but neither were they desolate and empty. Grand buildings had not yet arisen to be gaudy ruins, and statues did not look down in stony mockery upon destitution. Dublin was small; it was not grand, but it was cheerful; it was not liberal, but it was hearty. Its mansions were hospitable; they abounded with good cheer, and they shone with beauty; and both the good cheer and beauty were native. Life could be easily more orderly and more imposing than in those days it was in Dublin, but it would be hard to have it more brilliant, more intellectual, or more graceful. The Irish University, the Irish Parliament, and the Irish Bar, all centred in Dublin, and they were all that learning and oratory could make them. The public men of the day were familiar with the languages of Greece and Rome. Many of them equaled the greatest of ancient statesmen in grandeur of eloquence, and transcended them in grandeur of sentiment. They were men to be proud of; and now many who decry their measures, glorify their genius. Even Donnybrook Fair had its charms. Its song and dance, its capers and fun, its shows and juggleries, its whiskey-drinking and shillalahs, formed a grotesque comedy. It was the saturnalia of a people whose life was made up of strange and queer contrasts; it was the burlesque and the aggregate of their oddities. It was no lofty exhibition, but it was distinctive, vital, national. Subsequent changes gave the excluded masses the rights of citizenship, politics, discussion—in one word, Liberty.

Later came the inevitable and unseen events of potato-rots, famine, the decline of the population with pestilential rapidity, the bankruptcy of patricians, and the despair of plebeians. It was despair every way. The tragedy of fact was then present with a terrible reality; the whole island was its stage, and dying thousands sank in the catastrophe, not of fictitious, but of actual agony. All this was fact. No ardor could resist it, and no rhetoric could disguise it. O'Connell, who "never feared the face" of man, quailed in the presence of calamity and fate. His words were bold, but his spirit was sinking. He sickened; so did the people's hopes; that hope seemed to die with him in his death, and to be buried with him in his grave. Young Ireland put forth its voice; nothing was around it but popular despondency, and no multitude answered to its call. It was not indifference in the people, it was not inaction in the priests, which caused this want of response to the insurrectionary call; it was despair in both—the despair of instinct in the people, the despair of intelligence in the priests. And both were right. Both in their respective modes understood that to face the banded armies of the British empire, and the empire at peace, was simply to rush upon destruction. They forbore. Multitudes died of hunger; and all who could, began to quit Ireland. They came hither with increasing numbers, and with increasing rapidity. The aggregate swelled as it moved, and the momentum quickened with continuance. Hitherward they came; but though the movement may be seldom as it was then — though it may have alternations of suspension—hitherward the Irish will come. In fact, emigration is an inevitable social law for the British islands. They live by it, and they could not live without it. Their populations must disperse or perish. It was the same with the ancient Romans. Italy could not contain them, and so they diffused themselves throughout the world, by conquest or by colonization—rather, indeed, by both conquest and colonization. The Briton proper follows the example of the Roman; he conquers and colonizes; but Briton or not Briton, the inhabitants of the British islands emigrate; yea, and they will emigrate. But they do so in a special order. So far as this western continent is concerned, the Englishman cares little to come hither, except as an official placeman. The adventurous Scotchman generally settles in Canada, or some other British province. He does not, indeed, object to a snug place; and in some of the very snuggest of places, within the range of the British empire, you will find Scotchmen; nor are they undeserving of them. But independently of place or office, the Scotchman has many motives besides which impels him to emigrate. Any of them, however, seldom lead him to settle in the United States. To the United States come the hard-working Irish. If this is to *our* credit, it should *not* be deemed to their *dis*credit. We should assuredly not turn upon them with disapproval for the inclination which moves them to seek their fortunes within the sphere of this broad republic. We have land enough and to spare, and they have strength—for want of which the land is dead; for land, or anything that the land contains, can only live by labor. But, as I have said, hitherward the Irish come, and, with turns and changes, hitherward they will come. Every thousand that arrives is an encouragement for ten thousand others. The forerunners, by their example, encourage those behind them to follow. They supply them with funds to enable them to come; and by being here already, they strip exile of its repulsiveness in awaiting them with the welcome of friendship and society.

But instead of looking at these emigrants in the mass, I will take one of them as an individual—an individual of the working order—and trace him in four transitions of his course—namely, in leaving Ireland, in landing in America, in arranging for settlement, and in being settled.

Departure from one's native shore for ever is, under any circumstances, a serious movement, and is melancholy when most hopeful. To be able to quit with indifference the land of youth, of friends, and of all first emotions, I cannot

regard as a heroic virtue, but as a selfish vice. And the
iustinct of attachment to native things which makes it grief
to part from them, is no matter of education. It belongs
to the human heart, and it is a grief which is more likely
to be poignant in the breast of the laborer than in that
of the scholar. When we can consider how local and
restricted laborious life is, especially in olden countries, we
will not count the trial small which wrenches it away from
all its native associations. These native associations are of
great value; and, whatever the political economist may
assert, it is, I think, no common hardship that an honest
man, who is willing and able to work, cannot, if he so
desires, find subsistence in the country which bore him, and
a grave in the soil which holds the dust of his fathers. The
poor man's pride suffers by emigration, as well as his affections. Whatever the poor man can glory in, after his conscience, lies near him. The sphere of his life is not that of a
nation, not even of a county, scarcely of a parish; it is that
of his immediate neighborhood. Beyond that he is not
known, and away from that he loses consequence. *There*
the worth of his character, when worth it has, is understood, and there are the witnesses of his integrity. His
manners *there* are not grotesque, because they are in keeping with the manners of those around him; and the habits
which expose him elsewhere to mockery, are, where he was
born, the habits of associates. That fortune of an upright
fame, which was all the wealth he had, he loses for the time
when he quits his home. The distant man will not know
his claim—it may be, will be slow to learn it, or careless to
give it credit. He must depart; he must go he knows not
whither, and he must meet he knows not whom. He must
turn from the fields in which, while he had leave to toil in
them, summer was pleasant, and winter was not bitter.
Away in strange lands, he must look for another life, and

try, as best he can, to learn it. Generally, it is poverty which compels him to quit his country, and poverty has manifold disadvantages. Even the outside of it is often read by the most benevolent as they would read a bill of indictment. Poverty is not comely, and, like an idiot in a family, the tolerance of it is local. It is not so with wealth. Wealth is for all countries, and has friends everywhere. It is cordial and inspiring to all who come near it. Wealth is, indeed, a most admirable talisman for the discovery of gracious people. The rich man upon his travels must be hard to please if he does receive all the attentions he can pay for, and they must be dull, with a stupidity not often found in civilized regions, upon whom the charm which he bears has no power. Bright looks and welcome wait upon it, and though *heart* is not salable, smiles are ready, and smiles are sufficient for the passing hour. Fair apparel and a full purse are always pleasingly intelligible ; and the best letter of introduction is a letter of credit. Music is said to be a universal language, but of no music is this so true as of the music of the mint. It is a fine softener of the harsher passions. Even bandits become tender to the sound of doubloons. They treat with distinguished consideration the plethoric trader whose money-bag is as protuberant as his paunch ; but they pummel without remorse the miserable pretender whose purse is as emaciated as his jaws.

Practical philosophy in prosperous nations sets a direful mark upon poverty. Poverty, in the view of this philosophy, is a repulsive caitiff, a worthless villain, a most unmitigated scoundrel ; and a ragged wretch is a self-evidently ragged rascal. There is, however, a kindlier philosophy than this, and, I think, a wiser one, which believes that an honest heart may beat under a threadbare garment, and that even an emigrant clad in shreds may have a conscience of invincible integrity.

The Irish emigrant used to leave the shores of his country under considerable illusion, and although, of late years, much of the illusion must have been dispelled, some of it may still remain. General reports concerning America reached him with many exaggerations — exaggerations which, coming to his imaginative temperament from the far-off land of his fancy and his hope, he easily believed in the land of his sufferings and his despair. Private accounts were seldom more exact than general reports. The Irish settler in America, who had attained to any degree of comfort, wrote a glowing account of it to his relative or neighbor at home. Under the influence of novelty and contrast, the settler could not write with cool exactness. Under the influence of distress, and the desire to escape from it, the recipients of the letter found even more promise than the letter meant. Add to this that the writer was seldom master of expression, and that, if he were, the reader would rarely be able to enter into its precision. But it was not by words alone that such an encouraging illusion was excited, but by substantial evidence in the form of generous remittances. This evidence still continues. May it always continue, while there is an Irish heart in America to remember that there is any home in Ireland which needs it. May the *need* become extinct, but may the heart be ever lovingly the same. Now, as at other times, from every part of this wide country, the mails come burdened with rudely-directed letters. Many are those for Ireland, and all the many contain remittances. They tell not of the hardship with which the money was earned; they tell not of the sacrifices with which it was spared; they usually say— "We are well in health; we have work, we have good wages, we have comfort and plenty at the present, and we hope to be better off in the future." The dark side of the picture they conceal. Cheerfulness and help they give to their friends; their griefs and trials they keep to themselves. Take into account how often this is the import of letters from America. Silent on disappointment, exultant on success, it will not seem surprising that, in spite of facts to the contrary, imagination will still outrun discretion in the minds of those at home; it will not seem surprising that in such a country—a country from which money comes in so great abundance—money must be in quantity beyond measure, and that money so liberally bestowed must be easily acquired. Many a man, therefore, about to emigrate even still fancies that, if once in the land of Columbus, he has only to show himself to obtain employment, and that to have employment is to be on the certain road to wealth.

Perhaps some emigrants there yet may be who are under the old mistake of supposing a universal equality as characteristic of American society. If such there are, it will not be long after their arrival when they will be entirely cured of their blindness. If every error and prejudice under which men labor could be as rapidly and as effectually removed as this, our world would be one of transcendent enlightenment and wisdom. The emigrant will find grades and social differences here not unlike to those which he left at home. No citizen in this country of the male sex, and twenty-one years of age, but can do something in making a President. For any particular citizen, however, to be made a President is really a hard matter. Some great citizens, men of magnificent genius, had struggled for it all their lives, and yet had missed it. It is for this reason that, whenever I am in conversation with a very ambitious mother, I always advise her, in her hopes for a gifted son, to be moderate, and never to let her aspirations soar above the chief-justiceship. In testimony to the reasonableness of womanhood and maternity, I must say that I have seldom met a mother who was not willing to be content with this modest expectation. Every mother cannot be a mother of the Gracchi; neither can every mother be the mother of a President. In a word, and seriously, the man is most wisely prepared to come hither, who comes with the conviction that he will have to enter on an obstinate and hardy effort ; and the friend who aids him towards this conviction, gives him most efficient help.

The second stage of our emigrant's transition, that of his landing, is not a very cheering one. It is not a cheering subject for description. The emigrant, whom we must take to represent a very numerous class, is often ill prepared to leave, and, if possible, worse prepared to land. He has but touched the shore when many of his illusions disappear. The hard reality which he finds, is unlike the vision of which he dreamed. Frequently he stands almost penniless in the city into which he is thrown. He was, at home, it may be, unused to towns, and he finds himself instantly a stranger amidst a measureless wilderness of streets and throngs. The pressure of great masses surrounds him. The hum of care, of commerce, or of pleasure which fills the air about him has no sound in it that his fancy can interpret into welcome. But the emigrant is not always friendless; perhaps seldom entirely so. The same hospitable feelings which bind neighbors and relatives to one another in Ireland, are still more powerful when they come together in America. Shelter and food are often gratuitously given, and this not for days, but for weeks. A poor man will not turn out an acquaintance whom he knew at home, while he has space upon his floor and a slice remaining of his loaf. I am in possession of facts which convince me that there is ever going on among the Irish in this country a mutuality of assistance that strangers to the Irish character do not know, and cannot even imagine.

The vices of the Irish are open, passionate, uproarious,

often sanguinary; their virtues are silent, domestic, personal.
The vicious Irishman is marked by vices which attract
attention. He is soon *felt* in a community of order as a
disturbing character, and he is quickly brought to punishment. Undoubtedly he deserves it; and let him have it. I
have noticed carefully, and with close attention, variously
directed, the records of crime in the courts of this country.
It could not be disguised, if it were desirable to deny it, that
many of the criminals are Irish. But I have noticed that
they are here much as at home, the criminals of the impulsive
passions, seldom of the calculating ones. I have observed
that the murders they have done, have been generally
done in hours of insanity, and under the illusions of excited
blood and brain. Not the better, I admit, than other kinds
of murder, but different. When I have seen cases of astute
incendiarism, with no object but to cheat insurance companies; when I have read about instances of cool and planned
assassination, for the mere increase of property; when I
have noticed the execution of frauds that, by their genius
and augustness of perpetration, gave the miscreants who
contrived them infamous celebrity, I have rarely found them
Irish. Wicked and reckless, as to their passions, as many
of the Irish in America may be in their vices, I claim for
them a rare gentleness and kindliness in their virtues.
Among these virtues is their neighborly affection, their social
humanity. Such virtues abound among them; they abound
without notice, beyond notice, and they abound no less in
their emigrant than in their native relations.

Among the Irish abroad there is something almost Jewish
in their adherence to each other and to Ireland—except, indeed, that now and then contests arise among them, which
show that, like the Israelites, they have not in dispersion
forgotton their feuds. Still, the analogy is, on the whole, a
just one. The Irish in America forget much that separated

them at home; and they love as well as forget.   Were it not
for the aid that residents in America, from Ireland, afford
privately to recent comers, not a few of these comers would
every season perish.   I myself have known of zealous
Catholics giving shelter to deep-blue Protestants, and in a
small apartment—more than illustrating the prophecy of the
lion lying down with the lamb ; in the Ribbonman, in
charitable hospitality, holding "sweet communion" with the
Orangeman.   Personally, I do not know that the Orangeman has done the same by the Ribbonman, yet I doubt not
but he has; for party hostility, which seems to have no
medium of reconciliation at home, finds one in a common
sensibility for country abroad.   A numerous class must have
work near the sea-board, or despair.   Necessity thus crowds
the sea-board cities.   But even when the Irish emigrant has
funds, he is too apt to remain in cities until his funds are
exhausted.   He falls then under a like necessity with him
who was, on his arrival, destitute.   Nay, by becoming an
additional candidate in competition for leave to toil, he
doubles the difficulty on them both.

There is that in an Irishman's disposition which abhors
the wilderness.   I once knew an Irish Catholic who tried
his hand at turning Protestant.   He was a simple-minded
and unsophisticated rustic.   He had always been accustomed
to crowds and companionships, whenever his heart was
active, and without them his heart must sink.   On his first
day of going to the Protestant Church, the congregation
was miserably small.   The new convert became alarmed; he
turned from the porch, ran back as fast as he could, nor
stopped a moment until he felt himself warmly and comfortably at Mass, in the sweltering perspiration of a throng
which made his bones ache, but set his heart at ease.   I
also knew a Protestant who, as he advanced in years, became very anxious as to the prospective credit of his funeral.

His family had been popular, albeit they were Cromwellian. It was not the Bible portion of their trooper ancestor's spirit which came down to them, but the fighting, hunting, and drinking tendency of it. This was at least the part of it which this son of it inherited. His ancestor voted for penal laws, but never executed any. They fought duels, cracked jokes as they snapped pistols, and loved men all the better who had tried to shoot them, or whom they had tried to shoot. They were famous at fox hunts. The father of the individual to whom I refer had his stables covered with trophies gained in this heroic exercise, and was as proud of fox-tails as an Indian warrior is of scalps. The men of this family drank claret with Catholic priests whom they might have hanged, and winked at religious ceremonies which they had declared high treason. They horsewhipped peasants, but played football with them ; they would not have them free, but they made them drunk. They were vigorous and hardy fellows. Not a man of them was ever sober at night, or a sluggard in the morning. They were great Protestants, but poor theologians. They would have stumbled in the Commandments. They gloried in Cromwell; but they knew as much about the doctrine of the Westminster divines as they did about Melchisedek's father. But they were wonderfully popular, and all of them had big funerals. O'Connell and politics stopped this course of things, and the individual to whom I allude felt that the change was a sore grievance. He wished to walk quietly in the way of his fathers, and be as numerously attended as they had been to the grave. He had not their hearty zeal for Cromwell, nor their hearty hatred of the Pope. It was a sort of mixed feeling that he had; it was like his whiskey-and-water, half and half ; but the water part was his hatred of the Pope, and the whiskey part was his desire for the big funeral. As he could better do without the water to his whiskey than without the whiskey to his water, he could more easily become lenient to the Pope than be reconciled to the idea of having a slender procession after his body to the grave. He, too, was popular; for he was reckless, jovial, and social. In quieter times he might have died a Protestant, and yet had a mile-long funeral. It had in some manner, however, got into the popular mind that, at the last, he intended *not* to send for the parson, but the priest. This was his puzzle: If he sent for the parson, he would have but poor chance of an extensive procession, since he himself made, as he was a very large man, a considerable part of the small Protestant congregation. He was not only a large man, but was, in his way, and for the times, respectable. If he sent for the priest, he would have a burial worthy of his ancestors, and be carried to the grave, as they had been, with thousands in attendance. The wish for a big funeral was decisive, and he sent for the priest.

This strong social feeling of the Irishman has its evil side as well as its good. It exposes him to much peril, and especially in circumstances that are new and strange. In this country, peculiarly, it induces him to fix himself in cities, and he soon becomes so enslaved in them that he cannot quit them.

I have so far spoken of the Irish emigrant in reference to his departure from his own country, and his arrival in this. I have alluded, however, only to the emigrant as man. I must say a few words on the emigrant as woman, or, rather, as maiden. I wish I had not these few words to say, or, on this topic, any word. How I shall say them, is a pain, a difficulty, a perplexity; the very necessity to say them, confuses me with sorrow, fear, and shame. As, however, the necessity exists, and as the word must be spoken, it is better to speak it plainly. This word concerns the danger, the moral danger, that awaits young women in some of the ships to which they are trusted, or to which they trust themselves—a dreadful danger, which, if not escaped on the sea, prepares for them a terrible destiny on land. Of late years, we have had, from time to time, revelations showing that numbers of young women in emigrant ships have been made victims of the most heartless and hardened debauchery, not only by the crew, but frequently by the officers. Indeed, it is hard to see how the crew could incur such guilt without the participation or connivance of the officers. No deeper tragedy can I conceive than the destruction of hapless girls, desolate upon the ocean, and strangers between two worlds. No deeper baseness can I imagine than the villany of those who destroy them. There is in the innocency of a pure girl something so blessed, that I can hardly suppose that even a libertine would stain it. Indeed, a libertine, who had any moral feeling or imagination spared him by his vices, would guard it against its own weakness, and shelter it against himself. The grossness with which he was familiar, but which did not utterly kill his humanity, would by very contrast render this innocency holy in his sight. He would think of his sisters—possibly of his daughters. The thought would rebuke his passions, and, however transiently, sanctify his character. What shall we, then, think of men who receive into their care and keeping an unsuspecting rustic girl from the arms of a weeping mother, and the silent sorrow of a not less loving father; or it may be that the girl is an orphan, who has no mother to weep, and no father to grieve —what shall we think, I say, about the vileness of men who treacherously betray the helpless, and destroy with a destruction worse than death the being whom they were bound to protect, not merely by contract of bargain and payment, but by every merciful, every honorable, every manly impulse. Give the case distinctness. A young girl, fresh from the fields, with the bloom of health on her cheeks, and the peace of honest maidenhood in her heart, is committed to an emigrant-ship. She weeps as she quits her native land. She dreams sadly of her home, of those within her home, and, in her inward solitude of young affliction, she lovingly calls back her childhood's life. But the tears of youth are soon dried up. Then come the prophecy of hope, and the vision of a sunny future. Before she is well upon the wave, her imagination has already carried her across the ocean, and gives her, beyond it, many a pleasant picture, many cheering consolations—not the least of which is, the idea of the money that she will be able to send back to her poorer friends. But ere she reaches the New World, she is *not* what she was when she left the Old. By cunning, force, or guile, she has been blasted. She has lost innocence, she has lost her own esteem, she has lost her reputation; for in the ship, as on the shore, there are community and social judgment. Not long since, she had virtue, she had the courage and the joy which virtue gives; but she is now, and especially to her own remorseful thoughts, a worthless thing—a mere worn rag of human nature; and nothing is left to her but hopeless guilt, with its anguish and its despair. What need I dwell on the horrid fate which glooms over her arrival—the mad and short career, the early and the lonely death!

Is it right to call the wretches MEN who thus crush the weak, and work such havoc by their filthy lusts? Yet some of them are styled *gentlemen*. In the character of a genuine sailor there is much to admire. He is frank, generous, kind, and, when truly himself, he has a sincere respect for woman. Habituated though he often is with vice, it does not wholly brutalize him. He has times and seasons, in the solitudes of ocean, when he muses on home, on early days, on the girlish worth of his sisters, on the matronly sanctity of his mother; and in such times and seasons his better nature prevails. He believes in virtue, and he would sooner die than destroy it. These feelings do not always forsake him when he comes on shore. I was once crossing a street in New York. Two sailors were walking together. One of them made a rude movement towards a woman. "Shame! John," said the other; "remember that you have a sister!" But the mean creatures who in emigrant ships dishonor the name of humanity are no genuine sailors; and genuine sailors should always be considered as having no share in the infamy of these unmitigated scoundrels. If such scoundrels cannot be suppressed, then should no Irish girl not fortressed by a family, and especially by stout brothers, be committed to an emigrant ship. Better to stay at home, with any sort of privation, than run this deadly risk; better toil and starve than venture where all that makes life worthy may be lost. Who, knowingly, would put his healthy child into a plague-ship? But a plague-ship is safety itself compared with a corrupt emigrant ship; for the plague-ship can only kill the body, but the corrupt emigrant ship kills the soul, and kills the body too. Floating dens of iniquity must not be. No! by earth and heaven, no! By all that is just or true, civilized or human! by all that is dear in the home! by all that is honest and noble in society! by all that is generous in man! by all that is sacred in woman! they must be put down, they must be kept down —not merely by laws, but by that strong force of moral opinion which gives to laws their power, and without which laws are only solemn and formal mockery. The ship which has not adequate provision for health, order, and comfort— which has not all reasonable safety for decency and purity, should be regarded as a receptacle of corruption, and shunned with a universal fear. Since the Irish do not emigrate in local communities, or in kindred groups, Irish girls are those, of all others, to whom captains should be fathers, and to whom sailors should be brothers. Let ship-owners see to it. It concerns their interests as well as their characters. Indeed, emigrants in general, of all countries, that have not wealth, are both on the sea and on the land made to bear severities and hardships from which ordinary justice and common humanity might easily save them.

Being here, what should the emigrant aim at and prepare himself to be? This is our third topic, and must be briefly treated. If he has nothing but muscular labor to depend on, he must, of course, give himself to any honest toil which he can find to do. The merest drudgery which keeps us from dependence, and into which we carry an upright spirit and a manly purpose, is not a condition of shame, but of dignity. I would have no man or woman scorn the hum-blest calling which can be followed with integrity; neither would I have any discontented. I would not that a word which escapes me should seem to justify irritation with a man's providential station ; I would not that it should excite in him a reckless desire to change or quit it. The hardest task can be softened by cheerfulness and resigna-tion ; and if it supplies the means of fair subsistence, it is not to be despised ; it is not to be relinquished with haste ; it is to be fulfilled with loyalty, and to be held with cautious patience. Adventure, speculation, eagerness for riches, re-pugnance to common toil, contempt for sober experience, faith in golden dreams—these are among the most glaring faults of our age. Far be it from me to preach such dis-turbing doctrines. But, nevertheless, I would have the Irish emigrant look upward and look forward. I would have him not only seek for competence as to the needs of the day, I would have him seek for permanent independ-ence. However lowly the possession might be at first, I would have him become a capitalist, an owner of property.

A passage which I found in a newspaper, from the speech of a manufacturer in New York, at a banquet given to his work-people—most of them, by the by, emigrants—has so much good sense in it, that I take a fragment or two from it. "Before I part with you," said he, "let me give you a few words of advice. *Money* in this country is *power.* As long as you have money in your pockets, man or woman, boy or girl, you have a *friend* that will protect you, when other friends forsake you." The speaker then exhorts man and woman, girl and boy, to open an account in a savings bank, be the deposits ever so small, and to open it at once. I would preach the doctrine of acquisition in no sordid spirit; neither did this gentleman so preach it. But thoughtful and provident accumulation is not selfish covetousness, but disinterested carefulness. It is not a mean vice, but a noble virtue—a virtue which domestic and social morality imperatively demands, and which domestic and social life most blessedly rewards. I am no advocate for avarice or ambition. I would, indeed, excite the sentiment of aspiration, but it is aspiration following its purpose with earnest rectitude, and with manly perseverance.

As I would have the Irish emigrant prepare himself to become an American citizen, and in due time become one, I would have him, with all his heart and soul, enter into the genius of American citizenship. And speaking in the spirit of the American mind, I attach not the idea of firm, decisive citizenship to the condition of casual, dependent, and daily toil. I do not here allude to mere voting qualification, for much besides that is included in the character of a citizen. The American mind cannot join the thought of a perpetual state of hire with manly freedom. This is the source of too much of its arrogance, but it is also the source of its boldness, its elasticity, its self-resolve, and its self-reliance. The American accepts any work *for the time*—if it pays. He does it cheerfully, he does it manfully; but if it is at the bidding of another, he does not intend to do it always, or to do it long. The American journeyman intends to be an employer. The American clerk has it in his own mind that in good time he will be a capitalist. The American laborer, working on another man's farm, solaces his fatigue by calculating how long it may cost him, if he likes the location, to buy the owner out. The American waiter, while handing round Madeira, resolves that, when he gives dinners, he will be generous in Champagne. Lord Jeffrey once observed that, if a prize were offered for a new translation of the Greek Testament, some Yankee would begin the Greek alphabet, and win the prize while critical scholars in Europe were thinking over their versions, and resolving to set about them. Any man, therefore, who is satisfied with perpetual dependence, any man who is void of aspiration, and incapable of effort, is *not* in harmony with the spirit of American life, and with the genius of American society.

Property is of course of manifold varieties, and, in any form, gives the possessor stability and power. But I would desire to see the Irish emigrant more frequently than he is the proprietor of land. I may, however, want the experience which would give me any title to an opinion in this matter. My reasoning may be unsound, my views illusive, and my ideas unpractical, yet, presuming as it may seem, I would say to the Irish laborer in America, "If you have means, settle on your own spot of soil; dig for yourself; be your own master. If you have not means, try to acquire them, and to this purpose direct your energies and your earnings." Life upon the soil ought, I think, to be congenial to the feelings and the habits of an Irish emigrant. The moor, the hillside, the meadow, the copse, the wood, the mountain, the potato-garden, and the grain-field, were the scenes amidst which he was reared. Country sports were

the amusements of his youth—country employments the
toils of his manhood ; and when I myself go back and live
in memory, my dream is on the hill, looking around me for a
solitary shepherd, or, in the harvest-time, gladdened by the
multitude of mowers and reapers. As a tiller of the soil,
the Irish emigrant would often, I fancy, call to mind the
green pastures of former times, the song of the linnet and
the lark, the familiar cock-crow, the deep notes of the black-
bird and the thrush ; and though he could not have all of
these back again, he would enjoy, I should imagine, the life
which came the nearest to that which he had among them.
There is something, too, in the ownership of acres which
is grateful to an Irishman's pride. Though the acres which
a man first acquires bring with them no boast of heirship,
yet, if a man pines for a dream of ancestry, let him look
onward to his grandchildren, and be, as Sir Boyle Roach
would say, "a grandfather to himself."

To be serious, a hardy working man can find no position
with so much dignity in it, with so much of real independence, as that of a cultivator. Toil on land ennobles his
position, and removes his toil from all that would render it
inferior or invidious. Toil on a man's own land, be the
land ever so wild, is toil in a man's own right. It is the
action of a sovereign, and the man is "free," as has been
finely said, "from the centre to the stars." The advantages,
socially, morally, and economically, of such a position I cannot in this brief space exhibit, and there is no occasion, for
they are easily conceived. Were the Irish emigrant more
systematically than he has been a settler upon land, he would
have had a place in the social scale of this country more
favorable to his better qualities than that which he has
actually held. He would then have been a creator of wealth.
The agency which he has exercised in the national resources
would have been more readily observed, and more distinc-

tively acknowledged. The emigrant is, indeed, a creator of wealth in making a railroad as well as in tilling a farm, but his agency is not so clearly discerned. But when a garden is made to bloom where before only wild grass grew, *then* there can be no mistake.

In rural settlement there would also be the influence of *fixed* condition. Religious feeling and religious habits would exert their due power. The home virtues would be cultivated and matured. Education would do its work, and have noticeable results. A *fixed* condition, besides its positively good influences, would save Irish emigrants from many evil ones. Some of the worst temptations which beset the laboring Irish in this country belong to unsettled and undefined relations with society. Land would be a centre of steadiness. Land is the basis of all wealth, for it is the feeder of all life. The man who tills the soil which he fairly owns cannot be poor, if the soil gives any due return for his labor. Banks may break down; parties from opposite directions may prophesy ruin to the country; storms of eloquence may rage; laws may be made and un-made; but so long as the rain cometh down from heaven— so long as the earth is properly solicited to give forth her increase—so long as the farmer is allowed quietness for his toil, he will have seed for the sower and bread for the eater. That fixed occupation of the soil which I would recommend —that trust in regular industry which I would urge—that content in moderation which I would desire for myself and for others, are not in unison with the passionate spirit of our day. They are, however, the only means of a true prosperity, and, with all earnestness, I would wish to see the Irish emigrant acting in the temper of my philosophy. It would be his most effectual guaranty against distress— his most complete emancipation from hopeless and servile labor.

To the emigrant of some patience and a little means, there is land here open—land as teeming with abundance as the sun ever warmed or as the rain ever watered. Here it is in this mighty America, in its virgin freshness. It wooes the seeker by its freedom, and it waits for him with its bounty. Here it is, with its wide and sweeping verdure, lovely through its eternity of unused seasons. Here it is, with no despot or bailiff, with no distraints, no evictions—free as the air that blows over it, and rich as the dew that falls upon it. Here it is, with its floor of mountains, plain, lake, and river, with its roof of lucent sky, for the exile to find his home, and fearlessly to look upward through the immensity of the heavens. Practical difficulties, I know, are in the way, but none, I trust, which practical knowledge cannot remove. If wisdom and experience do not remove them, the power of necessity must.

If such an outpouring exodus should ever again occur like that in 1847, it must consolidate itself into system, shape, and order ; it must take such shape and method as will compel isolated individualism to give place to collective and associated forces. The Germans, the Swedes, the Norwegians, come in bodies. This takes solitude from the wilderness, lays hold upon the desert in the strength and charity of mutual affection and companionship, plants at once upon it the living germs of society, and awakens it with the sacred voice of the temple and the home. Let it not be said that the Irish cannot do likewise—that they cannot travel together in agreement, or dwell together in unity.

But say what we please as to theory, the Irish emigrant will settle as character, capacity, chance, and circumstances determine ; and after a few years, he will be found in every occupation of trade, business, labor, and profession. But I will keep to my idea, and close with the supposition that he settles upon land. I do not overlook the trials which the emigrant must meet in any space that is free and open to him. His shanty will be bare and rough, but surely it can be hardly worse than that which a railroad laborer inhabits. His toil will be severe, it may be long, but the reward is noble in a permanent and settled independence. I look beyond a few years on the space whereon he has been working. I see no more the groundling hut. The wilderness has sprung into bloom. A comely dwelling is embosomed amidst offices and orchards. A domain is conquered and possessed. Crops and cattle, rich fields and full barns, evince the patient royalty of fortitude and toil. Here the needy friend may come without fear of trespass. Here the stranger may enter, and find no empty welcome. Here there is no terror of an approaching rent-day, for God alone is the landlord. God made the earth that so it may be used. Thus it is prepared by man, and then it is a beautiful heritage for the children or the successors of him who thus prepares it. The barren place is made a garden. Children sport where the bison fed ; herds of oxen fatten where deer had roamed ; and the house-dog bays where wolves howled. The man, come whence he may, who contributes to this work his share of thought and muscle, does much to make society his debtor. The fine action of genius is very pleasant, but the hard effort of labor must come first. The pioneer and the settler must be in advance of the artist and the author ; the sounds of music must come after the echoes of the axe ; the painter must be in the wake of the hunter ; the ploughman must be before the poet ; and the hut must be the herald of the temple.

IRISH-BORN CITIZENS.

As an Irishman, as an American citizen, with many ties which bind me as sacredly to the land of my adoption as those which bind me to the land of my nativity,.I speak here to my kindred countrymen in our new country. We have community by the land of our birth; we have no less community in this land which has given us an hospitable heritage. The ancient land is full of imperishable memories —of memories which through centuries have kept the nation's brain excited and the nation's blood on fire. The ancient land is full of sublime retrospections—retrospections of thought, of sanctity, of action; and none but its basest and most unworthy children ever become insensible to the venerableness of its character and the dignity of its fame. Ireland has, throughout the world, given, in all modes of genius, a good account of herself—in song, story, eloquence, history, philosophy; in all sorts, too, of nobleness and vir- tue, in the kindliness of peace, and in the bravery of war. I am not here to dwell on the ancient glories of Ireland, or to repeat the sadly monotonous tale of her misfortunes. While recollecting both, my immediate purpose is to speak of some fundamental relations which, as citizens, we have contracted and hold to the nation and government of the United States.

First, there are industrial relations. As the great ma- jority of Irish who come to America are of the working class, they naturally settle in the Free States, or in States where slave labor does not predominate. Very naturally, I say, the Irish come to the Free States, because, in the first place, the labor market in these States is more ample and more profitable ; because, secondly, labor does not, in the Free States, subject a man to contempt and degradation. Thus, independently of all politics or parties, the Irish have come mostly to the Free States. Yet I have often heard much of the moral blame of slavery charged against the Irish, as if they had imported the Africans, who were torn by force from their native soil to minister in eternal bondage to the white man's lust of gain. Now, it is a singular fact that no country has been so free from guilt of injustice to the African as Ireland. When the slave trade was most profitable—when millions of money were made by it in Liverpool and Bristol—when Cooke, the actor, told his audience, in Liverpool, a piece of his mind thus : " Miscreants! there is not a brick in your town that is not cemented with Negro gore "—no Irish body of merchants would engage in it. An attempt was once made in Belfast to establish a slave-trading company. There was a meeting of capitalists ; a paper containing the terms of agreement was ready for signature. A venerable man arose and said, in slow and solemn tones, " May the lightning of God Almighty's anger blast the arm of the man who first attempts to sign that accursed document." The document remained unsigned, and Ireland was saved from the guilt of man-stealing, and from the guilt of the multitudinous murders of the middle-passage. Even before slave holding was thought a sin, Ireland had small concern in it ; and on the twenty millions of West Indian redemption-money, she made the least demand. And all the world knows that the most eloquent denouncer of slavery who ever lived, the great orator who always made impassioned and electric speech the servant of justice and humanity, was an Irishman—I mean the heroic and dauntless O'Connell.

Until recently, both the great political parties of the country fraternized on the question of slavery, and both alike canvassed for the votes and favor of the South, as the South did for those of the North. Men of Massachusetts hobnobbed with men of South Carolina, and there was no talk between them on the moral or political iniquity of Negro slavery. In what ratio the Irish vote went with one party or the other, I do not know, and I never cared to inquire; but slavery, one way or the other, could not have influenced it, since it is only of late that the question of slavery came openly into politics.

The interest of the Irish, and also, I think, their inclinations, have led them to settle in their greatest numbers in the Free States; but their toil has been important to the whole nation. They, of all immigrants, have contributed the most to that free labor by which the country has grown in prosperity and power. By their bone and muscle have these great highways been built up which have become the wonder of the world. And only by means of these highways have the successive additions been made to the country of those wide and fertile domains which are truly its greatest wealth. Strong Irish workers have been of measureless benefit to the country; but also the country has been of measureless benefit to them. It has given them chances of life and manhood, when all such chances had been lost in the land of their nativity. The son of an honest railroad laborer may, with virtue and talent, become capitalist, advocate, judge, senator, governor, President. Each party reciprocally benefits the other. America wants labor; the Irish need employment. In this mutual relation both are fairly equalized. The abstract impersonation of the Irishman may say—" I have made your railroads, your canals; I have been the instrument of all your hardest toils." But then the abstract impersonation of the American reply— " Yes, it is all true ; I acknowledge the obligation. On the other hand, however, I had prepared the way for you. I had saved the capital from which you have had and have wages. We have, my friend, a common interest, we have a common country; but it is country more than interest that unites us. We are fellow-citizens, and as such we must cordially live and work together. Let no vile disturbers breed strife between us ; let us not fall out by the way; but let us seek strength in united and earnest brotherhood." Boasting on either side is unbecoming and uncalled for. Mutual esteem and mutual respect are the generous feelings to be cultivated and maintained between the Irish-born citizens and those who, by precedence and priority of parentage, are natives of the land.

We look next at some of the social relations to the country held by the people of Irish birth. I have heard the Irish in America accused of being clannish, and as having society only among themselves. It should be considered that immigrants are necessarily strangers to natives, and strangeness, at first a feeling, may become at last a habit. Nothing is more natural than that immigrants should have much society among themselves. It is natural that, for a long while, they should feel as in a strange land ; and how can they more easily relieve this feeling than by holding communion with those who share their native memories, and with whom they can interchange native sympathies? But the fact is, that of all citizens from abroad, the Irish are the least clannish. They live among native citizens, among them spend their earnings, speak the same language, and are one with them in all the large and generous comities of life. There are no citizens from abroad that, less than the Irish, separate themselves from what is native and national, and it is often the complaint of Irish parents in this country that they cannot hinder their children from becoming more American than the Americans. No man is more cosmopolitan in spirit than an Irishman, or a man of the Irish race. He is quick, ready, cheerful, companionable—willing to please, and easy to be pleased. He hates isolation ; and wherever his lot may happen to be cast, he quickly makes himself at home. Irishmen, and men of the Irish race, are met with all the earth over. They are found in all grades of social station, and mental and moral condition—in all sorts of employments, intellectual or mechanical, secular or sacred. But to no country to which the Irishman goes from Ireland does he bind himself so heartily as to the United States. And this is no wonder. The United States gives him, if I may so express myself, a second nativity. He is born again into the sense of a new home and a new hope. He may fail, he may be disappointed, he may suffer grievously and bitterly; but no sensible Irishman will ever charge his failure, his disappointment, or his suffering on the American nation, its people, or its institutions. America, though distant, is not foreign to Ireland and the Irish. Much of their blood and bone, of their life and love, are on its soil. They may rightfully claim their share in the living substance of the American people. If home is most truly where our affections are, where those are to whom our affections attach us, then America must be to vast numbers of the Irish people most really their home. Among the masses in Ireland there is a spirit of affection which looks on America as a land of promise, and the same spirit among them here makes America their second country. With some unavoidable difficulties, it is to them truly a country. But these difficulties will become less and less with successive generations. There are fair chances for the industrious and the thrifty. The thoughtful and the worthy are as sure in this as in any country in the world of honorable recognition. Talent of every kind and degree, come from where it may, can find and make for itself means of usefulness and activity. Genius the national mind is ever ready to admire, and that with no grudging temper, and with no stinted measure. There must be struggles, hard struggles, to all who come into a new land and strange circumstances. Character is tested by these struggles, and the merit of those whom they prove, and who bear them well, fails never of its reward. Those who endure patiently, manfully, and wisely are sure in the end to conquer. The Irish in America have not been inert, unsympathetic, or unaspiring. They are a strong element in all the activities of the nation. They have contributed their share to its wealth and power. They had their part in making its past history; they are now having a larger part in making its future history, and the future, I trust, will not same the past.

Of the crimes and vices which darken and disturb social life, the Irish have also their share, and, I hope, not more than their share. But if the Irish have their part in the crimes and vices of society, they contribute also their portion to the sanctities and virtues by which society has life, strength, and security. It is further to be taken into consideration, that the crimes and vices to which the Irish are exposed are such as obtain an immediate publicity, and therefore, by their constant iteration in police reports, lead to profound misjudgments on the moral character of the Irish in America. It has been, of late years, the habit of certain speculative moralists to excite much alarm concerning the "dangerous classes," as these moralists term the vicious and the criminal who come from among the ignorant and the poor. But are there not "dangerous classes" which also belong to the educated and the rich? One unnatural murder, one instance of base and brutal lust, one great fraud, one huge breach of trust, one astounding but well-contrived bankruptcy, among those to whom the world has given credit for intelligence, honor, and refinement, are crimes that outweigh thousands of petty larcenies, thousands of ordinary felonies, not merely in the gigantic magnitude of their immorality, but as fearful evidences of social corruption. Crimes of this kind shake the very foundations of public virtue, and are infinitely to be dreaded. Society has a right to guard itself against those who would injure it, whether they are high or low; it has a right to secure itself against them, both by means of prevention and penalty. But the moral character of a race or nation cannot be justly judged by that of the vicious and the criminal, whom it repudiates and gives over to punishment. Irish vice and crime is such as quickly meets its doom; Irish goodness and virtue, or indeed any goodness or virtue, do not thus openly come into public notice. In the social body as in the individual, we feel disease more than we feel health; and so, in communities, vice is ever more observable than virtue; and yet communities would die if virtue were not, upon the whole, their permanent condition. I say nothing to excuse what may be evil in the Irish, or to discredit what may be good in others. While in all people there is enough of good to encourage social faith and hope, there is enough also of evil to tax all moral forces in the work of social improvement.

I come now to consider the most important and serious relation which the Irish-born citizen holds to the nation and government of the United States—the most serious and important that any citizen can hold to any nation or government—I mean the civic or political relation. This is the highest which he can hold, because it makes him a living member of the body-politic, endows him with certain advantages, and imposes on him correspondent duties and obligations. It is true that the government, and all that are entrusted with national authority, have duties and obligations towards the citizen. Among the most sacred of these are, respect for his legal rights, and security to him, and liberty in the legal exercise of them. These principles are recognized, in theory at least, by every civilized government, whatever be its form—whether it be a despotism, a limited monarchy, or a democracy. So there are certain essential ideas implied in all governments, such as supremacy, unity, and perpetuity—supremacy of authority, unity of jurisdiction, and perpetuity of duration. Without these, organized order and regularity of function would be impossible. Authority which is final must be somewhere, and it must be known and acknowledged, or there would be uncertainty and contest without limit. The want of strong, definite, recognized, central authority in feudalism, covered Europe for ages with private wars. The theories concerning the origin of authority in government does not in any way interfere with its nature; it is alike supreme, whether we ascribe a divine right to it, or hold that it derives its right wholly from the people. When the people have once organized their will into the best forms which reason, experience, and wisdom can construct, then they have shaped for themselves an organism of supreme law to which they owe their allegiance, their submission, and their respect in all concerns properly within the limits of human government. The forms into which the ruling authority is organized may be changed, may be modified, may be improved, but authority there must still be. The administration of it may be criticised, may be praised or blamed; the agents of it may be displaced or punished; but this does not touch the essence or existence of the authority. It is a necessity of government, whether the government is one of choice or of coercion—as necessary as supremacy of authority is unity of jurisdiction. The laws must be the same in origin, so far as they apply to the same nation, and they must be of uniform execution. Thus, in this country, State laws are made within each State, and within each State they are executed. One State cannot make laws for another; nay, one part of a State cannot make laws for another part. The State authority is for State purposes, supreme within the State, and in so far, and no farther, it is sovereign.

The laws of the nation are national, and, for national purposes, are supreme, and have through all the States a universal jurisdiction. Each State, of course, contemplates its own perpetuity. So does every nation; and so, according to universal instinct and necessity, does the nation of the United States. Without such a conviction, all government would be paralyzed. There could be no loans, no treaties; no prospective arrangements for the future, not even the enactment of a law, since every law looks to the future, and not to the past. It is true that, in relation to God's time, the continuance of the longest empire is not as the beat of a second, Egypt's millenniums are not as the stroke of a pulse, or Rome's fancied eternity as the duration of a sigh. As God alone is great, so God alone is eternal. But with man's time it is different; and without the conviction of permanence, nothing great could ever have been achieved, or even conceived of; the human mind would always have been dwarfish; States or Governments could never have been imagined; mighty thoughts of individuals or peoples could never have come into the birth of beauty or of majesty; but man must always have existed as a wretched and brutal savage. So, too, in comparison with God's government in the universe, the stability of all human government is a thing of transient vicissitude. The stealthy and silent clutch of the destroyer may seize the strongest in the dark, when he has not the least suspicion of his danger. The proud emperor of Babylon, "king of kings,' feasted with his nobles when Cyrus came on him in the night and trampled his glory in the dust; and the descendant of *that* great Cyrus was himself hurled from his lofty throne by a young upstart from the mountains of Macedonia. Still, man acts rightly and wisely in following, as best he can, the laws and principles which God has for his guidance implanted in his nature.

Now the nation and government of the United States, like every nation and government, suggest to our mind the three ideas on which I have enlarged—supremacy of authority, unity of jurisdiction, and perpetuity of duration. It is as a nation the United States have been regarded by other countries of the world, and on the principles here stated they treated with the Federal Government as with a government which had supreme authority—of course, in government thus considered, I include Congress—to treat with them; as a government which was one and complete in itself, so far as these relations were concerned; and as a government which rested on permanent foundations—not here to-day, and gone to-morrow. Not only the Powers of the world thus regarded the nation and government of the United States, but the poorest emigrants from Europe. It was not of this State or that they thought, but of the American Nation. Owing fidelity to the State in which they might happen to reside, still the feeling uppermost and most present in their minds was that of being American citizens. The great mass of the Irish come hither with the intention of permanent residence, and they are seldom long in the country before they make declaration of that intention upon oath. This intention and this oath imply not only an acknowledgment of the supreme civil authority, but also a belief in its perpetuity; for surely none would think of making any nation the home of themselves and

of their posterity, the government of which was uncertain
and feeble, and which could afford no security to liberty,
property, or person.   No people of any sense would put
themselves within the power of tyranny or amidst the miseries of anarchy.   Faith in a government of strength, of
order, and of law is necessary to all social confidence, all
industrial energy in the present, and all hope in the future.
But people do come, and war has not hindered them.   They
come deliberatively and aforethought, and thus testify their
full confidence in the worth and security of the national
government.   They do this, too, upon oath.   To a man of
the least conscience and intelligence, there is much in this
that is very solemn—much to remind the adopted citizen
of his obligation, and to bring it more directly home to a
thoughtful mind than it comes even to a native citizen.
The foreign-born assumes citizenship; the native-born in-
herits it.   The one has it from his fathers; the other takes
it on himself.   With the native-born, it is involuntary; with
the foreign-born it is deliberative.   If loyalty in the native-
born has more in it of instinct and sentiment, loyalty in the
foreign-born is enforced by all the sanctions of honesty and
honor.   And taking it for all in all, the Federal Union has
deserved this loyalty from its foreign-born citizens.   It has
secured to them a political equality throughout the Union
as the members of one great nation; it has been a check
on the excesses of party and of faction—a safeguard against
local prejudices and theological antagonisms.   I speak here
of constitutional principles as organized in the political
nationality of the United States—not of this or that administration, of such or such act or acts of Congress, of this
or that set of measures.   National unity has been of incalculable advantage to the foreign-born inhabitants of the
United States.   If dependent on the several States, and
separately, for their civic position, it would have been ex-

tremely precarious, variable, and uncertain. In many cases
it might have been vexatious, annoying, and humiliating.
But any such narrow tendencies in the States the liberal
spirit of the national constitution disallows or counteracts.

It is indeed true that each separate State has much power
within it, both in its own concerns and in those of the
nation; but there is a safeguard against any arbitrary use
of it in the vast extent of the country, in the facility of
removal, and in the aggregate good sense of the national
legislature. But let the State circumscribe him as it may,
the naturalized foreigner has still the rights and dignity of
an American citizen.

Foreign-born citizens have not been wanting in national
loyalty. In all the trials which this country has gone
through, from the first struggle for national independence
to the present war, there has always been a foreign element
in zealous union with the native. It ought not to be otherwise. The country in which people choose to live, whose
benefits they enjoy, whose honors they share, whose hopes
they bequeath to their posterity, has a rightful claim to
their aid and service, even to the sacrifice of life. To
answer this claim may be simply fidelity to duty, but it is
fidelity to a sublime duty, and, when the duty is bravely
accomplished, it amounts to heroism. Of such heroism,
both in deeds and sufferings, among foreign-born citizens—
and not least, among the Irish—history will contain immortal record. I ask no exclusive honor for the foreign-
born, Irish or otherwise, in the present melancholy war.
The native and the naturalized have been heart to heart
and hand to hand on its blood-deluged fields, and amidst
its dark and deadly tempests of iron and fire. They have
alike shared in its victories and defeats, in its hardships,
sicknesses, in the sharp agonies of wounds, and in the slow-
consuming waste of fever. Many of the native, of youth

of the richest gifts and promise, have fallen in the bloom of their life, in the blush of their coming noon; and beauty, and genius, and talent, and scholarship, and worth, goodness, nobleness, and honor have been taken from the earth for ever; and the men that would have been the authors, the artists, the orators, the legislators, the merchants, the magistrates of the land have gone to their final sleep in bloody shrouds. But they "sleep well." They met death in the ecstacy of courage and patriotism; their souls went forth in the cause of their country; and all the glory which this world gives to eloquence and poetry is not worthy to be compared with the fame and the love with which their memories will be cherished. So, too, numbers of the mature, who earned high positions in peaceful occupations, have given up their lives, and are at rest before their time. Their places on earth and in their homes will know these young men or their elders no more; but their images will live in silent hearts; and though the grief of these hearts has been such as cannot speak, they are comforted in the heroic deaths of their well-beloved. Yet tens of thousands who died unnoted, died as bravely; and they, too, left their memories in wounded and bleeding hearts. The Irish, who form a numerous portion of the laboring and able-bodied population, have contributed largely to our armies. Should we question the individuals who make up any Irish congregation or assembly, we should find that most of them had associations with the army, either by friends or kindred in the service, or killed—ay, by thousands killed—men who will no more bound with fearless enthusiasm to strains of martial music—will no more be awakened by the morning drum—no more obey the trumpet's significant sound—no more listen to the ear-piercing fife—no more have any part in "the pomp and circumstance of glorious war." Still, these —not the officers alone, but the most obscure private—had those to whom they were dear, and by whom they were loved—parents whom they helped or supported, wives and children, brothers and sisters, or some to whose life-long companionship they looked forward with the fondest hopes. Not in this country alone did the loss of them fill lowly dwellings throughout the land with affliction, but brought sorrow, and tears, and wailing into many a thatched cottage in Ireland—from Dublin to Galway, from the Giant's Causeway to Cape Clear. The Irish, both in command and in the ranks, have earned for themselves a place of soldierly and patriotic honor which will be generously, I trust, and not grudgingly given them in the future history of this country. I had always confidence in the national loyalty of my countrymen; but I contemplated only foreign enemies; I had no idea that the nation's foes should be they of its own household. The Irish have been faithful as a mass to the nation and the government, and without hesitation they have shot down their own countrymen in the ranks of the enemy, by his own will or by force. I do not say that in battle they could well do otherwise. What I mean is, that in doing this work they did it without shrinking, and without scruple. In such a contest as the present every strong man counts; and even of the man who goes into it as a substitute, we should not meanly think, for he shows at least one good quality—a quality most excellent in war—that of courage—at least, contempt of danger; and if we are to have mean thoughts of any one, it should be for the man who, without very sufficient reasons, sends a substitute—shuns himself the danger, and keeps quietly and comfortably at home. Honor, as Falstaff reasons, cannot set a leg or an arm, or take away the grief of a wound; it hath no skill in surgery. Honor is but a word, and a word is but a breath; therefore, he'd have none of it. A very wise conclusion, we may think, for one who wishes to live and die in a whole skin; but, in truth, the reasoning is false, and the conclusion is as foolish as it is base. The selfish may think of Patriotism as Falstaff thought of Honor; and if they prefer to live with the contempt of their country to the risk of dying for it, they may enjoy their ease and their opinion, but no true man will envy them in either.

Much discourse on the present war would here be very absurd. Historically, politically, morally, critically, financially, in fact, in every aspect of it, it has been discussed most thoroughly, and will continue to be so discussed, while it lasts, in every place of speech and in every form of print. I could not omit the topic; but as I have nothing new to say or suggest, my remarks will be as brief as I can make them. The necessity of brevity may seem to make my statements dogmatical, but *that* I cannot help, and cannot avoid. I think the Southern leaders of their own will brought on the war, and I think they desired to bring it on; I think they were prepared to bring it on. The election of Mr. Lincoln did not so much subvert their power in the Union as break their monopoly. This was the turning-point at which they decided to carry out their foregone conclusion. They had still great power in the country, but they had not the *whole* power. Having lost controlling sway in the Federal Union, they hoped for an absolute sway in a separate Confederacy; they hoped also to extend this Confederacy into a mighty empire. So, when the country was at peace with all nations—when it had recovered from severe pecuniary distress, and was in the stoutest vigor of monetary strength—when gold came to us by the ton, and Heaven had blessed us with a most abundant harvest—when our commerce had begun to amaze the world, and our power excited its fear and compelled its respect—when the increase of our greatness and prosperity seemed even to outrun desire, these men of guilty discontent invoked the

demon of disunion, and with him all the miseries that accompany and follow civil war. The war was inevitable, and
was begun by the South. Mr. Lincoln was constitutionally
elected, and became chief magistrate in the traditionary and
appointed mode. He was no radical or revolutionist; he
was rather conservative and conciliatory; and the South
made this election the occasion of the bloodiest civil war
which history records. Mr. Lincoln was elected; and
think of Mr. Lincoln as we may, intellectually, morally, or
politically, we cannot think it crime that he accepted the
"greatness thrust upon him." Being elected, what could
he do? Was he to consent to divide that Union which,
in the sight of Heaven, and in the presence of assembled
thousands, he had just sworn to maintain? Was he to
subvert that constitution which he was made President to
defend, to uphold, and to obey? He had no choice. The
war began with the South. The President, as best he
could, had to meet it. Loyal millions agreed with him.
The war, on the part of the North and of the national
authorities, was evidently unexpected; and it was as evidently prepared for on the part of the South, or of its
leaders. Suppose the Federal Government had at once
assented to peaceable separation. It would have been a
submission to dictation; for it was in this spirit that the
Southern leaders acted from the first; and such submission
would have justified all the contempt which the champions
of the South have invariably lavished on the people of the
North. The people of the South have long been, in their
own esteem, the patricians of the nation, and those of the
North, according to their estimate, plebeians and peddlers.
Would Northern churls dare to meet Southern chivalry?
They have done it; they have vindicated the character and
manhood of the North, and shown that, if the North loves
wealth and life, it loves the Union and a complete nation

ality better. For these it has spent and will spend wealth and life, nor think the spending vain. When the war began, many in the North supposed it would be a short one; some said thirty days, others went as far as ninety; but it really required no prophetic sagacity to foresee that the war would not be one of days, or of weeks, or of months, but of years. Such prophecy was, at first, regarded, not merely as false, but as ungracious, if not disloyal; and yet it is hard to see what interest any one not a contractor could have in making it. Both parties were obstinate, determined, and, in some respects, fairly balanced. If the North had more men and money, the South had the advantage of a defensive position, of local knowledge, of a people almost ready-made soldiers, of officers among the most educated in the nation, with two or three commanders, as experience proved, of original and extraordinary military genius. The North had on its side solid character, steady bravery, a cause made noble by a sense of right, and made sacred by venerable traditions, and by the memory of great names. But the best moral qualities, though sure in the long-run to win, are not always the most successful in the beginning of a war. No cause could have been more just than that of Germany against Napoleon, and yet the French scattered its armies for years upon their fatherland as chaff before the wind. The battle of Leipsic did, indeed, reverse the battles of Jena and Austerlitz, but the reversal was a good while in coming. The people of the South, as we hold, had a bad cause—all the more, their natural and undoubted bravery had the fierceness of desperation. They became revolutionists, innovators; they took the fatal choice, and were not likely quickly to repent or come to reason; they cast their lives upon the die; they trusted their fortunes to the " God of battles," who stands *now* in our prayers for the "God of peace;" they drew the sword, and they cast away the scabbard.

We are now in the third year of the war, and the end is not yet. We have still much to bear, and much to for-bear. We have to guard against divisions and despondency; also against spasmodic exultation. We need the ardor of hope as well as the enthusiasm of courage; we need the bravery of patience as well as the bravery of action. We are in the midst of a stupendous struggle. How awful its magnitude is, will be seen in history through the perspective of centuries. It is no time for paltry spites, or for vituperative accusations; it is no time for bandying bad epithets, or for calling each other names; this work is fit only for angry fishwomen or unruly wives. Even with respect to the enemy himself, let us beat him with good blows rather than with bad rhetoric. "Let us deliberate," said some one in the French National Convention. "Deliberate! deliberate!" shouted the fiery Mirabeau; "deliberate, while Hannibal thunders at the gates of Rome." So, while we are in this mortal strife, it seems unmanly and as unworthy to say, in word or act, "Come, let us have a war of words that shall outsound the war of blows; let us be heroes of the tongue; let us have glorious political scolding-matches. We may be the contempt of nations, but we shall be demigods in our own esteem. Posterity will immortalize us; will build monuments to our memories, and inscribe statues with our names." In the mean time our speechless soldiers languish in hospitals, grow dispirited in passive vigilance, or bleed out their heart's life in mortal battle. There is no need that we should give up our opinions, but only for the time put some generous restraint upon the will. An honest physician who watches over a patient in a critical condition will throw theories of physic to the dogs, and do that for his patient which his best skill and the danger of the moment requires. If he calls in other doctors, he and they will feel the solemnity of the occasion, and try to meet it, with grave and thoughtful knowledge. They will not, like the quacks whom Le Sage so admirably describes in "Gil Blas," dispute about their systems, and let the patient die. Let us think of Presidents as we may, the country, to our thoughts, should be eternal. Presidents, as the fates may order, will run their course of four years in wisdom or in folly; but the desire in the heart of an American citizen should be, "Let the Union live for ever." Every American citizen, native or adopted, should stand by the country, and stand by it at any cost. The country is worth the cost, and though the individual may lose his life, or suffer much, the integrity of this magnificent country is the grandest inheritance that any man can leave to his posterity.

In the course of my remarks, I have entered into no discussion on the conduct of our military affairs, in the Cabinet, the field, or the camp; on ability or want of it in command; on victories or defeats, on their causes or their consequences. I am no military critic, or, indeed, political either. My vanity in either of these relations is perfectly invulnerable. I am even better off than was Achilles, since, as I never have been in the national council, no public scribe can impeach my statesmanship, and as I have never been in battle, I could never have got a wound in the heel, even in running away. I have entered into no discussion on the complications of politics which had preceded this war, and which have become more deeply entangled and involved as the war has advanced. I return to one simple position. It is the duty of every man to stand by the country in its peril, and it is also his interest. All honorable minds, in shaping their manner of existence, look to praise as well as to profit, and the most honorable minds think not so much of the praise, as of the merits that shall deserve it. And when the day comes, as come it will, when this great American nation shall have vindicated its majestic integrity, the late posterity of those who fought or died to gain it will have a fame grander than even Shakespeare has given to those who battled on the field of Agincourt; and when the last fight of our sad struggle is fought, the elegant young men who show themselves in our towns, but who take no dangerous part in the strife, and gentlemen who dine pleasantly of days and lie quietly abed o' nights, shall think themselves accursed they were not there, and hold their manhood cheap.

But some people say, Why not let us have peace? or, at least, why not propose some terms of peace? No humane or Christian heart beats that does not desire peace. We must, however, count the cost of peace as well as the cost of war. When two parties go into contest, one must succumb to the other, or subdue it. We must have the better of the South, or the South must have the better of us. They or we must dictate the terms of reconciliation or reconstruction. If *we* dictate the terms, they must be those of the Union, one and indivisible. If *they* dictate the terms, they must be those of disunion and independence. What likelihood is there of agreement? I see none at present. The South is not, as yet, either powerless or hopeless. It will have independence or nothing. It has not either here or in Europe given the hint that it will be content with less than independence. Even the timid and cautious suggestions in favor of compromise thrown out in a few places South have been generally scouted with indignant reprobation, and this too in districts of the South which, we are told, are suffering incredible hardships. According to all human appearances, the cost of peace now would be the loss of the Union. Are we prepared to pay that price? If we are, we ought to have paid it long ago, and spared humanity the countless miseries of a fratricidal and desolating war. Perhaps some would say, in the words of a celebrated politician, "Let the Union slide;" others perhaps would say, "Let the South go." This cannot, must not be. Great as the extent of our territory is, there is not room, at least on this side of the Rocky Mountains, for two separate governments. Suppose that all the space which the Southern people occupy was nothing more than a natural wilderness, ought the people of this nation to allow a foreign power to plant itself on the soil? How much less ought they to permit an antagonist and angry rival force to build itself up against them. That force would command a vast sweep of ocean boundary, and the outlet of the most important system of rivers in the world. It would be against reason and against nature that twenty millions, always increasing, should allow themselves to be girded all about in a sort of geographical imprisonment by a nation which begins in bitterness, and which would continue always to be in opposition to us. It would be political insanity not to hinder this, if we can. Between us and such a power there would never cease to be inflammatory irritation and jealous rivalry. We are too near each other to live at peace, as two countries, or, as such, to have safe or durable conditions of alliance. The present lamentable strife will, I know, leave deep and red scars behind it. Time, however, will heal them, when we are again united ; but let us be permanently divided, then late generations will find these scars sore and fresh. At any cost, we must do our utmost to prevent such a result; and we are justified in doing so, not merely by political foresight, but also by the instinct of self-preservation.

To let a nation erect itself beside us and against us, with means to work us mischief in *that* wherein it agrees with us as well as in *that* wherein it differs from us—to let a nation arise, with unlimited space for extension—to let it gather its strength into a force which towards us would long be the force of enmity, with a hatred all the more obstinate and implacable, because it would be the hatred of revolted kindred—this would be a combination of madness and folly, for an example of which we might search all history in vain. Loyal citizens, native or adopted, are bound by duty and by interest to save the country from so ruinous a catastrophe. Surely it cannot be, while the land contains bravery and fortitude to fight, and to keep the faith of manhood and integrity. Generations yet unborn will bless the memory of those whose heroism and suffering held safely for them, amidst mortal anguish, the inheritance of a common country.

Moreover, this contemplated empire is to be a slave empire. Over slavery in the States, separately, the nation had no legal control. It was properly a municipal, not a national institution; and the communities among which it existed had a right to deal with it as with their other purely local concerns. We should be no more entitled to make war on the people of the South on account of slavery than we should on the Hindoos on account of Brahmanism; on the Tartars or Chinese, for Buddhism; on the Turks, for pollygamy; on the Abyssinians or Ethiopians, for eating raw beef. I have myself never had but one opinion about slavery, and that I have had since I could think. It is, that slavery is radically unjust. And I believe that, in the progress of human improvement, a time will come when it will be as great a wonder that men ever bought and sold men as that they ever cooked and eat men. Opposition to slavery has been with me a matter for which I claim no merit. It grew with me from instinct into thought, from thought into passion, from passion into faith; and I gladly hail the day, however distant, when no man on earth shall bear the name or burden of a slave—when the human countenance, and the divine image in the human soul, shall be everywhere recognized as the sufficient title of a free birth-right. This faith I have ever held as a matter of individual moral conviction. I have never connected it with politics or party; I have never hesitated to declare it. I have never held slaveholders simply as such, as under one sentence of universal condemnation for their inheritance from an evil past in which, at one time, all the nation shared. But the establishment of a consolidated slave empire is a matter which involves the whole South. It would be a new and voluntary creation—a shocking and ghastly political spectacle in the presence of the civilized world. It would be the first instance in all history in which an empire was openly and professedly founded on the principles of slavery; the first instance in which a revolution orignated in the interests of slavery. Many are the wars and the revolutions which the world has witnessed; but it has been given to civilized men in our day to glorify bondage, and to try to make the spirit of it the new life of a new nation. Many rebellions there have been, defeated or successful; but professedly, at least, they have been for liberty, never for slavery; always they have been to break fetters, not to bind them; to extend the area of human freedom, and not the area of human chains. The would-be architects of this proposed empire plainly announce that the foundation and the corner-stone of their structure is the perpetual enslavement of millions in America, partially or wholly, of the African race. The establishment of such an empire would be a measureless misfortune, with its remorseless charter of eternal bondage, its multiplication of markets for the home trade in human beings, and its murderous commerce abroad for a foreign supply. This would be to roll the world backward with a vengeance. Nations there have been in the pagan past who had no scruple in robbing men of freedom, but they did not boast of slavery. The ancient Romans, proud and oppressive

as they were, honestly, in their laws, admitted that slavery
was a coercive and not a natural human condition. We do
not find that ancient literature sought inspiration from
slavery, that eloquence gloried in it, that the drama exalted
it, or that it was celebrated in ballad, song, or epic. Even to
those heathen men, it was to their better feelings a moral
and a social disgrace, which no poetry could beautify, which
no art could ennoble. Modern and Christian genius has had
for it a still profounder repugnance. No freeman in the
midst of freedom could sing the blessings of the chain, nay,
nor could a humane master sing them in the midst of
slavery. The slave himself may sing to lighten his toil or
to relieve his heart, but *he* must be a pitiless miscreant who
could find music in the bondsman's fate to enliven the
banquet or the ball. And yet I have seen comments in
Northern journals which left it to inference that Southern
slavery is better than English free labor. Now, no one
who reads English papers will deny that social statistics
there present a frightful picture of ignorance, brutality,
misery, vice, and crime ; poisonings which beat the skill
and cunning of Italy in the Middle Ages ; domestic vio-
lences and murders in most horrible varieties ; infanticide
reduced coolly to a system, as if babies were begotten and
born only to be buried, so that their parental murderers
might have wages for killing their own offspring in paltry
burial fees. In the statistics of English vices and crimes,
some vices and crimes exceed belief. They are not only out
of nature, but often seem to have no possible motive. They
seem to be the offspring of an epidemical moral and social
insanity, or as if some fiend, the most expert in cruel and
licentious temptation, had England given to him by the
father of sin to be for a time his especial province.

All this is lamentable and terrible. But would slavery
cure it ? If slavery is a remedy for vice and crime, where

must we limit the application of it? The vice and crime of England, or of any country, are not confined to its destitute or to its laboring classes. If the laboring classes are to be enslaved to prevent them from doing wrong, and to give them the security, the blessedness, the Eden-like innocence and enjoyments of a Southern plantation, what is to be done for the naughty middle and aristocratic classes—as, for instance, when a British girl, who can speak excellent French, poisons her unsuspecting lover in an affectionate cup of coffee; when a sporting duke plays the rogue upon his son, and leaves to him the inheritance of beggary; when a titled scamp becomes the plague of his family, and eats out, or drinks out, or games out the provision of all his brothers and sisters; when a nobleman allures his son into a solitary rural ride, and tries to assassinate him in order to become his heir; when a middle-aged couple first murder their landlord, and then their three children? But enough of this, and too much. Would slavery be a remedy? If so, it must not be confined to the working or to the destitute classes. It must not be confined to toilsmen, or aristocrats, or vicious grocers; it must also extend to authors and authoresses. French literature used to be accused of finding its most exciting interest in the breach of a certain commandment which it is not necessary to quote; but of late English literature has its greatest stimulus in commenting on that commandment which says, "Thou shalt do no murder." But all the most popular English fiction of the present day deals with murder; it lives in an atmosphere of death; it goes away from the open light, from the blessed day; it prowls through the gloomy concealments of nightly conspiracy and crime; and Romance, which used to be our delight, becomes our fear; reading it now seems like serving on a coroner's jury, or being present at any number of remarkable hangings. The Newgate calendar is flat and stale as compared with our present murder-literature. It is as if we should put Jonathan Wild the Great on a level with a common pickpocket. And ladies are the most famous in these blood-and-thunder novels. Midnight meetings, and all the works of darkness, seem to give them a very strange delectation; but how far they can think it edifying to their universal sisterhood, from fifteen to forty, to have their brains saturated with thoughts of guilt and death, to have assassins and their victims be the shadows in the day-dreams of virgins and of wives, and bloody spectres haunt the visions of their nights, *that* is a matter to be settled with themselves. Perhaps, as none more crave to see a man hanged than women, women, as the next best thing, like to write about it. It is a sad sign of the times. Money is made by these novels of murder. It is a pity, for most of us would rather see women associated with love than with murder. But slavery would be no remedy for the morbid social and moral condition which give these lady quill-drivers the materials for their nightmare compositions. Slavery is no remedy for any disease that flesh is heir to.

I have spoken freely, I have spoken plainly, and I have spoken on my own personal responsibility. If I have asserted strongly the necessity of the war, just as strongly do I lament that necessity. I rejoice, but with no savage or arrogant exultation, in our victories; for if the Duke of Wellington said, with respect to foreigners, the saddest thing next to a defeat is a victory, how sad then is the best alternative when the victory is over our own misguided brothers, with whom we had been once united in the spirit of kindly companionship. I am not vindictive against the South. I admire its courage; I admire many instances of genius which have been displayed in the course of the war, and still more many instances of generosity and humanity. I think that when the history of the war comes to be written, that it will be seen by posterity that no civil war of equal magnitude has ever been conducted on both sides with more reverence for the sanctities of honor and of life. People will not now agree with me; but these people who do not agree with me, cannot have studied the history of the civil wars of the Romans, or those in the Middle Ages; they cannot have studied the history of the Thirty Years War in Germany, or the history of the insurrection in Ireland in the year seventeen hundred and ninety-eight, and above all, they cannot have studied the history of the first French Revolution. Still, both in speech and action, passions hating and hateful have, as it was inevitable in such a war, displayed themselves, that, as it had been hoped, could not have been excited in the nineteenth Christian century. Neither side is a fair judge of the other in this matter; *that* supreme verdict the God of eternal justice knows; and He who is the Searcher of hearts will hold every individual soul to its own personal account. The cruel, the blood-thirsty, the rapacious, the lustful, on whatever side they be, will have to meet the dread sentence of an infinitely righteous Creator.

But to conclude: We naturalized citizens, from Ireland or elsewhere, have a simple duty. We walked hopefully in the brightness of the nation, and we rejoiced in its light; we must not despond or grumble in the interval of its trouble. We shared, or had our chance to share, in its good things; it is right that we should also share in its evil. Our blood has been prolifically poured on the battle-fields of the country, and there is no danger that we shall dishonor the memories of those who shed it.

IRISH CHARACTER, MENTAL AND MORAL.

I AM to speak on Irish character, mental and moral. I begin with Irish mental character. That part of the mind which we call intellect ; that part of the mind which deals with thought and argument, reasoning and ideas, is, in the Irish, quick, sharp, strong, and active. The Irish mind combines readily and rapidly. It delights in analogies and analysis, in criticism and controversy. Hence, perhaps, the success of the Irish mind at the bar, in the pulpit, in the popular assembly, in all those positions which demand the spontaneous transmission of thinking into speech—thinking that is never far from passion, and speech that usually is instinct with the spirit of imagination. The logic of the Irish mind takes naturally, therefore, the form of rhetoric or oratory. The action of the Irish understanding, united as commonly it is with fancy and emotion, quick to yield to the influence of sympathy or antagonism, kindles readily into eloquence—into eloquence of persuasion and conviction, or of contest and invective. But the Irish intellect has also shown its force in profound and abstract thinking. It is much given to mathematics. So dispersed used to be this kind of knowledge in Ireland in my time, that small local almanacs were full of questions, from mere crambos and puzzles in arithmetic and algebra up to the higher regions of geometry and the calculus. The gentlemen who conducted the trigonometrical survey of the kingdom declared that they found youngsters in abundance to do their calculations at a halfpenny a triangle. The Irish intellect is not less given to metaphysics, as many subtle and deep thinkers bear witness, from Scotus, among the greatest of early scholastics to Berkely, the father of modern Idealists.

From the earliest Christian times know to Western Europe, the Irish mind has been celebrated for its devotion to theology, for its attainments in ecclesiastical learning; and during a long period these were the only studies which constituted literature. Ireland, in this respect, was the school of Europe; and not the school only to which strangers came for instruction, but the school likewise from which native students went forth in all directions as teachers and apostles. It was once the fashion to sneer at such statements, but the fashion has had its day. A deeper scholarship has silenced the ridicule of shallow scoffers, and nothing in the past of nations is now better ascertained than the antiquity of Ireland, and the intellectuality of its early civilization. Particularly it has been so within the sphere of western culture. Irish learning was from the first found in the colleges of the continent, as afterwards Irish statesmanship was in its cabinets, and Irish valor in its camps. Beautiful ruins that abound in Ireland are mournful monuments of its former zeal in the cause of letters as well as of religion; for the structures that are lovely even in their desolation were those that once gave shelter to priest and student when Ireland was, as Dr. Johnson calls it, "the quiet habitation of sanctity and learning." These architectural remains show what grand and goodly dwelling-places Ireland reared for her men of prayer and her men of thought—show with what love and pomp she cherished the sublime ministry of the soul — show her enthusiasm for divine things, in noble forms of art as well as in sacred inspirations of soul. The barbarism which was fatal to scholarship and scholars; the barbarism which desecrated the sanctuaries of devotion and intelligence; the barbarism which gave force and will the place of faith and reason ; the barbarism which turned the college into a barrack, which pulled down the Almighty's temple, and built up the robber's castle—none of *this* was Irish ; this came first from the wild outlaws of northern seas. The Danes began the havoc, which other ravagers and spoliators successively and ruthlessly continued. The Irish, in the worst of their own conflicts, reverenced the shrines of worship and of study. The savageism to which neither laws nor letters, human or divine, were sacred, was foreign. The savageism was not Irish which destroyed buildings and burned books, which spared nothing in its fury, which swept as a devastating tempest over all that the labor or the zeal of mind had created or ennobled. The intellect of Ireland has survived many persecutions, and come clear and bright out of much stormy darkness. *That* intellect oppression could neither crush nor kill; it has a living force, which renders the spirit ever superior to the senses. But all this, it may be said, has reference only to the mind of a select few. The mind of the mass, it may be urged, has in the mean time continued in contented ignorance, and given small evidence of capacity. The very laws, which were made by Protestant rulers in Ireland against the education of the Catholic people—laws enacted for the purpose of closing every avenue by which intelligence could be cultivated—do of themselves refute both parts of this objection. For if the people had been already in contented ignorance, no laws would have been needed to hinder them from instruction, and if the people had been void of natural capacity, such laws, instead of being the refinement of cruelty, which they were, would have been the most laughable of absurdities. Surely to forbid schools and schoolmasters under direst penalties to a people who had no desire for schools or schoolmasters, and no fitness for them, would have been an audacity of drollery which even Irish farce has never dared. Such was not the case. The people, even the humblest of them, had both the desire and the fitness for education. A few generations ago, in Ireland, Protestant laws, as I have said, forbade Catholic education — confronted every endeavor after it with terror and penalty. If by stratagem such education was achieved, it was shut out from every sphere of activity or ambition. Now that, in the face of such threatening, and despite its execution, the Irish of all classes should still protect the schoolmaster—should still respect his office—should still, by every means of ingenuity, avail themselves of it—should still, for the sake of knowledge, brave the danger of spies, of informers, and the stern consequences of confiscation, imprisonment, or death, is an example of vigor in the life of mind which the history of few nations can show.

The Catholic Irish, in those hard times when education was thus forbidden them, carried their literary studies into the silent fields, and amidst bushes and brambles conned Homer, Virgil, Euclid, or the spelling-book; and this was the origin of what has been called "the hedge-school." The old Irish hedge-school should be held in immortal honor, as the last refuge of a people's mind, and as the last sanctuary of persecuted intellect. The Irish who dared all penalties for their faith, dared no less for their understanding. They were as zealous martyrs for scholarship as for conscience. Even while the penal laws were still in force, peasants who spoke Latin could be found among the hills of southern Ireland; and at all times classical studies have been popular among the Irish. Within the short period in which there has been in Ireland any comprehensive system of popular education, even the poorest of the people have made remarkable progress, and the time is fast hastening, when few, even of the poorest, will be liable to the odium—as odium it is considered—of not knowing how to read or write. Yet I do not esteem mere knowledge of reading and writing in itself as highly as many do. When *that* knowledge is not carried into thoughtful and practical application, it often satisfies only the vanity of conceited and pretentious ignorance. In any event, the mere knowledge of elementary reading and writing is no standard by which to judge in certain conditions of society the amount of a people's intelligence. Here is how I should estimate, until within the present century, the mental stock of a quick-minded farmer in Ireland, and his active accomplishments, even if he were not able to read or write. I leave out the proper business of his rural profession, which, if skillfully conducted, implies no contemptible quantity of knowledge, experience, industry, acuteness, and good sense. Independently of all this, such a man usually spoke two languages, English imperfectly, it might be, but Irish in all its wealth. In either Irish or English, he could tell a story; in either he could sing a song; and to the song he could sometimes add a tune on the bagpipes or the fiddle. Play indeed he might not, but he was sure to dance, and to dance with every ingenuity of step; he could dance any measure, from a single reel to a treble hornpipe. He was fully indoctrinated in all the science of the shillalah. He pulled it, a juicy sapling; he trimmed it, set it, seasoned it, greased it, polished it, coaxed it, petted it; it was thus disciplined, trained, highly educated, and became admirably fit for use; then, as frequently as occasion offered, *he was not* the boy to leave it idle, or to manage it unskillfully. He knew well how to govern it with his fingers and thumb, to give it breath with his mouth, to play upon all its stops, and to make it the occasion of vociferous, if not of "most eloquent music."

He was acquainted with all the local traditions; could recite the chronicles of every family. For every marked spot he had note and name. He was acquainted with the legends and the myths of every olden ruin. He was at home in the romance of witches, ghosts, fairies, and giants. He was also well informed in the "Arabian Nights," in "Gulliver's Travels," in "Robinson Crusoe," in the "Seven Champions of Christendom," in the "Seven Wise Men of Greece," in the "Wars of Troy," and in many classics of the same sort too numerous to mention. He was tolerably versed in the history of Ireland; he was familiarly ready with its great names, from Partholanus to St. Patrick, from Con of the hundred battles to General Sarsfield, and from Ossian, sublimest among the bards, to Carolan, the latest of them, and the sweetest. He was tolerably instructed in the doctrines of his religion, and he could cunningly defend them. He rather courted than avoided controversy. He was usually more than critical, and less than complimentary, on the characters of Henry VIII., Anne Boleyn, Archbishop Cranmer, and Queen Elizabeth. His version of the Protestant Reformation was not a favorable one; and certainly his ideas of Luther and of Calvin were exactly the opposite of eulogy. Now, taking all this together, it forms a respectable amount of faculty and acquisition; and though it might not be singly owned, except by a very marked individual, it was yet collectively shared by the average of the population. Grant as much to the average of ancient Greeks, and the classical enthusiast would speak of it with abundance of laudation. Mr. Grote sets a very high value upon less. "If we analyze," he says, "the intellectual acquisition of a common Grecian townsman from the rude communities of Arcadia or Phokis, even up to the enlightened Athens, we shall find that over and above the rules of art, or capacities requisite for his daily wants, it consisted chiefly of various

myths connected with his gens, his city, his religious festivals and the mysteries in which he might have chosen to
initiate himself, as well as with the works of art, and the
more striking natural objects which he might see around
him—the whole set off and decorated by some knowledge
of the epic and dramatic poets. Such," continues Mr. Grote,
"was the intellectual and imaginative reach of an ordinary
Greek, considered apart from the instructed few. It was an
aggregate of religion of social and patriotic retrospect, and
of romantic fancy blended into one indivisible whole."

Reading and writing, as critics now very generally admit,
were not known to the ancient Greeks, when early poets
chanted in their public assemblies mighty songs about gods
and heroes. It is even maintained that these poets could
not themselves read or write. Even in later times, when
reading and writing became accomplishments among the
especially educated, great multitudes, without these accomplishments, had among themselves an instinctive and traditional education. It was this mental force of nature, and
its marvellous susceptibility and plasticity, which constituted
the essentials of Grecian genius. Reading and writing became instruments for *this* genius, but they did not give it.
Genius it was which gave reading and writing to the Greeks,
as it was genius which gave them inspired rhapsodists
before reading or writing had ever been thought of. When
reading and writing had become perfect, it was still their
genius that gave the Greeks their great men, that enabled
the Greeks to *understand* their great men. It was this
genius, and not mere reading and writing, that gave the
Greeks the loftiest drama which nation ever had—the
most perfect architecture and sculpture of which human
imagination ever dreamed. It was this genius which made
the Greeks the masters of mind and method, the conquerors
of barbarism, the creators of art, the originators of science,

and in beauty and philosophy the teachers of the world.
Yet multitudes to whom this genius was native, out of
whose intuitions it sprung, who could feel it in its noblest
power, could still neither read nor write. Put, then, the
Christian faith of Ireland against the pagan faith of Greece,
the sublime doctrines, the immortal hopes and fears, the
spiritual ideas, the impressive worship of the one against
the carnal fables, the bounded conceptions, the conventional
rituals of the other; put the tragic story of Ireland against
the patriotic struggles of Greece. As to imagination, put
the wild and deep passion of Ireland against the graceful
and the fair poetries of Greece; put tradition against tradition, legend against legend, myth against myth; give
Grecian sculpture to the eye, give Irish music to the heart;
let the Grecian temple speak to the love of beauty, let the
Gothic church speak to the instinct of the soul; put, I say
the one against the other, then, for all that gives active life
to mind, the Irishman, to whom I have directed attention,
is surely not behind the Greek whom Mr. Grote describes.
Yet the Irishman to whom I refer is but a quick-minded
peasant, while the Greek to whom Mr. Grote refers is a
townsman, and of ordinary education. To those higher
powers of Greek genius which left ineffaceable impression on
the civilization of the world, this comparison has, of course,
no application; but in mere vividness, in *that* intellectual
irritableness to which mental activity is a necessity, there is
no small resemblance between the Greek mind and the Irish
mind, and also, for the delight which mental activity in itself
bestows, both minds appear to have been similarly constituted. No mind, not even the Greek, has ever had a more
disinterested love of knowledge than the Irish mind; no
other mind has ever had more passion for study, and without any reference to its gainful applications. In no country
more than in Ireland has scholarship been sought for in

defiance of such appalling obstacles. Hunger, cold, weariness, sorrow, loneliness, sickness, have been braved for it.
Many a hero of the mind has struggled with death itself in
battle against the ignorance which poverty or persecution
had enforced. In no other country has men made nobler
efforts than in Ireland to obtain education for themselves
or for their children. Many a man in Ireland who arose to
professional eminence had the schooling which prepared
him for it at the cost of his father's sweat, and many a loving
sacrifice has been made in the home to meet the expenses
of the college. I do therefore deny, and I deny it most
strenuously, and with all my soul, that the Irish have ever
been content with ignorance, or indifferent to knowledge.

The imaginative element in the mental character of the
Irish is that which comes now under observation.

This element in the Irish character is diffusive. It pervades the whole mind, and it pervades the whole people.
There is in the Irish mind an idealism which, more or less,
influences all its faculties, and which naturally disposes the
Irish to what is intensive and poetic. Many of the faults
and failings in Irish character may perhaps be traced to
this peculiarity. It may have led to that want of balance
and compactness which, not without justice, is attributed to
Irish character—to want of directness, force, and persistency
—to want of that sustained purpose which alone conquers
and succeeds. This interfused idealism has hindered it from
grasping the prosaic and the practical with sufficient firmness, or of holding to them with persistent tenacity.

A sense of ever-present soul in nature pervades the Irish
popular imagination. This imagination personifies objects,
and endows them with intelligence. It goes behind the
visible world, and, whether at noontide or at night, it discerns another world for the mind. Could the traditions,
the tales, the legends, the countless stories, droll and

dreadful, which make the unwritten poetry of the people, have been in due season collected, they would have formed a body of popular romance which only the "Arabian Nights" might have surpassed. They would besides have had a moral truth, a spiritual depth, a sanctity and a purity of which Oriental genius is peculiarly deficient. Then how the comic, the beautiful, the pathetic, and the tragic, are embodied in creatures of the Irish popular imagination, as, by turns, they are capricious, fantastic, melancholy. There is the Leprachawn, the mocking imp that delights in solitude and sunshine; the tiny shoemaker that, whenever seen, is busy with his hammer and his lapstone. The cynical and cunning cobbler knows where pots of money are concealed which would make everybody richer than the richest of the Jews. Oh, how many times, in those golden days of youth which are given *once* to the most wretched, and are never given *twice* to the most blessed, have I looked for that miniature Son of the Last—watched for his red cap amidst the green grass of the hillside—spied around to catch the thumb-sized treasure-knower, that I might have guineas to buy books to my heart's content, or wealth enough to go, like Aladdin, and ask for the caliph's daughter. But I must honestly confess that, though no one ever looked more diligently than I did for a Leprachawn, I never found one. There are the fairies that love the moonlight, that affectionately sport around beauty, and watch over childhood. There is the Banshee, the lonely and fearful spirit-watcher of her clan, the loyal visitant who attends the generations of her tribe, wails over the hour of their death and sorrow, and who, under castle window or through cottage door, sings her lamentations for the long-descended. The imaginative element is so native to the popular Irish mind, that those writers of Irish fiction truest to this element have best revealed the heart of the people's life.

An Irish peasant used once to be recognized in a certain class of literature only in condescension or in ridicule, and some of his own native writers put the grossest burlesques of him in novels and on the stage. Lady Morgan took the peasant kindly into her protection, but her especial heroes and heroines were of the nobility and gentry. Miss Edgeworth was earnest and warm-hearted, and to her genius every Irishman must refer with reverence and affection. She evidently loved the people, felt with them, and often "caught their living manners as they rose." She had pity for their sufferings; she had charity for their sins; she entered into the spirit of their goodness as well as of their follies; and their grief, wit, drollery, and oddity, she could happily depict. The broad comedy and the immediate pathos of their life are often most effectively and dramatically presented in her writings. But that imaginative, that ideal element which lies in the very soul of the people's life she failed to reach, and so far she failed in that genuine representation which traces outward characteristics to their inward sources. William Carleton, born himself into peasant life, knew it in the core of its heart; and genius inspired the knowledge of experience—a genius of power in its order, strong in passion, in humor, and in pathos, in the comic and the tragic. The light and darkness of rural character, in all their minglings and degrees, are to be found in Carleton's stories of the Irish peasantry. But whether in coarse merriment or deadly sorrow, in the sanctities of virtue or in the madness of crime, there is ever the presence of the imaginative element in Carleton's pictures of Irish character; and in this Carleton is true to fact and true to nature. With the grace and sweetness of her sex, added to an exquisite genius, Mrs. S. C. Hall illustrates the same principle in her descriptions of peasant life among the Irish. Banim and Griffin, of astonishing grasp in tragic conception, dealing mostly with the darker forces of Irish nature, show the action of imagination in the passions and the deeds of all their leading characters. I have here purposely brought into view the literature for which native and primitive Irish life alone has supplied the inspiration and the material.

In reference to the artistic direction of Irish imagination, I have only time to specify Music and Eloquence, and these I select as the most national and the most characteristic. Music is universal. It is not absent from any human heart. Every country has it, and in it every country takes delight. But the countries of strength, of wealth, of work, and of prosperity are *not* those which most or best cultivate it. The people of such countries are too busy in building ships and cities, in founding or ruling empires; they have other occupation than to give their thoughts to song, or train their hands to instruments. Music has indeed sounds for mirth and gladness; but its inmost secrets are hidden in the heart of sorrow—its deepest mysteries are reached only by the serious and meditative spirit. So it is that the best religious music is deep and pathetic—so it is that Christianity has so profoundly inspired music, for Christianity, born of a tragedy, has never lost the sense of its origin; it carries always in its bosom the solemn ideas of death and immortality. So it is that, as the lyric utterance of humanity, music has most of soul when it is the voice of memory, and of those relations to the future and the infinite which, in revealing at the same time our greatness and our littleness, sadden while they sanctify. Music too is peculiarly the art of the subjected and the unhappy. It is no wonder, therefore, that it should have attained so much excellence in Ireland. A sentiment of grief seems to breathe through the whole of Irish history. The spirit of Ireland is of the past, and the past to Ireland is a retrospect of sorrow. Irish music is alive with the spirit of this impassioned and melancholy past—a past which has such pathos in it as no words can utter, and for which music only has expression. Irish music is thus the voice of melancholy, with variations of war song and prayer, of dance sounds and death sounds. It is the lyric sighing of solemn and reflective musing, of troubled affections and of mourning nationality—a low long litany for the dying, without the resignation which belongs to the requiem for the dead. The bards which reached the deepest sources of this music, struck their harps amidst afflictions; in later times they composed it as if under the shadows of ruins, where the weeds had grown upon the castle tower, where grass was rank in courtly halls, where echoes of the lonely wind were in the vacant spaces of dismal valley or of haunted cave, and where the pallid ghosts of saints and warriors seemed to listen to the strain. Grief is always sacred ; grief invests even the most savage people with dignity; but when genius weds itself to grief—when genius breathes the historic sadness of a cultivated nation, it makes art as immortal as humanity. So it is with Irish music; and herein is the secret of its depth, its tenderness, its beauty, and its strength. In wedding this music to expressive verse, Moore has drawn life for his own genius out from the soul of his country; and while the memory of Ireland shall last, the melodies of Moore will be sung.

In speaking of Irish eloquence, I enter on no critical disquisition. This has been done so often and so well, that there is nothing more to say, and I will not, therefore, tax your patience with the repetition of a rather out-worn theme. I would merely observe : Irish eloquence, like Irish music, has much of its character from that law of human experience which connects intensity with adversity — to which we must also add the ardor, the enthusiasm, and the impulsive sensibility of the Irish temperament. Thence the **language of the people,** on most occasions of excitement, breaks readily into eloquence—eloquence always intense, and often exalted. Rich in terms of endearment, the Irish give full and musical expression to the affections, whether in affliction or in happiness, with most energy, of course, in affliction ; and sometimes in cases of- peculiar grief, their phraseology is burdened with all that is terrible or tender in the utterance of the smitten soul. But in passion dark, deep, and strong it is that the Irish are most powerful in the intensity of emotion and in the force of mind. And this never consists in mere sounds or in parade of sentiment. The Irish character is not sentimental. For *that* it is too imaginative and too impassioned. Exuberant as the Irish are in diction, the diction which comes from their fervid moods is earnest with import. When they use bold words, the occasion justifies their use ; and when the occasion calls for the boldest words, the boldest never fail them. They do not endeavor to suppress gladness or grief. In a dogged silence, or to counterfeit insensibility in pretended cynicism, they allow feelings to fill the heart, and out from the fullness of the heart they speak.

It was natural that such a people should have orators, and the orators born of such a people were made greater by the confidence which they had of the people's admiration and sympathy. This unity of sympathy and confidence brought the orator and the audience together in the electric interchange of passion and of thought. The orator inspired the audience ; the audience inspired the orator ; and both the audience and the orator arose to the consciousness of a higher nature. Yet the orator never took liberties with his audience. Grattan came to the Dublin hustings, to meet a Dublin crowd, in the full majesty of his eloquence. Curran taxed his utmost wealth of pathos, of imagination, of argument, and of humor, before a country jury. To multitudes, gathered from the cottages and farmhouses of a laborious population, O'Connell spoke the best speeches which he ever uttered. To rural throngs upon the open hillside, or under the straw-roofed chapel, the artificial, yet impassioned Shiel delivered some of his most elaborate and most fiery appeals. From the inner essence of Irish character came to birth, voice, and might the turbid power of Flood, the deep thinking of Plunket, the Shakespearean sweep of Burke, with all the other men of flaming tongues, in whose burning hearts the fire of a generous nationality was kindled. If Irish genius gave nothing to the world but the eloquence of such men, in that alone it has given to the world an immortal contribution.

Irish moral character is my second topic, and it must be rapidly treated. On this, as on other points, I am necessarily obliged to limit my attention to the broad characteristics of the national masses. The conditions of a lecture on so large a subject allow only reference to essentials of a people's life. Such essentials are to be sought mainly in the aggregate majority.

There is a good deal of what is spiritual in Irish character, and there are no exorbitant tendencies to what is sensual. The Irish nature is in a great degree a religious nature. Taking the Irish as a mass, they are devout, believing, patient, showing in the saddest hours, and under the heaviest calamities, an immovable trust in Divine providence. Habitually, they are zealous for the doctrine of their Church, faithful to its ordinances, and those among them who are the most earnest in their convictions, and the most observant of their ecclesiastical duties, are sure to have most of those essential virtues which all Christian creeds require in the Christian life. As the great body of the Irish people consists of Roman Catholics, in speaking, therefore, on the religion of that great body, of course I refer to the Roman Catholic. Independently of the form or the matter of belief in any religion, we respect those who adhere to it in sincerity, devotedness, and at the cost of loss, suffering, and sacrifice. These are in themselves moral qualities, and have in themselves an independent moral value. These qualities, all that is best in our nature, compel us to admire. We may not agree with the religionist, but we give honor to the man. We can conceive of a man holding what we con‑ sider dangerous error; but he may have an integrity, an honesty, a humanity, a heroism which his error does not reach or vitiate; while we must withhold all esteem from a man who professes what we regard as sacred truth, if we have reason to think he does so in guile, falsely, for gain or for ambition. I can see good, and acknowledge good in men of various beliefs. If this should bring on me discredit from them all, I cannot help it; I must even risk the gen‑ eral excommunication; but I would rather be outlawed for charity than be enthroned for intolerance. I honor the sincere devotedness of the Catholic Irish to their faith. I honor the zeal with which they have always confessed it, and the constancy with which they have suffered for it. Not in the quiet order alone of religious virtues do we find the Irish devoted; in the heroic order also of such virtues they have shown the spiritual value of the soul. I admire all in man that shows unselfishly the triumph of the spirit‑ ual over the sensual. I admire the Mohammedan conscience which strengthened the Moors to quit, for its sake, their beautiful paradise in Spain, and in burning Africa to seek for desert homes. The Hollanders are not a poetic race; rather sluggish and worldly they seem to our usual appre‑ hension; but as I look at them banded against Philip the Second, for their country and their creed, they are a nation of demi-gods. Nor are the once persecuted Protestant Dis‑ senters of England, whipped, imprisoned, and despoiled, less lofty to my thoughts. No warrior in the hour of most

praiseworthy victory is to my mental vision clad in more
genuine glory than the cropped-eared Puritan, whom the
savage servants of savage laws exposed in a pillory to the
inhuman insults of a cruel rabble; and though I have not
sympathy with his general type of character, my heart as
well as my admiration is with him in his courageous tribulation. So it is with the French Huguenot, preferring ban-
ishment to hypocrisy. So it is with the Scotch Presbyterian,
for love to his idea of truth perishing among the lonely
hills, or struck down in bloody battle, counting nothing loss
but the loss of his integrity, and nothing gain but the glory
of his cause. My imagination carries me back even beyond
all these. My spirit wanders amidst gloomy regions and in
dreary times. With pitying brotherhood, I follow the
hunted and the persecuted to their places of concealment,
of imprisonment, or of death; and whatever my opinion
may be of their creeds, I honor the heroism of their conscience. If suffering, then, for the sake of conscience can,
in spite of differences, compel respect, Irish Catholics have,
indeed, a sacred claim to it; for sharp and long was the
suffering which they bore. Even now, since multitudes of
them are the poor workers of the world, and Protestants
often the rich employers, adherence to their faith is not seldom a testimony to the power of conscience over interest.

Passing from the spiritual to the ethical and the practical
in Irish character, I desire to be neither eulogist nor censor,
but, with independent judgment, according to my knowledge
and ability, to state the truth. In constitution, Irish character is sensitive, excitable, with passions that readily take
fire and that burn deeply. Nationally considered, this character has been evolved out of an agitated historical experience, out of disordered centuries, out of social conditions
which were alternately in the storm of anarchy or the stillness of exhaustion. I will not compare Ireland with other

countries. Such comparisons are to no purpose. Let Ireland bear her own burden, and let other countries bear theirs. The national life in Ireland has never had time to compact itself, or been in a condition to consolidate its strength. Disturbed relations have generated fierce passions and occasioned fierce crimes. They have more or less infused disorder and disease into the social constitution. Wrong tempers and evil deeds I will not charge on circumstances alone, for that would be unwise advocacy and immoral logic. It is, however, only simple fairness to take circumstances into account in the judgment which we form of Irish character, or of any character. But under whatever circumstances wickedness appears, let it still be accounted wickedness, and let no amount of temptation save it from that moral condemnation which every violation of Divine law merits. This is what a man should feel for himself, and what, for father, mother, brethren, wife, child, or country, he ought not to belie.

No one will deny that much crime has been committed in Ireland, or that Irish character is capable of crime which may be dreadful and deadly. Generally, it is the crime of passion, wild and strong, or of confused ideas of justice, or of the reaction of an aroused indignation against oppression, or of low and exceptional natures, brutalized by ignorance and vice, or of disordered brains, maddened by stimulant or despair. Seldom is Irish crime mercenary, seldom is it solitary. Even in crime, the Irishman is social. Fearful and dark his crimes may be, but rarely are they individually conceived, and rarely perpetrated by individual agency. Commonly they are the result of shared and collective motives; in extremely few cases do they originate in silent and secret malice. So radically indeed is the individualism of guilt foreign to an Irishman's character, that whenever an Irishman's guilt *is* concentrated into self, it is

a guilt which seems the most to put off the man and put
on the demon.

Making thus all admission that severest criticism can
demand, I may speak with freedom on some moral excel-
lences in Irish character. Honesty I claim as a leading one.
Amidst all the disorders of Irish society, property has usually
been safe. Stores of luxury have been left unmolested
amidst a starving people; and a man loaded with money
need not have been afraid to spend the night in a mountain-
hut, though the peasant and his family had gone supperless
to bed. Seeing the millions worth of wealth that humble
Irish have constantly in trust, and that is most religiously
preserved, I will not turn aside to answer the petty accusations of petty minds. There are those who complain about
the loss of a pin who themselves neglect no opportunity to
cheat; there are those who lay stripes on the indigent
pilferer, but who gives smiles to the millionaire successful
in gigantic fraud. Truth I claim also for the Irish—truth,
I say, in its largest and most essential meaning. What is
piety but truth in relation to God? What is fidelity to
religious conviction but truth in a high and holy sense?
Take, as a general case, the most miserable Irish beggar,
ready to perish of hunger, and, was he persuaded that
denying his faith would make his fortune, he would put
away the bribe and die. What is honesty but truth? and
the Irish have at least a nation's share of the virtue. But
I must admit that, "to be honest as this world goes, is to
be one man picked out of ten thousand." What is domestic
purity but truth, blessed and beautiful truth—truth of the
heart, truth of *word*, truth of *look*, the sacramental truth of
dearest life? The Irish have their portion of such truth.
Let us not desecrate the idea of truth by confining it to
what is merely verbal, and let us not praise that as truthful
virtue in which there is no temptation to deceive. Why

should the rich, the powerful, the independent lie? What urgency have they to do so? Let not such judge. Let those who have been tempted, tempted sorely—tempted by indigence, by fear, by habits of subjection—let those who *know* what the struggle means, and what the victory costs, be the jurors to those who have been tempted, like them-selves, and let such pass the righteous sentence on the wretched ones who fall. But the Irish tell such lies, especi-ally the needy Irish, and above all the servant girls. What sinners and exceptions they must be in the midst of sur-rounding truth. How guilty they must be, with such brilliant examples everywhere before them—such examples of sim-plicity, of sincerity, of veracity, and of integrity. What severe conscientiousness in our parties and in their leaders. How scrupulous our press. How full of probity our statesmen. How rigorously verity rules the lips of our orators. How genuine is all mercantile commodity, and how abhorrent to falsehood is the word of seller unto buyer. How patriotio and disinterested all government contractors and officials. Of what unbending rectitude are all our moneyed corpor-ations. How honorable, and how, like Cæsar's wife, above suspicion, are all their agents; and no one of them ever runs away with the whole capital in his pocket. The man-servants and maidservants that could be capable of a *lie* in such an age of truth, are surely the most hardened of trans-gressors. May the Lord have mercy on their souls. Yet, occasionally, untruth is noticeable in their betters—at least, what simple people might consider untruth. Joseph Sur-face Goliathan, Esq., has no respect to the sanctities of his home; he has no respect to the sanctities of other men's homes; but he burns with a sense of indignant virtue on finding out that Biddy went to meet her lover when she said she went to see her aunt. Yet Joseph Surface Goliathan, Esq., thinks lies, breathes lies, eats lies, drinks lies, sleeps

lies, dreams lies, buys lies, sells lies, pays lies, and has lies
paid him—is himself a conglomerated lie, will die in falsehood, and his ashes, after death, will be consecrated by a
lying epitaph.   For much and many, Joseph Surface Goliathan, Esq., is a representative character.   I do not defend
Biddy's lie ; and because Goliathan is a big liar, that is no
reason why Biddy should be a little one.   Let the lie, big or
little, white or black, be fore ver hateful and shameful.   But
then the Irish do so blarney.   For my part, I regret to
observe that good old blarney is dying out, and giving place
to surliness which is not more honest because it is boorish.
Blarney, as we call it, had its source in kindness, and its
inspiration from those emotional and imaginative elements
in which native Irish character used to be so rich.   It was
the melody of speech, and showed that Irish manners had
a soul of sweetness in them, as well as Irish music.   It has
lingered longest among the poor ; for as old traditions, old
tunes, old dialects, old fashions, and shall I say—old clothes?
—stay longest among the poor, so do old civilities and old
courtesies.   It were a pity that gracious speech should be
among "the old things" which have passed away ; and it is
a great injustice to accuse gracious speech of insincerity because the man is poor who uses it.   Why should such
speech be deemed elegance in brilliant costume, and falsehood in threadbare or homespun—compliment with a simper, and cajolery with a brogue?   Must the word be suited
to the coat?   If so, then coarse utterance must accompany
coarse raiment, then the garment, and not the man, must
regulate expression.   But the action too should be suited to
the word ; then the rude in dress should not only be rude in
phrase, but also rude in deeds.   If, however, there sometimes are men in plain clothing who are more than
courteous, there are also men in fine clothing who are less
than civil.   The excess on one side is certainly better than

the deficiency on the other; for surely it is preferable to overdo the gentleman than to emulate the ruffian. Blarney is therefore an excellent thing in its way. If variety is the spice of life, if wit is its salt, blarney is its sugar. There are two B's which bring great reward to those who cunningly understand their secerets—and these are Blarney and Bunkum; blarney for the individual, bunkum for the public; indeed, bunkum is merely the bigger of the B's—it is blarney expanded to the utmost possible compass of windy magniloquence.

The Irish are said to want thrift. Thrift may be defined as the art of saving, and in this art the Irish in America, at least, have achieved notable distinction. How but from thrift are kept in motion these unbroken tides of remittances which flow into Ireland as regularly as the Atlantic waves? How arise those goodly structures throughout the country devoted to Roman .Catholic worship and institutions? All comes from the thrift of Irish labor—labor that, in the mass, is of the humblest order and of the smallest pay. Still there is a surplus, and the funds of American savings banks show how ample; but ample though it is, it amounts to little out of what the Irish spare from their earnings. The Irish, however, do not spare selfishly; they do not spare to be rich, to be capitalists, to have individual importance grounded upon wealth; they spare through the force of sentiment. One sentiment is that of religion, and another is that of kindred. The toiling Irishman calls no surplus his own till he has made contribution to his Church, and to the utmost ministered to the needs of his immediate relatives. The Irish used to be called idle, and accused of having no spirit of industry. The accusation will not stand in America. The laboring Irish in America are the severest of toilers. Theirs are the heat and the burden, theirs the cold and the struggle, theirs the utmost of exposure and

danger unto death.   The terrible fatigues from which others
shrink, they cheerfully endure.   They labor and complain
not.   Life and limb they constantly risk ; and though limbs
are often lamed, and life is often lost, still they battle bravely
on with Fate in the heroism of unpraised exertion.

But "Work or Die" seems to be now sounded alike in
the ears of all.   We are living in a new age, and in a
troubled one.   This new age brings with it new conditions,
new duties, and new trials.   The men who belong to the
age must accept its conditions, be faithful to its duties, and
be equal to its trials.   "Work or Die" is, I repeat, the
watchword of the age, and he who does not heed it must
take the consequences.   And now, in this dark and troubled
crisis, in this calamitous and awful struggle, we have additional calls on our energy, fortitude, and principle.   We
shall not, I hope, be found wanting in the hardest trials
which honor and duty may require, but bravely do and
heroically suffer whatever is given us, as soldiers or citizens,
to do or suffer in behalf of the nation's dignity, welfare, and
restoration.   Stern as these demands are, they are noble ;
hard conditions, but grand discipline ; trainers of manhood,
teachers of power; and they who grow by their culture become the masters of circumstances, and the makers of
destinies.

IRISH SOCIAL CHARACTER.

I WISH it once for all to be distinctly understood, that I speak in this lecture of Irish social character as I knew it in my youth, long and many years ago, or as I heard of it from tradition ; I speak also of it in its distinctive national qualities, as developed among the masses of the people, or in such individuals as fairly represent those masses.

The Irish nature is eminently social. This may in part be owing to instinct of race, and in part to the influence of circumstances. Ireland is a small country, and for generations it has been thickly populated. I cannot recollect that, in any part of Ireland, I was ever for many minutes away from the sight of a human habitation. Of late years, the case, I understand, is different, but it is not of late years that Irish character has been formed. Always living thus in close companionship, it can be seen that not only would the social qualities become active, but the exercise of them would become a necessity of life. Accordingly, Irish character is abhorrent of seclusion, of isolation, and of solitude. It opens, expands, and grows in the communion and crowd of numbers; it droops, desponds, and withers in loneliness, or amidst a few. In good or evil, in gayety or grief, in kindness or in wrath, the Irishman longs for fellowship. In the hour of injury, he calls for condolers in his wrong; in the hour of success, he calls for congratulators on his triumph. In adversity he yearns for sympathy; in prosperity he draws together sharers of his plenty. In marriage he cannot dispense with the wedding gathering; and he would be grieved to anticipate other than a crowd at his funeral. Among his fellows, the Irishman must live; among them also he would die. Living or dying, his heart answers to that divine announcement, "It is not good for man to be alone."

In speaking of Irish social character, I will, first, trace it in its emotions; and, secondly, in its activities.

The first position, therefore, is the social character of the Irish in its emotions.

I may distinguish the love of kindred as one of the most powerful among these emotions. This with the Irish is tender, strong, far-reaching. No one that knows Irish character or Irish life has failed to observe in both the energy of the home affections. Warm and refined among the rich, they almost deepen into passion among the poor. In the barest cabin, no suffering, no affliction, no struggle for existence ever hardens, enfeebles, or extinguishes the instinctive inspiration of domestic attachment. In circumstances wherein it might seem that humanity itself would die, these attachments in the Irish nature preserve their vigor; for often, when the faith and hope of earth are lost in misery, and clouds are so thick upon the ways of Providence that the spirit is almost ready to perish in despair, love in the father's and mother's heart is yet a light from heaven that brightens affection with divine trust and with human sanctity. Rarely have Irish fathers and mothers been wanting in that love. Much and often it has been their need. Children never give back love equal to the measure of it which they receive; but compared with other nations, Irish children are not those that give back the least. And among the Irish how constant and how enduring is kindred love. The Irish parent claims by affection, as the Roman parent claimed by law, a perpetual ownership in his child; and the Irish child willingly allows the claim, which the Roman child soon learned to evade. An emigrant in America who is or might be himself a grandfather, will bow to the demands of his father in Ireland; and exacting, even unreasonable, as these parental demands often are, children thousands of miles away as obediently regard them as they did the commands which ruled their infancy. Such affections are not in the Irish mere animal instincts; they have much in them of spiritual as well as of social sentiment. The parent is jealous of his home with a goodly jealousy; and the peasant and the peer alike share this feeling. The man who digs a rood is as sensitive to the purity of his cabin as the man who owns a county is to that of his palace; he is no less zealous to guard it; and insult or wrong to it he is quite as ready to avenge. But yet I cannot say that everything is best in every Irish home. I know that much in many a poor Irish home is not there for its good, as indeed there is in many other homes, both poor and rich; and much there could sometimes be changed for the better. Wisdom and order are not always there in the measure of affection; and affection itself is not always sure against passion.

Even married love, which should be as the sacredness of God, or the weakness of woman, which should be to man as the holiness of heaven, does not always protect the wife from the violence of the husband; and when early and native feelings have died away in distant lands, and depravity has killed all generous impulse in the heart, and burning drink has put the flame of madness in the brain, it does sometimes come to pass—hard it is to say—that the Irish wife finds her murderer in the Irish husband. Such terrific facts occur. I add nothing to their simple statement, for comment they do not need; exceptional they must be with any people; and they do not impeach, therefore, what I have to say on the better nature of the Irish. Their love to kindred is, as I have asserted, tender, strong, constant, and far-reaching—far-reaching certainly, for *he* must indeed be a subtle and learned genealogist who could define the point of relationship at which the claim of an Irish cousin disappears, the point at which the claim would be denied. From the immediate claims of kindred, Irish affection never loosens itself. This to the Irish is as continuous as existence. It endures undismayed and undiminished in every fortune. Whatever else they may be, the Irish are loyal to those whom they left at home. The images of those far off come into their nightly dreams, and into their daily fancies. In the crowds of England, in the wilds of America, in toil and exile through the world, thoughts of kindred arise at the turn of every recollection. Then the moistened eye and the silent prayer bespeak affection, sublimed by faith. The hard-bought earnings are hoarded by pious thrift, and are wafted with unselfish love to those to whom "the untrammeled heart ever fondly turns." Generous and holy in the divine strength of human nature is this affection to kindred. "Lovely it is, and of good report." I have not spoken on the devotedness of Irish woman. To the honor of woman, it must be said that *her* goodness is less the result of circumstances than that of man—less dependent on culture or on race. Kind and generous affection is more the quality of her sex than the distinction of her nation. Other charms she may want or lose, but this is hers everywhere and for ever. Her face may be dark on the plains of Africa, her person may be worn in an Irish cottage, "the loveliness which made men mad" will pass away with years, but those blessed charities which glorify the soul can be erased by no blackening sun, can be extinguished by no privation, can be exhausted by no age ; they are as enduring as they are fair. I allude to woman in Ireland because of the trials which there encompassed and exalted her. The fidelity of woman's nature has its noblest manifestations in adversity; and of this training it had in Ireland a long martyrdom. In blood and struggle, in sickness and hunger, in every calamity which that country of successive woes has been heir to, woman has borne a hard share of the burden. Pure in her home, constant in her toil, uncomplaining among many wants, as wife, mother, daughter, sister, friend, in every relation, in every sphere, true to all her godly instincts, she has ever been a guardian and a ministering spirit. Strong in meekness, in charity, in patience, she has been a support to the feeble, a comfort to the weary-hearted, and against the unruly and the evil-tempered more than a conqueror.

Love of country in the Irish is not less than love of kindred. The feeling of country has to the Irish, as it has scarcely to any other people, the strength of an affection. It seems compounded of many loves—of the domestic love, which is born in home, and of which home itself is born, of the passionate love, which enraptures the heart of youth and of maiden, and of the transcendent love, with which the religious sentiment, and every sacred, every unselfish inspiration sanctifies the soul. Like every deep and genuine affection, it is not clamorous or arrogant, and does not readily expose itself. To no people is praise of their country more dear than it is to the Irish; but it is only dear to them as it comes from the heart, and their own instincts tell them when it is the heart that speaks. No people love to talk of their country more than the Irish; but they will not confidingly do so with strangers; they will only do so when they are sure of sympathy, and that is hardly sure to them but from each other. They will not submit to the risk of mockery or of indifference that which is to them so cherished and so pure. The uneducated especially, doubting their ability of language to do justice to their feeling, are careful that the beloved and ideal island shall not suffer from their infirmity. This ideal lives ever in the Irish mind· it is steeped in the endearment of the heart, and shines in the light of the Irish imagination. Wherever the Irish go, they bear this within them ; and sometimes it is that alone which hinders exile from being a hapless wilderness. The undying love which Ireland holds in Irish memory seems to be strangely different from what circumstances might suggest, did we not know the strength of the disinterested affections, and that love has never its motive in mere profit or mere pleasure. From no country do so many of its inhabitants emigrate as from Ireland, and emigrate with no expectation to return. The Swiss who leaves his country to fight in some foreign service, has at least the illusion that he may come back with money and renown. The Scotsman usually calculates that when he has made his fortune in some British colony, he will, in the evening of his life, spend it comfortably at home. Usually the Irishman quits his country with no hope that it shall again give him a local habitation or a name ; but so far as he is loyally Irish, that country is dear to him in every fortune ; he never scorns, and he never forgets it. He may be unworthy, and disgrace it ; he never will be unnatural, and defame it. Not to be condemned, but generously to be praised, is that tendency in the Irishman to remember endearingly the land which the sense of kindred has hallowed. In that land his fathers rest ; its grass is green, it may be, on his mother's grave. Shall he forget the land which the ashes of his parents consecrate, when both are at peace from their labors and their sorrows? When he does, let his word have no value, let his friendship have no honor, let his presence have no homage ; let him be the scorn of his own country, and let no other country trust him.

As the Irish disposition is quick to do kindness, it is
quick equally to feel kindness. Gratitude is therefore a
characteristic feeling of the Irish nature. It is as strong as
it is sensitive, as permanent as it is fervid. Even a trifle is
often greatly esteemed and long remembered. Ordinary
goodness, even simple justice to a servant, dependent, or
tenant, has not unfrequently been repaid with the devotion
of a life, or even with the sacrifice of life itself. Domestic
history in Ireland is full of such instances. In that history a
Caleb Balderstone would be no singular or imaginary character. Characters as droll, as faithful, as quick to invent for
the honor of the family, ready also to suffer or to die for it,
the domestic history of Ireland has had in plenty, and of
both sexes—a history rich in many a sublime tradition of
humble heroism. It is not in the domestic sphere alone, or
in merely personal relations, that the Irish are of ardent
gratitude. They are as much so in national concerns. In
truth, for those whom they regard as benefactors, private or
public, they are prepared to undergo any toil, to bear any
suffering, and to feel all that the most loyal affection can
inspire. Catholics as the people in the mass are, religion
has not hindered them from giving love and honor to such
Protestants as evinced earnest sympathy in their affairs.
When Bedell, during the dismal insurrection of 1641, was
prisoner among the insurgents, they behaved to him with
all tenderness ; allowed him full liberty of worship. When
he died, he was buried in consecrated ground, according to
the ritual of his own Church, and with the attendance of its
minister. Now Bedell was not only a Protestant bishop,
but a zealous Protestant proselytizer. Yet so profound was
the faith in Bedell's personal goodness, that in murderous
and gloomy times he not only enjoyed security, but was to
the last honored and beloved. Popular enthusiasm made
the Protestant Dean Swift a demi-god ; and generations

after his body had been dust, his name was cherished in the popular memory with impassioned admiration. Curran, who, of all forensic orators, blended most musically together the Irish heart and the Irish imagination, was a Protestant ; but to that heart, to that imagination, he was, and will ever be, of all such orators, the brightest and the dearest. Grattan was a Protestant, and he was to the Irish a leader and a hero. O'Connell was indeed a Catholic, and though this was, I admit, in his favor, it was not this alone which made him the mighty agitator that he was, and the national tribune of the people.

In whatever character you find the sentiment of gratitude, you will be sure to find that of reverence ; for both sentiments imply the same moral and sympathetic susceptibility of nature. Gratitude is *heart* active in memory ; reverence is *heart* active in faith and in imagination. Reverence is as noticeable in the social character of the Irish as it is in their religious character. Indeed, the religious element is traceable in many of their social forms. Most of the popular salutations include a prayer or a blessing. It must not bo said that these are mere words, without soul or meaning. However frequently repeated, they are never void of living import. It is in the spirit of reverence that the Irish are loyal to tradition and the past. Hence their homage to persons in whom tradition and the past are represented ; as, for one instance out of many, to the members of old families. It was not wealth or prosperity that used to move the feelings of the Irish, but those intangible associations which, though nothing to the senses, are real to the mind. There is something of the "mystical" native to Irish feeling; and this gives worth to what is spiritual and remote, above what is material and at hand. The merely moneyed man, proud and powerful in his wealth, drives out from his new mansion in his new coach, attended by servants blazing in

new liveries ; but to the Irish fancy there is no pomp in this
glare, and no charm in this splendor. Some poor gentleman walks out from a dilapidated old rookery, dressed in
rusty black, you know by instinct that no bank in Christendom, much less in Hebrewdom, would advance a pin on his
autograph ; yet there is dignity in his manner which passes
the show of dress, and an air of serene self-respect which
not all the funds of all the Rothschilds could bestow. He is
poor, but he knows that his poverty is respected. Nay, in
the kindly tribute which he receives from the people as he
moves among them, of willing deference, his rank is more
than recognized. Who may such a man be? He is perhaps
the successor of some anciently far-off noted O' or Mac—the
last, it may be, of some venerable name. While he lives,
men will, as he passes, bare the head, and women will bend
the knee ; and when he dies, a procession miles in length
will accompany his body to the grave.

I now enter on the second division of this lecture, and
speak on Irish social character in some of its activities.

The activity of the social sentiment we observe among the
Irish peculiarly in their hospitality. Hardly is there an
occasion among them which deeply moves the heart that is
not celebrated with a gathering of guests. Thus it is at
weddings, at baptism, and once it used so to be at burial.
So it is if the member of a family is about to leave it, with
the prospect of long or final separation ; so it is on the
return or visit of such as had been formerly inmates of the
household. Not only is the friend of by-gone years received
with collective welcome, but let him give his name, his
word, his sign to the merest stranger, that stranger will, in
like manner, be received. The Irish delight to give to
entertainment the gladness of a feast. A cordial joy of
soul flows into mood and manner, and all they say and do
has a festive spirit. Whenever the Irishman calls his

friends and neighbors together in order to have a pleasant time, all his nature seems to say, "Rejoice with me." He is every inch a host, and every inch a generous and a merry one. It is not merely that he does his best, and gives his best, but he is happy in the doing and the giving. He is not only happy in himself, he communicates also his happiness to others. His guests share in his expansiveness, and spontaneously enter into his glorious freedom of jubilation. Herein is a gracious charm, which can add sweetness to the humblest fare; without which, the most costly luxury is tasteless and unseasoned. I have sat at rich men's feasts, where good digestion did *not* wait on appetite. Coldness dulled both appetite and digestion; and much would I have preferred mirthful humor over a laughing potato, to gormandizing grimness which satiated but did not satisfy, and guzzling solemnity that inebriated but did not cheer. "The hospitality of other countries," says Curran, "is a matter of necessity or convention—in savage nations, of the first, in polished, of the latter; but the hospitality of an Irishman is not the running-account of posted and ledgered courtesies, as in other countries; it springs, like all his qualities, his faults, his virtues, directly from his heart. The heart of an Irishman is by nature bold, and he confides; it is tender, and he loves; it is generous, and he gives; it is social, and he is hospitable." A genial temper animates hospitality, I think, in all grades of Irish life. And this is another instance in which the peasant and the peer are kindred in their nationality. But the peasant once in Ireland exercised a peculiar and sacred order of hospitality, strange to the nobility and to the wealthy. Such hospitality is mentioned in the Gospel—hospitality which reckons among its guests the poor, the maimed, the lame, the blind, and which has its recompense in heaven. These classes in Ireland had not merely a share of the humble man's feast; they had also their pittance out of his scarcity. Daily he divided with some of them his food, and nightly he shared with some of them his roof. None more than the humble Irish seemed to keep constantly in mind that Christ was supplicant in each person of the destitute; and well did their treatment of the destitute anticipate that last address—"I was anhungered, and ye gave me meat; I was thirsty, and ye gave me drink; I was a stranger, and ye took me in; naked, and ye clothed me; I was sick, and ye visited me; I was in prison, and ye came unto me." So it used to be in Ireland. I cannot speak of the present; I speak only from my own observation; and so speaking, I can speak only of the past. But it belongs, I believe, essentially to the Irish character to *be* to want, or suffering extremely, merciful and tender. This is not by mere training or habit. Irish character is kindly and pitiful by nature. Its compassion is not local, but human. It makes no question of creed or country. It has no hesitation because of unfamiliar hue on the stranger's face, or of foreign accent on his tongue. So far as look or language speaks a fellow-creature's want, the Irish heart is quick to understand the speech, and the Irish hand, if means it has, is prompt to relieve the want.

Again: The transition is direct from the activity of sentiment to the activity of passion; and this, as a manifestation of Irish social character, leads me to speak of internal divisions and antagonisms in the social life of Ireland. To enumerate the injuries which these have done to the country, to describe the misfortunes and the miseries which they have inflicted on the people, to tell of the discredit which they have cast upon the national character, would be to recite the darkest chapter in the history of Ireland; but the chapter would be long as well as gloomy; and here some passing words are all that our space will allow; they are all, however, that our occasion needs.

In early times, the Irish had been for ages divided among themselves; and when, at length, there came assailants from without, want of union was want of strength. Originally broken up into small princedoms and chieftancies, they maintained from generation to generation the strifes which thus originated. The modern factions and the bloody fightings which grew out of them were constantly changing their names; but just in the degree that the cause was mythical or unknown, the hatred was fierce and real. But fighting, when not seriously envenomed, has, with the Irish, its comic as well as its tragic aspect; and aristocratic fighting has it as well as vulgar fighting. In proof of this, one has only to read Sir Jonah Barrington's chapter on "Duelling." These heroes of the pistol here chronicled were as cool with reference to their own lives, as they were indifferent to the lives of others. A hero with extremely slender legs had one of them broken by the ball of his antagonist; he held up the shivered limb, declared that he would never fight another challenge with such an opponent; "because," said he, "the man who could hit *that*, could hit anything." A person in one of Carleton's stories says of his father and himself: "It plazed Providence to bring us through many hairbreadth escapes with our craniums uncracked; and when we consider that he, on taking a retrogradation of his past life, can indulge in the pleasing recollection of having broken two skulls, and myself one, without either of us getting a fracture in return, I think we have both reason to be thankful." The makers and administrators of the law were as given to fighting as the people. Legislators fought, judges fought, sheriffs fought, barristers fought, magistrates fought, and from such the people had not only example, but direct encouragement. I will give you an instance from the traditions of a locality with which I was once familiar. Colonel Lane was a man of rank, and one of his majesty's justices of the peace for the County of Tipperary. Upon a certain fine morning, Larry O'Loughlin, bandaged about the head, called on his honor, and demanded a warrant against Timothy Tierney, to the illegal use of whose blackthorn kippeen Larry charged the fractures on the palace of his brain. "Larry, ma-bouchal," said his honor, "I didn't expect this of you. I'm ashamed of you, Larry. You are both neighbors' chilther. The dacent fathers to both of you are my tin-nants, and honester men there are not in the whole barony of Slievarda. Upon my conscience, I'd think it an etarnal dishonor to give a warrant against either of you, or to see you in the dirty coutintions of a court of justice. But I'll tell you what I'll do for you. I've as purty a coach-house as you'll find in the county. I'll send word to Tim to meet you there, say this day week. Give the lawyers to bother-ation. Fight it out as respectable boys ought to do. My huntsman, Dan Cregan, and myself will see fair-play. Shake hands, then, in pace and quietness, and be good fellows to the end of your lives." The Irish are not less given to intellectual contention. No legislature in the world has ever exhibited such brilliant gladiatorship as the Irish Parliament. What masters of invective its members were! Did the Billingsgate of genius ever surpass Grattan's attacks on Flood and Corry? Listen to what he said at the hust-ings to an opponent who attempted to impeach his vote in electing a representative for Dublin. Was ever more abuse put into fewer words? "Mr. Sheriff," said he, "when I observe the quarter whence the objection comes, I am not surprised at its being made. It proceeds from the hired traducer of his country, the excommunicated of his fellow-citizens, the regal rebel, the unpunished ruffian, the bigoted agitator—in the city a firebrand, in the court a liar, in the streets a bully, and in the field a coward; and so obnoxious is he to the very party he wishes to espouse, that he is only supportable by doing those dirty acts which the less vile refuse to execute."

The Irish temper goes easily into argument, but it does not so easily restrain itself within the bounds of logic. This tendency and its defect, Carleton observes with acute perception, and puts it into truthful and humorous illustration. I take a case in dispute between two hedge-schoolmasters in the administration of a Ribbonman's oath. "I'll read yez that part of the oath," says one, "which binds us all," etc. "I condimn *that*," observed the other master; "I condimn it as being too latitudinarian in the principle, and containing a paradogma; besides, 'tis bad grammar." "You're rather airly in the morning wid your bad grammar," replied the other; "I'll grant the paradogma, but I'll stand up for the grammar of it." "Faith if you rise to stand up for *that*," replied his friend, "and doesn't choose to sit down till you prove it to be good grammar, you'll be a standing joke all your life." "I believe it's pretty conspicuous in the parish that I have often, in our disputations about grammar, left you without a leg to stand upon at all," replied the other. "I would be glad to know," this other inquired, "by what beautiful invention a man could contrive to strike another in his absence?" "Have you good grammar for that?" "And did you never hear of detraction?" replied his opponent. "Does that confound you? Where's your logic and grammar to meet proper ratiocination like what I'm displaying?" "Faith," replied the other, "you may have had logic and grammar, but I'll take my oath it must have been in your younger years, for both have been absent ever since I knew you. They didn't like, you see, to be keeping bad company." "Why, you poor cratur," said his antagonist, "if I let myself out, I could make a hare of you." "And an ass of yourself," retorted the other.

"Hut, you poor Jamaica-headed castigator," brawled the opponent, "sure you never had more nor a thimbleful of sense on any subject." "Faith, and the thimble that measured yours was a tailor's one, widout a bottom to it, and good measure you got, you miserable flagellator."

The Irishman's readiness for a fight, mentally or bodily or his joyfulness in either, cannot be doubted. Much on this has been said in satire, and sung in song. Yet not alone in sport must we speak of Irish courage. It is noted in deeds sublimely brave—in deeds which give men the majesty of gods. In stern trial, such courage has been equal to those supreme hours which try the souls of heroes —on field or sea, in camp or fortress, in every rank from the leader crowned with glory to the soldier or the sailor without a name.

But Carleton is not best known in his broader pictures of Irish life. He is still a greater master of its subtlety and its pathos. I agree with a writer in the Dublin University Magazine, that "broad humor is not the characteristic of our people." They have, indeed, broad humor, because they have all sorts of humor; but the humor the most peculiarly their own is keen, quiet, sarcastic, suggestive—in which the word has always meaning more than meets the ear.

Ere I quit this topic, I would further devote a few words to the relation that, in my time, used to exist between Catholics and Protestants in Ireland. Where party did not interfere, it was charitable and kindly. Among the people in general, where an evil spirit was not excited, the relation was friendly, and often it was even affectionate. I have known the most intimate cordialities to exist between Catholics and Protestants in Ireland; and doubts of one as to the ultimate salvation of the other have often seemed to me to mingle, in a strange sort of manner, the mirthful with the serious. "I wonder," says Rafferty to Regan, "that

Catholics here in this Ireland of ours are so poorly off, and that so many of us true believers go to the bad?" "Well," says Regan, "if you don't know the reason, it's small blame to you. Nature, you see, didn't give you the gumption. I'll excogitate it for you, you spalpeen. Being mimbers of the thrue docthrine, you obsarve, we're persecuted, like Lazarus and Melchisedek. The ould boy is always a timptin' of us, and he niver laves us aisy; but as for thim Protestants, you see, they're well-behaved, becase the ould boy lets them alone; and he lets them alone becase he's always sure of them." There was, however, one Protestant whom Rafferty did not like to consider as within the power of the ancient sinner. "Regan, asthore," said Rafferty, "do you think that the ould dark vagabone can ever catch a howld of the dacent man Jack Hayden?" "Jack Hayden, forsooth! He's had howld of better men, and I don't see what should make a differ for Jack Hayden." "I'm sorry for him," said Rafferty; "a better neighbor than Jack Hayden, man niver smoked out of the same pipe with. He was always ready in a fight to help a friend with his stick, and on the rint-day he was quite as ready to help him with his money. Ah, shawn agrah! what shall I do, if I haven't you near me in the next world? for a good fellow you were to me in this. But I have comfort for you, shawn, my brother. When all the clothing and blankets which you gave every winter to the poor will be wet and wrapped about your sowl, the niver a blast of the bad fire can come near you, though Satan and all his sarvints were bursting their cheeks in blowing of it."

I come now to my closing topic, and that is the activity of the social imagination among the Irish in wit and humor.

A nation is entitled to the credit of wit when it has produced a great many individuals eminent for wit; a nation is entitled to the credit of wit when the spirit of wit enters into common life, and into ordinary intercourse. In both these respects the Irish are, I think, entitled to the credit of wit. But how is this to be illustrated? Shall it be from the wit of eminent individuals?

Among the individuals whom the Irish celebrate most for their wit were Swift, Sheridan, and Curran. The wit of Swift was fierce and sarcastic. Inflamed by political passion, it became terrible invective, as when he said of Lord Wharton, "He is without the sense of shame or glory, as some men are without the sense of smelling, and therefore a good name is no more to him than precious ointment would be to these." The wit of Sheridan sparkles through his dramas, and sparkles so constantly and so brilliantly as to become almost an excess of light. In society his wit was sportive, and was usually in spirit or in fact a practical joke. The wit of Curran, like his eloquence, was ideal. As his eloquence was the ideal of fancy, intellect, and passion, his wit was the ideal of intellect, fancy, and oddity. I quote a characteristic saying ascribed to him. A companion walking with him in Hyde Park, London, observing an Irish acquaintance of theirs at some distance, with his tongue out, said to Curran, " Why, think you, does that fellow so keep his tongue out?" " I suppose," answered Curran, " that he is trying to catch the English accent." Now the wit of these men has become literary, and may be read in books, or it has become traditional in famous sayings. The marked passages in books which might be quoted are hackneyed; so are the sayings; both the passages and sayings are over-rated and worn out. Social wit, especially, is peculiarly difficult to illustrate. So much depends upon utterance, upon circumstances, upon the grouping of persons, upon contrasts of character, which no description can impart, that often the very endeavor to exemplify social wit destroys it. Social wit is a subtle essence, which you cannot condense;

an etherial spirit, which you can neither localize nor fix.
Sir Jonah Barrington lived in Ireland in the most witty
period ; yet, among the characters whom he celebrates, the
most amusing is Sir Boyle Roche, and he celebrates him
only for his blunders. He was a man, however, of brilliant
blunders. His blunders were good, and his correction of
them was still better. On such occasions he was doubly
witty. He was witty in the original mistake ; he was still
more witty in the subsequent amendment ; and he was sure,
by an increase of absurdity, to fix attention on the point
which most deserved it. We are all now familiar with his
famous address to the House of Commons. "Are we to
beggar ourselves for fear of vexing posterity? Now, I would
ask honorable gentlemen, and this still more honorable
House, why we should put ourselves out of our way to do
anything for posterity, for what has posterity done for us?'
Explaining this, he said, "By posterity, I do not at all mean
our ancestors, but those who are to come immediately after
them." "Mr. Speaker," said he on another occasion, "if
those Gallican villains should invade us, Sir, 'tis on *that very
table*, may be, these honorable members might see their own
destinies lying in heaps atop of one another. Here perhaps,
Sir, the murderous ruffians would break in, cut us to mince-
meat, and throw our bleeding heads upon that table to stare
us in the face." Arguing once for the suspension of the
Habeas Corpus, he observed, "It would surely be better,
Mr. Speaker, to give up not only *a part*, but, if necessary,
even *the whole* of our Constitution, to preserve *the remainder*." But there was a good deal of wise bravery in his
blunder when he said, "The best way to avoid danger, is to
meet it plump." That was a good thing which Barrington
said to Lord Norbury—"He has a hand for everybody, and
a heart for nobody." Norbury himself would have been a
wit, had he happened to have had a *heart*. Terribly appal-

ling it was for Norbury to say, when passing sentence of death on a man for stealing a watch. "My good fellow, you made a grasp at *Time*, but, egad, you caught Eternity." The reputation of O'Connell as a wit is lost in his greater one as a tribune. That was a bitter saying of his against the London Times. "The Times," he observed "lies like a *misplaced* mile-stone, which can never by any possibility tell the truth." A priest having remarked to him that some traitors to the people were poor bargains to the Government. "My dear friend," he replied, "you have no idea what carrion finds a ready sale in the market of corruption." The wit of O'Connell is in strong contrast to that of Curran—the contrast of the real to the ideal, of the practical to the imaginative, of prose to poetry, and of passion to fancy. In Curran's wit there is ever insinuated imagery; in O'Connell's lacerating invective.

The sense of the ludicrous is often excited in Irish life by a certain unconscious oddity. I remember once in Dublin laughing heartily at a caricature which hit this point very happily. It represented a poor fellow, all in rags, under pelting rain, and a tattered umbrella over his head, while he is at the same time saying to himself, "It's devilish lucky I thought of my umbrella." A touch of the tragic was added to this, when Baron Power, of the Exchequer, went to drown himself, and the weather being wet, he too carried an umbrella. There is a strange incongruity in the idea of a man about to close his days in water guarding against a shower. The unconscious oddity of Judge Henn, in his ignorance of the law, has, however, nothing but the ludicrous. "How, gentlemen," said Judge Henn to a pair of disputatious lawyers, "can I settle it between you? You, Sir, say the law is one way, and you, Sir, on the other side, as unequivocally affirm that it is the other way. I wish to God, Billy Harris (the clerk of the court), I knew what the law really is."   "My Lord," replied Billy Harris, if I possessed that knowledge, I protest to God, I would tell your Lordship with a great deal of pleasure."   The faculty of medicine is sometimes at fault in this humorous way, as well as that of law.   A doctor pressed the judge to order him his expenses.   "On what plea," said the judge, "do you claim your expenses?"   "On the plea of my personal loss and inconvenience," replied the doctor.   "I have been kept away from my patients these five days, and if I am kept much longer, how do I know but they'll get well?"   But that peculiar form of mental confusion called "a bull," Mr. Edgeworth, in his famous "Essay," shows is not confined to Ireland, and that to the most striking instances of such mental blunders Ireland has no undivided claim.   If the most complete intellectual bull was made by an Irishman, Sir Richard Steele, the most complete practical one was made by an Englishman, Sir Isaac Newton.   When Sir Richard Steele was asked how it happened that his countrymen made so many bulls, he replied, "It is the effect of climate, Sir.   If an Englishman were born in Ireland, he would make as many."   But Sir Isaac Newton put a better bull than this into fact, for, having made a large hole in his study door for his cat to creep through, he made a small hole beside it for the kitten.

The truly broad humor of the Irish mind was to be found in my day among the peasantry, and on this point I will quote testimony from the North British Review, which fully corroborates my own early experience.   "In genuine humor, whether of the mirthful or the satirical order," the writer avers, "the Irish peasantry are superior to both the English and the Scotch.   An Irishman is not, as it is often supposed, a mere blunderer into fun.   No man can seek occasions for humor.   But when occasions come, the Irishman is prompt and ready.   "An Irishman," the writer tells "thus describes his cold reception by an old friend : 'I saw Pat Ryan t'other side of the way. I thought it was Pat, and Pat thought it was me ; and when I came up, shure, it was neither of us.'" "A poor old Irish cripple," says the North British Reviewer, "sat begging at a bridge, urging his appeal to the charity of passengers with the eager and versatile eloquence of his country. A gentleman and lady, young, gay, and handsome, with that peculiar look of gratified and complacent consciousness which indicates the first few weeks of married life, crossed the bridge. They regarded not the petition of the beggar, so, just as they passed him, he exclaimed, 'May the blessing of the Lord, which brings love, and joy, and wealth, and a fine family follow you all the days of your life.' A pause. The couple passed heedlessly on, and the beggar, with a fine touch of caustic humor, added, '*and never overtake you.*'" This is almost as good as what the pavior said to Dr. Abernethy. In the necessity of his work, the pavior had gathered stones around the doctor's door. "Take these stones out of my way," said the surly doctor. "Where shall I take them to ?" asked the pavior. "Take them to hell," roared the great surgeon. "Wouldn't they be more out of your honor's way in t'other place ?"

But Irish popular humor, in my time, appeared never so much in the oddity of cunning as in the native drollery of some local individual. Every district had its comic character, its chartered libertine. The most remarkable character of this kind that I used to hear of I will call Darby Quirk. Darby had been negligent of his religious duties. The priest sought him out in order to remonstrate with him on this neglect. "Why do you stay from Mass?" said the priest. "Because of my respect for religion," answered Darby. "Your respect for religion ?" "Yes, your river-ence. Do you think I'd have the audacious contimpt to go into the beautiful and holy temple with such a tarmagant of a coat.   Look at this coat, your riverence; wouldn't it wear every bit of religion out of me, if I had as much in me as there was in St. Patrick?   If I had the patience of Job, it would soak every drop of it out of me, and, faith, it would have been worse for the patriarch a good deal than the wife he had.   It would take the bishop himself to work out his salvation in it, and after all he'd have to do it with fear and trembling.   It is a pinance to get into it, it is a pinance to get out of it, and the wearin' of it is worse nor the treadmill.   But in the temptation of swarin', it's the worse of all.   If your riverence was in *this* coat, nabocklish, but you'd sware like a throoper.   When I want in the morning to run my arm through the sleeve, up it dashes through the back; thin I whispers quietly: 'Botheration to you!' Next I thries the other hand, and it's where the pocket used to be I find it.   Thin I grinds my teeth at it and feels the oaths coming up my throat; but I stops them, your riverence, if I can, at Adam's apple, and only mutthers to myself, 'Sweet bad luck to you!' and 'The curse of Cromwell on you.'   At last, when I gets my body into it, and begins to square my elbows, smash it goes, from the collar to the skirts.   Thin I shouts aloud what I daren't tell your riverence — till your riverence buys me a coat that 'ill be dacent to go to confession in.   In a respictable coat, yer riverence, I'd be a credit to you; I'd be the jewel of a Christian, and a pattern of the parish."   Darby obtained a new coat, but whether he became the jewel of a Christian, or a pattern of the parish, never could I learn.

A story I used to hear of the alleged twofold tendency of Irishmen to blunders and to bumpers.   I stole the substance of it from some one, and where *he* stole what I made it from, I never knew; but I have so often seen *my* version of it in the newspapers, that I am now almost ashamed to venture on a new edition of it. And yet it is so characteristic of things that *were*, "when George the Third was king," that I must even give it. 'Tim, asthore," says Shamus, "I dhramed a quare dhrame last night." "What was it?" says Tim. "I dhramed I went to see the king." "Suppose you did, what did you say to the king?" "I said, 'God save your majesty!'" "And what did the king say to you?" "Misha, what could he say but, 'God save you kindly, Shamus!' and thin, with an uncommon polite look, he said, 'How does the world use you, and how is the woman that owns you?' 'Och, as to the world, your majesty, it's not so bad; and as for the woman that owns me, she's bravely, thank your majesty, and is mother of a dozen chilther.' 'Just the case of my own owld woman, Shamus, mavourneen, says his majesty. 'And now, Shamus, ma bouchal, as we are on family concerns, and as I would like to have some advice from you in *that* respect, do you think a dhrop of the crathur ud harm you?' 'No more, your majesty, than the flowers in May.' 'Would you like a small taste on the present occasion?' said his majesty. 'Would a duck swim, your majesty, or does the cat know the way to the dairy?' 'What will it be, Shamus?' 'Punch, your majesty,' says I. 'Hot or cowld?' says he. 'Hot, your majesty,' says I. 'Och, niver bother it,' says he; 'the queen has gone to bed, and the cook is fast asleep; but wait awhile, I'll go down to the kitchen myself and bile some water.' Shure I awoke while his majesty was away, and wasn't I spited that I didn't take the liquor cowld."

Irish humor is direct, individual, and imaginative. It does not deal merely in extravagance and exaggeration—it does not deal in cant words or phrases—it does not become suggestive of laughter from mere accident or repetition. It may be broad and wild; so it constantly is; but it is so by inward idea, and not by outward excess. In Irish humor

the substance changes as the form changes, and in every
new instance of the ludicrous there is a new mood of mind.
That which is most popular is luxuriant, hilarious, sometimes riotous in mirth; sometimes on the verge of poetry;
often there is satiric meaning in its drollery, and a sharp
sting in its assumed simplicity; always, it is full of life.
Humor in the mirthful Irishman is genial and exuberant.
It diffuses itself through his whole nature. It is not an
effort, but an inspiration. It is vivid, rapid, careless. It
illuminates his face, moulds his gestures, hangs around him
in his costume, lurks in the turn of his lip, in the twinkle of
his eye, and seems to laugh at you from his hat that hangs
upon a peg. It is warm with the fires of humanity. It is
aglow in his blood; a gala and a festival in his faculties.
This geniality of temperament has been to the Irish for
many ills of life a wonderful compensation. Sad as their
circumstances have been, they have manfully sustained
themselves against fate. They have never allowed distress
to drive them to despair; but, in patience and perseverance,
they have still outlived misfortune. They could joke over
their potatoes, and sweeten the big one with the little one.
When taint or blight left neither the big nor the little one,
multitudes encountered famine unto death, and they died,
in their extremity, without bitterness or blasphemy.

Pathos and humor have a common source in the centre
of strong feeling. The same sensibility which brightens the
eye with laughter in one moment, fills it with tears in another. It is by the same sympathy of life that we weep
with those who weep, and that we rejoice with those who do
rejoice. Melancholy and mirth, grief and gladness, are the
offspring of *heart;* and wherever there is much heart, there
will be much of mirth and melancholy The heart which
is most alive to the holiday of pleasure, is also most alive to
the visitation of distress. The element of *heart* enters

largely into Irish nature, and this nature shows that the tragic in life has not been less in its experience than the comic. I might say, much more has the tragic been in it; for the history of Ireland has been one long tragedy, continued from century to century. The history of Ireland has been a history of sadness, of suffering, of disturbance, and of disease. On the side of the *governing*, of power without grandeur, of coercion without conquest, of strictness without method, and of severity without wisdom ; on the side of the *governed*, of passion without force, of subjection without submission, of resistance without achievement, of pathetic complaint and wild excitement, of writhing pride that, maddened by defeated struggle, gnawed the chain which it failed to break. All this bitterness of historic experience has not been without effect on Irish character.

The native Irish character is not the thing of levity which it seems in its gayer moments. It does not always caper for want of thought, but often because of thought—of thought which it cannot silence; and the loud laugh does not so frequently bespeak the vacant as it does the burdened mind. This is human nature. Character which has been formed in an atmosphere of melancholy, will be the most subject to boisterous merriment. This too is Irish nature; and, accordingly, the spirit of melancholy is ever in the centre, let what may be on the surface. There is gravity behind the smile; bitterness may be felt in banter; a sting is in Irish sarcasm; sadness is insinuated in an Irish joke, and wails through the fantastic frolics of an Irish jig. It might seem, then, as if a genuine lecture on social life in Ireland should consist of thoughts steeped in the heart of sorrow, and of words written with scalding tears. I can well feel that such a lecture might be appropriate and just. But I have spoken and written much on the serious aspects of Irish life; so I take one opportunity to dwell on the humorous side of it.

But whether on the serious or the humorous, I feel that in speaking about Ireland, as I knew it, I am speaking of *the past.* I feel too that I speak in the *spirit of the past.* I cannot help this. Others may have "a Young Ireland;" to me, Ireland *is,* and must always be, "Old Ireland." I see her through the mists of memory; I see her with the mists of ocean resting on her hills, with mists of time resting on her towers; I hear, as afar off, the eternal music of the waves around her coast; I hear in her valleys and her caves the songs of the winds soft as the sounds of harps; I recall her in many a vision of lonely beauty, brightened by the sunshine on river, lake, and dell; in many a vision too of sombre glory in the battle of the tempests against her mountain summits and her rock-bound shores. I bring her *national* life back to my mind in heroic story, in saintly legend, in tales passionate and wild, in the grand old poetry of the supernatural and solemn imagination, which people love to whose spirits the soul of the immortal whispers, on whose ears there linger the voices of the mighty *past.* I bring her *domestic* life back to my heart in her gracious old affections which so sweeten earthly care, in her gracious old phrases into which these old affections breathe; for never did fondness deepen into richer melody of love than in "cuishla machree;" and never did the welcome of hospitality sound in more generous eloquence than in that of "cead mille failthe." All these come back to me through the spaces of years; and my heart answers to them with "Erin mavourneen." If I forget thee, Ireland! let my right hand forget its cunning; if ever I do not speak of thee lovingly and reverently, let my tongue cleave to the roof of my mouth.

GERALD GRIFFIN.

GERALD GRIFFIN, the brilliant novelist and poet, forms the subject of this lecture.

His parents belonged to respectable Roman Catholic families in the South of Ireland. His father was a fairly educated and intelligent man ; his mother was a woman of talents, and of considerable reading. She was also a woman of strong affections, of deep sensibility, of earnest religious feeling, and of great elevation of character. "She was, says her son, the biographer of Gerald, " a person of exceedingly fine taste on most subjects, particularly on literature, for which she had a strong original turn, and which was, indeed, her passion." Alluding to her sensibility, he observes :

"This sensibility, the restless and exhaustible fountain o so much happiness and so much pain, she handed down to her son Gerald in all its entireness. She was intimately acquainted with the best models of English classical literature, took great delight in their study, and always endeavored to cultivate a taste for them in her children. Besides that sound religious instruction which she made secondary to nothing, and which in her opinion was the foundation of everything good, it was her constant aim to infuse more strongly into their minds that nobility of sentiment and princely and honorable feeling in all transactions with others which are its necessary fruits, and which the world itself, in its greatest faithfulness to religion, is compelled to worship She would frequently through the day, or in the evening, ask us questions in history; and these were generally such as tended to strengthen our remembrance of the more important passages, or to point out in any historical character those traits of moral beauty that she admired. 'Gerald,' I heard her ask, 'what did Camillus say to the schoolmaster of the Falerii?' Gerald instantly sat erect in his chair, his countenance glowing with the indignation which such an act of baseness inspired, and repeated with energy, 'Execrable villain!' cried the noble Roman, 'offer thy abominable proposals to creatures like thyself, and not to me! What though we be enemies of your city, are there not natural ties that bind all mankind, which should never be broken?'"

A generous Roman spirit, Christianized and softened, also shows itself in her letters to her children and to others. Her husband, Patrick Griffin, was an easy-going, cheerful, home-loving man, with a tendency to oddity and humor. This couple had many children; and one of the younger was Gerald, who was born in the city of Limerick, December 12, 1803. It will be seen that he inherited from his parents the finely-tempered and richly-mixed nature which is the soil of genius. Gerald received a portion of his childish instruction from an odd sort of pedagogue in Limerick named M'Eligot.

"My mother," writes the biograper, "went to the school with the boys on the first day of their entrance. 'Mr. M'Eligot,' said she, 'you will oblige me very much by paying particular attention to the boys' pronunciation, and making them perfect in their reading.' He looked at her with astonishment. 'Madam,' said he, abruptly, 'you had better take your children home. I can have nothing to do with them.' She expressed some surprise. 'Perhaps, Mrs Griffin,' said he, after a pause, 'you are not aware that there are only three persons in Ireland who know how to read.

'Three?' said she.   'Yes, madam, there are only three—
the Bishop of Killaloe, the Earl of Clare, and your humble
servant.   Reading, madam, is a natural gift, not an acquirement.   If you choose to expect impossibilities, you had
better take your children home.' "

This man was a true philosopher of the Dogberry order :
" To be a well-favored man is the gift of fortune ; but to
write and read comes by nature."   An amusing anecdote is
told of another teacher of Gerald's.   "Mr. Donovan," said
one of the scholars, "how ought a person to pronounce the
letter *i* in Latin?"   "If you intend to become a priest,
Dick," said the master, in reply, "you may as well call it *ee ;*
but if not, you may call it *ee* or *i*, just as you fancy."

One way and another, at home and in school, Gerald acquired a respectable education, including, if not a scholarly,
at least, a gentlemanly knowledge of classical literature.
Owing to the removal of the family from the city, the youthful lot of Gerald was to live among the lovely scenes of the
country near it, along the banks of the magnificent Shannon.
By the influence of these on his senses and his fancy, by
meditation and self-communion in the solitude of fields and
woods, or in the solemn stillness of grand old ruins, he had
the training which was best suited to his character and
genius.   The influences on his mind, of natural beauty and
of ancient traditions, may be traced in all his writings, both
of poetry and of prose.   He had equally a passion for nature
and a passion for the past.   Earth, air, water, skies, suns,
stars, " the dread magnificence of heaven," held over him a
genial sway; so did the olden times of an olden race, by
myth, legend, and heroic story.   And this spirit of nature
and of the past did not fail him, even in the gloomy bareness
of a London garret.   Even there, the divine vision of God's
works was present to his imagination ; and songs of national
inspiration came in sweet, sad music to his heart.   Gerald,

while very young, began to understand his proper mental destiny, though he lived to lament that he had ever given way to it. He would not be a doctor, but a poet; and so, while yet a mere boy, he set about composing tragedies, ballads, songs, tales, and sonnets.

The elder Mr. Griffin, though a worthy and industrious man, did not prosper in the business of a brewer in Limerick; nor does it appear that success attended his exertions in other occupations. Accordingly, he, his wife, and a portion of their family, emigrated to America, about the year 1820, and settled in the County of Susquehanna, Penn., some hundred and forty miles from the City of New York. Gerald was left to the care of an elder brother, a physician, living and practising at a short distance from Limerick. He first began in Limerick his literary career by fugitive contributions to a newspaper, and, for a short time, undertook vicariously its editorship. In Limerick also he first made the acquaintance of Mr. Banim, afterwards celebrated as the author of the "Tales by the O'Hara Family." But this local and provincial sphere Griffin felt to be too narrow for his talents and ambition; so, a few weeks before the close of his twentieth year, he found himself in London, without friends, with little money, but with much confidence. He had a manuscript tragedy which was to lay the foundation of his fame and fortune; and, when that was firmly laid, he formed the heroic resolution to reform the stage, and, artistically as well as morally, to bring about a revolution in the opera. I heard lately of a zealous Christian who enthusiastically declared that, when he should go to the other world, his determination was to labor to elevate souls to *his own level.* I did not learn what he thought that level was to be; but whatever he anticipated concerning it, the spiritual Quixotism of his infinite, eternal, and ghostly mission was not wilder or bolder than the intellectual and æsthetic Quixotism of Gerald, when he determined to raise the drama and the opera of London to his own level. I have no means of judging what the success of the good man alluded to may be in the other world, but I have Gerald's own honest and laughable confession of the folly and the failure in this world of his noble and disinterested plan. I say nothing on the modesty or humility of either of these self-constituted reformers. I only trust that our philanthropist of the next world may not have to be so lamentably disappointed as Gerald was in the stony-hearted world of London. Though Gerald conquered at last in a struggle which was all but fatal, he suffered in London miseries that are almost incredible. To this struggle I shall again return.

It is a circumstance worthy of mention, that Banim and Griffin, strictly members outwardly of the Roman Catholic Church, began at one time to doubt the truth of Christianity. Both, on studying the works of Paley, were not only confirmed in the faith of Christianity, but became inwardly more devoted Catholics. I do not attempt to account for this, which to some may seem a paradox. I allude to it in order to make a simple remark. It has been the fashion of late to stigmatize Paley as merely a utilitarian sensationalist and worldling; but I think that many have gained moral and political insight from his works which they could never otherwise have gained. My own philosophy, intellectual and ethical, is almost the opposite in its principles to that of Paley; but I honor the man who did, for the progress of civil and religious liberty of his own day, a manly work, who did it too in a manly way, and in most manly English.

After Gerald Griffin had stamped his name in English literature, he alternated for awhile between Ireland and London; took a tour in Scotland, of which he kept an interesting journal, and then returned home for life; but that was not for long. Only a brief period lay now between him and the grave. When he had attained to fame, and was surely on the way to wealth, he at once and for ever turned from the literary life in which he had so determinedly fought and so bravely conquered. He became a monk among the Christian Brothers—an order dedicated to the education of the poor—a vocation which, so long as life was left him, he fulfilled with exemplary goodness and wisdom. This was not long. He died in the monastery of the Christian Brothers, in Cork, on the 12th of June, 1840, in the thirty-seventh year of his age. So lowly did he think of himself as to his spiritual state, that he shrank from entering into priestly orders. When he had decided to live a monastic life, he regretted all the years he had given to literature as wasted, or worse than wasted. Had he the power, he would have exterminated works in which his genius lives for the honor of his own name and the credit of his country; also for harmless pleasure, even for the edification of countless thousands. He did destroy, before his friends could have had any suspicion of his intention, a large quantity of manuscripts, which may have contained works that possibly were better and riper than any he had published. This loss to literature his brotherly biographer very naturally laments; and if he had had any knowledge of the author's purpose, he would have done his utmost to prevent the loss.

A strangely romantic and poetic episode runs through the last ten years of Gerald Griffin's life. Gerald Griffin, like Charles Lamb, seemed to have had a special regard for the Society of Friends. He became acquainted, in Limerick with a Mr. and Mrs. ——, who belonged to that religious body. There sprang up between the couple and the poet the strongest mutual attachment. The feelings of the poet towards the lady, though evidently of reverential purity, were colored, nay, beautified, by the difference of sex, and amounted to an enthusiastic, an impassioned friendship. His letters to her are very numerous, very eloquent, and often very elevated. His last letter, presenting her with an old desk, on which all his literary work had been accomplished, is tender and musical with pathos and affection. Shortly after he became a monk, she called to see him. When her name was announced, he was walking in the garden. He turned pale, hesitated, but at last, though with strong emotion, refused to see her. A form of the anecdote which lurks in our memory adds that, when this message of denial was given to her, she burst into tears. Some most affecting lines addressed to her were found, after his death, among his papers.

Gerald Griffin was of the very best personal appearance The following passage, in which his brother, a physician, describes a visit to him in London, will give a more truthful and vivid impression of it than could any second-hand summary of ours.

"On my arrival in London from Edinburgh, in the month of September, 1826, I found him occupying neatly-furnished apartments in Northumberland street, Regent's Park. I had not seen him since he left Adare, and was struck with the change in his appearance. All color had left his cheek; he had grown very thin; and there was a sedate expression of countenance, unusual for one so young, and which, in after years, became habitual to him. It was far from being so, however, at the time I speak of, and readily gave place to that light and lively glance of his dark eye, that cheerfulness of manner and observant humor which, from his very infancy, had enlivened our fireside circle at home. Although so pale and thin as I have described him, his tall figure, expressive features, and his profusion of dark hair, thrown back from a fine forehead, gave an impression of a person remarkably handsome and interesting."

My limits confine me to this meagre outline of Griffin's life. His biography is written by a fraternal hand, with such affectionate and modest eloquence as to show that the writer was kindred in genius as well as in blood with the gifted brother of whom he wrote. To that biography I refer my hearers ; and I can promise them all the interest which the struggles of a heroic literary experience, admirably recorded, can impart.

I now offer some observations on Gerald Griffin's character, personal and literary. I do this, because I conceive that some peculiarities in his character tended to increase his difficulties in London, as these difficulties, in turn, tended to bring out his character, and help us to understand it.

He was, in the first place, of a very reserved temper with strangers. The English were wholly strange to him; and, of all English, Londoners would be, to a temper such as this, most forbidding : yet Gerald Griffin, while only a boy, plunged into the crowded wilderness of London. And this reserve would, at that period (1823), be rendered colder, more cautious, more sensitive, by the consciousness that, as a Roman Catholic Irishman, his position would be regarded, politically and socially, as one of inferiority. Whatever embarrasses ourselves embarrasses also those with whom we come into contact. Whatever tends to keep us apart from others tends equally to keep them apart from us, and the distance is thus doubled. The reserved temper of Griffin, together with his inexperience of the world, and particularly his ignorance of English character, would, as I have said, naturally increase all his difficulties in London. It is not likely that such a youth would easily or readily conciliate publishers or managers, who, though often servile to the successful, are as often haughty to the untried, and account their independence impudence. Gerald wanted that pushing manner which has a certain vulgar power in it, that frequently carries mediocrity into notice, into a gainful notoriety, and a "Brummagem" popularity. Neither had he that jovial buoyancy which, by a joke, story, or a laugh, sometimes wins favor from the most selfish or the most worldly. Courteous, amiable, and by nature gay and cheerful as Gerald was, he was, notwithstanding the amount of humor that was in his genius, no laugher-at-large, and, in his own person, no laugh-maker. A great force of purpose gave his character a tendency to austerity; but his stoicism was one of high principle, the instinct of personal dignity softened by Christian feeling and by gentlemanly grace.

This independent personality in Gerald Griffin, which might, as we have supposed, embarrass his intercourse with strangers, did so, as we are informed, with friends. He kept his relatives in Ireland ignorant of his condition, and he did not inform those in America of his troubles until he was well over them. Not that he kept silent either. On the contrary, like poor Chatterton, when his wretchedness was darkest, he was writing the most hopeful letters. In these dismal circumstances he refused the generous offer of pecuniary assistance from Mr. Banim, a fellow-countryman, a fellow-Catholic, a fellow-author, and a most intimate friend. A kind acquaintance of Griffin's, with whom he used to dine frequently, was obliged, by difficulties in business, to reside within what are called "The Rules"—a space of sanctuary allowed by the Court of Queen's Bench to a certain class of debtors. This affectionate friend, at the risk of close imprisonment and heavy penalties, ventured to pass the forbidden bounds, and, sheltered by darkness, made his way to Gerald's obscure lodgings. He found him there, past midnight, hard at work: he had not a single shilling left, and, for three days, he had not tasted food. "Good God!" said the friend, "why did you not come to see me?" "Oh!" said

Gerald, quietly, "you would not have me throw myself upon a man who was himself in prison." The friend, however, saw that he had immediately all that his condition required. While Griffin was thus starving, he was obliged to refuse invitations to luxurious dinners, and the society of cultivated minds, because his clothes were ragged; for the same reason he had to skulk out of nights in order to take some exercise and breathe fresh air. The letter in which he afterwards describes these sufferings to his mother is one of the most pathetic compositions to be found in the personal histories of men of letters. These sufferings from bodily want, exhausting toil, and an overtaxed mind, brought on a dangerous illness—nervous debility, and irregular action of the heart. It was only a sudden visit of his medical brother that saved his life; but from the results of this illness he never entirely recovered.

Stoic though Gerald Griffin was, he did not neglect to seek the aid of such influence as a high-minded man might honorably accept; but disappointment, disgust, and failure were all that his exertions brought him; at least, they brought him no such success as would compensate for the pain and labor of making them. So he determined to stand upon his own talents. If *they* were not sufficient to maintain his claims, then his claims had no real foundation. "It is odd; but I have never been successful, except where I depended entirely on my own exertions." If these should not sustain him, he resolved to abandon the struggle. He did not abandon the struggle, but persevered with courage and determination. There was no giving in. "That horrid word 'failure!'" he exclaims. "No; death first!" He was no dreamer or visionary, but a hard and honest worker. No man within a given time wrote more than Griffin, or more variously. He was ready to do any reputable work which was given him to do, and to do it well. He had the most elevated ideas of literature, both as an art and as a profession, as he had also of the dignity and duties of a literary man; it was genuine elevation, and modest because genuine; it was not the assumption of puffed-up self-conceit, or the pomposity of flattered vanity. In Griffin's view, it was noble to do work which it was honest and of good report to do; and therefore he never shrank from the humblest tasks, when higher ones came not in his way. He never failed in confidence; but it was confidence founded in strength—the strength of Christian patience, of conscious genius, of a firm will, of a determination not to be conquered; and, after much tribulation, he won no inglorious victory.

Perhaps no adventurer of letters ever endured more hardships in the same length of time, in London, than Gerald Griffin did, and endured them with less moral injury to his personal or literary character. Griffin seems to have escaped all the hurtful influences which pain, want, and uncertainty so often and so fatally have upon character. He kept himself free of all meanness, all coarseness, from low companionships, from degrading and degraded habits, and came out of the trial a young man with his home-born purity unsullied, a Christian with his faith more confirmed, a gentleman unharmed in his honor or refinement, and a writer who won success and the public by his own independent genius, bearing his triumph with true and graceful modesty. When I call to mind how many able, brilliant, and even amiable men the literary life in London has morally prostrated or destroyed, I cannot but give high praise to Griffin, that he did not yield to temptations before which strong men have fallen.

It would be interesting to compare fully Griffin's experience in London with that of other literary adventurers who had tried their fortune there before him; but I must resist

the allurement. Johnson would come first to mind. Griffin.
as a youth, had the same courage which Johnson showed
at maturity. He held the literary vocation in as high esteem,
and followed it with the same affection and devotedness.
Like Goldsmith, he eschewed patrons, and hoped for nothing but from the public and the publishers. He had not
the open, easy, careless good-nature of Goldsmith; but
neither had he his imprudence and improvidence. He had
a regard for his personal dignity, in which Goldsmith was
deficient; and he took care, as Goldsmith did not, to guard
this dignity. Savage, Chatterton, and Dermody may suggest themselves to many: but Savage was a charlatan;
Chatterton was a man of genius by the gift of God, but
chose to become an impostor by the instigation of the devil,
and preferred infamy to fame. He "perished in his prime"
by a double suicide : first, the suicide of his inner life; and
secondly, the suicide of his outward life. Dermody was
only a clever sot—a pot-house poet. To none of these has
Griffiin any moral relation. To Chatterton he was mentally
related in the early unfolding of striking talents, and inci-
dentally in having come near to the chasm of despair, into
which Chatterton, being void of faith, took the fatal leap.
The biographer of Gerald Griffin compares his literary character with that of Crabbe, to the disadvantage of Crabbe.
The remarks about Crabbe I regard as hardly just or
generous. Besides, they are unnecessary; for there is no
need that we should accuse Crabbe of servility, in order that
we should glorify Griffin for independence. Both were true
men, and neither in worth nor fame does one stand in the
other's way.

Does it not seem, however, as if the desperate struggles of
such remarkable persons would be a warning and a terror
to indigent young men against literary ambition; at least,
against their plunging themselves with blind impetuosity

into the dark whirlpools of mighty cities? But these young men see, in the lottery of the game of literary ambition, only the winners and the prizes. They think not of the losers or of the lost. Lucian, I believe it is, who tells us of a sailor that, having escaped from shipwreck, went into the temple of Neptune to make a votive offering. "Some individuals," said the priest, "seem to scoff at the power of Neptune; but look around, and behold the numerous tributes of those whom he has saved." "But where," asked the sailor, "are those whom he has drowned?" And so, if some, after London misery, have reached the glory of literary reward, what conception can we form of the wretchedness of the obscure thousands who sank into its gloomy depths never to be heard of more?—many, indeed, self-deluded, many vain, ignorant, and presumptuous, but also many of as true genius as those who succeeded. Might not one suppose that, before entering such a career, a young man would say to himself, "Where will it end?" And, end where it may, does the gain bear any proportion to the risk, while the chances of loss are incalculable, and loss itself is often deadly? Have not men, too, who gained all that genius could desire, confessed at last that, in substance, experience was much the same in literary life as it is in common life? Never was there a man more covetous of literary distinction than Gerald Griffin; and yet, before he had reached half-way to the eminence it was in his power to attain, he wearied of the aspiration which had carried him so far. Notwithstanding, the charm will work; and, in order that some may rise into the open day of fame, thousands sink into the thick night of poverty and despair.

But is it not so in all nature? The whole of life is risk; but risk does not therefore paralyze life; because, through life, hope ever goes along with danger. If danger deterred from action, the world would soon be at an end; it would have no armies, no navies, no commerce, no travel, no explorings of sea or land ; it would cease even to be peopled, for men would not run the risk of establishing and supporting homes, or women that of marriage and child-bearing If Jove's brain travailed with Minerva, if the mountain labored, as fable tells us, with a mouse, so will brains, till the end of time, palpitate with literary gestation, whether the result of parturition be wisdom or folly, mice or Minervas.

I proceed to some remarks on Gerald Griffin's genius and writings.

Griffin was certainly a man of genius—a man having a certain inborn aptitude, which is not the result of education and industry. This sets him who has it apart, not only from ordinary, but also from merely able men. For the mysterious something wherein this difference lies, we have no other name than genius ; and, though it cannot be formally defined or explained, its presence in any product of mind is recognized with unfailing certainty. It became active in Griffin while he was very young. Indeed, when Griffin gave up literature, he was still young ; so that Griffin was always a young author, and yet we might say that he was also a ripe one. From the first, he displayed a certain masculine vigor altogether different from the feebleness which sometimes characterizes the compositions of young writers who afterwards become remarkable for their strength. The early power of Griffin we see in the fact that his tragedy of "Gysippus" was written in his twentieth year ; his romance of "The Collegians," in his twenty-fifth. He had an inventive and bold imagination : to this his power and variety in the creation of character bear witness. He had great fullness of sensibility and fancy, as we observe in the picturesqueness of his style, and in his wealth of imagery. He delighted in outward nature, and is a fine describer of it; but, like Sir Walter Scott, he never describes for the sake of description, but always in connection with human interest and incident. He excels in the pathetic; but it is in passion that he has most power—strong natural passion, and such as it is in those individuals in whom it is strongest and most natural—individuals in the middle and lower ranks of life, especially in the middle and lower ranks of Irish life. It was in these ranks, and in Irish life, that Griffin found the spirit and the substance of his characters. He was a rapid and productive writer, and as much at home in criticising as in creating. He passionately loved music, and, by instinct, taste, and knowledge, was an excellent critic of it, as he was also of literature. His genius, too, was of the most refined moral purity, without sermonizing or cant; and when we reflect that guilt, and sin, and passion, low characters, vulgar life, and broad humor are so constantly the subjects with which it is concerned, this purity is no less remarkable than it is admirable. Every such case elevates literature, and makes it the source of a new pleasure; for it practically proves that the utmost freedom of genius may be exercised without offending the most rigid or alarming the most sensitive.

The poems of Gerald Griffin fill one large, thick volume of his works. Besides the tragedy of "Gysippus," they consist mostly of lyrical pieces gathered out of his several fictions through which they are interspersed. They are characterized by sweetness, feeling, and fancy. I regard Griffin's lyrics as his best poems, and his simple songs as his best lyrics. I think that, had he chosen to write Songs *of* Ireland, and Songs *for* Ireland, though he might never have attained the indescribable refinement of Moore, his songs would have had in them more music of the heart, and more homely nationality. Many of Griffin's songs have been popular; often sung and often quoted—such as "Old

Times, Old Times," "A Place in Thy Memory, Dearest,"
"My Mary of the Curling Hair," "Gilli-Ma-Chree," and
others.

Here is a song which I venture to quote. In spite of its
Irish phrases, the most English ear cannot be dead to the
spirit of its beauty. It is pathetic and original. It does
for the bride's young life what "John Anderson my jo" does
for the wifely faith of age—it breathes the unsensual and
unselfish affection of woman's heart. Love is usually celebrated in song for passion and for youth; Burns celebrates
it for purity and old age. In the one case, love looks to the
future; in the other, it looks to the past. So, usually, the
bride is made joyful in giving her life to her husband; in
Griffin's song, she is made sad in separating it from that of
her old parents. The thought is good, and true, and natural—more exquisite even than that of Burns; for in his there
is no future; but in Griffin's, the hope of the future is for
a time lost in the dutiful feelings of the past.

The mie-na-mallah ° now is past,
    O wirra-sthru! O wirra-sthru!†
And I must leave my home at last,
    O wirra-sthru! O wirra-sthru!
I look into my father's eyes,
I hear my mother's parting sigh—
Ah! to pine for other ties—
    O wirra-sthru! O wirra-sthru!

This evening they must sit alone,
    O wirra-sthru! O wirra-sthru!
They'll talk of me when I am gone,
    O wirra-sthru! O wirra-sthru!
Who will cheer my weary sire,
When toil and care his heart shall tire?
My chair is empty by the fire—
    O wirra-sthru! O wirra-sthru!

° Honeymoon.
† Similar to the English phrase, "Ah, the pity of it!"

How sunny looks my pleasant home !
  O wirra-sthru ! O wirra-sthru !
Those flowers for me shall never bloom,
  O wirra-sthru ! O wirra-sthru !
I seek new friends, and I am told
That they are rich in land and gold !
Ah ! will they love me like the old ?
  O wirra-sthru ! O wirra-sthru !

Farewell, dear friends, we meet no more,
  O wirra-sthru ! O wirra-sthru !
My husband's horse is at the door,
  O wirra-sthru ! O wirra-sthru !
Ah, love ! ah, love ! be kind to me ;
For, by this breaking heart you see
How dearly I have purchased thee !
  O wirra-sthru ! O wirra-sthru !

Here is a lyric, "The Bridal Wake," of so weird a pathos as to remind one of Burger's genius :

The priest stood at the marriage board,
  The marriage cake was made,
With meat the marriage chest was stored,
  Decked was the marriage bed.
The old man sat beside the fire,
  The mother sat by him,
The white bride was in gay attire,
  But her dark eye was dim.
    Ululah ! Ululah !
The night falls quick, the sun is set :
Her love is on the water yet.

I saw a red cloud in the west,
  Against the morning light :
Heaven shield the youth that she loves best
  From evil chance to-night !
The door flings wide ; loud moans the gale ;
  Wild fear her bosom fills ;
It is, it is the Banshee's wail
  Over the darkened hills !
    Ululah ! Ululah !
The day is past ! the night is dark !
The waves are mounting round his bark !

The guests sit round the bridal bed,
　And break the bridal cake ;
But they sit by the dead man's head,
　And hold his wedding wake.
The bride is praying in her room,
　The place is silent all !—
A fearful call ! a sudden doom !
　Bridal and funeral !
　　　Ululah ! Ululah !
A youth to Kilfieheras' ° ta'en,
That never will return again.

To show how early and how vigorously the poetic faculty became active in Gerald Griffin, I quote the following sonnet, written when he was but seventeen, and also to show how profoundly his mind was inspired with religious thought :

I looked upon the dark and sullen sea,
　Over whose slumbering wave the night's mist hung,
　Till from the morn's gray breast a fresh wind sprung,
And sought its brightening bosom joyously :
Then fled the mists its quickening breath before :
　The glad sea rose to meet it ; and each wave,
　Retiring from the sweet caress it gave,
Made summer music to the listening shore.
So slept my soul, unmindful of thy reign ;
　But the sweet breath of thy celestial grace
　Hath risen.　Oh ! let its quickening spirit chase
From that dark seat, each mist and secret stain,
Till, as in yon clear water, mirrored fair,
Heaven sees its own calm hues reflected there.

Some two years after the author's death, "Gysippus" was performed in Drury Lane Theatre, and was received with much applause—the great Macready acting the principal character.　As a poem, this play has been much admired ; and it deserves admiration.　I admire it much myself for its generous and elevated sentiments, its dra-

° The name of a churchyard.

matic style, with its absence of long and formal speeches, with its dialogue, sharp, natural, and rapid. I admire many of the situations and incidents as striking and pathetic; still, as a whole, I do not think that it reaches those depths and mysteries of life and passion which it is the province of great tragedy to fathom and reveal. But, then, it is the tragedy of a boy; and who can tell what the boy might have become, had he devoted his manhood to compositions for the stage? As the fact stands, we have Gerald Griffin's fullest power in his prose fictions.

Gerald Griffin is a delightful story-teller. The merest matters of fact and the wildest legends are alike at his command; and he tells with the same ease and the same fascinating interest a story of ghosts, fairies, witchcraft, or a story of guilt, grief, passion. His stories are of great variety; but they are all characteristically Irish; and Ireland has no need to be ashamed of them. The *spirit* of them is national, but the genius in them is individual. Gerald Griffin's own mark is on them. Nor are they mere copies— as Crofton Crocker's are—of fireside stories which the people used to tell among themselves, and tell them, too, much better than Croker has told them. I am hardly surprised at Griffin's vexation, when finding himself placed by a writer in the *Literary Gazette* by the side of Crofton Croker. "Only think," he exclaims, "only think of being compared with Crofton Crocker!"

Griffin's stories consist of three series—"Holland-tide Tales," "Tales of the Munster Festivals," and "Tales of the Jury-room." "The Holland-tide Tales" are supposed to be told by a group of persons met together for the sports of that evening; those of the Jury-room, by jurymen who cannot agree upon a verdict, and who pass the night pleasantly, after a smuggled supper and mountain-dew, in telling stories. There is no attempt at connecting the two stories in the volume which bears the title of "Tales of the Munster Festivals." In the Holland-tide series, "The Barber of Bantry" is a very exciting story of circumstantial evidence. A number of events conspire to prove the barber to have been the murderer of a man who, with a large sum of money, took refuge in his house in a dark and stormy night, and who was never seen again. After many years, the barber is arrested on what seem to be infallible proofs of his guilt.

"It will surprise you, Mr. Magistrate," he says on his examination, "to learn that, notwithstanding all this weight of circumstance, I am not guilty of the offence with which you charge me. When I have proved my innocence, as I shall do, my case will furnish a strong instance of the fallibility of any evidence that is indirect in a case where human life is interested. All the circumstances are true—my extreme necessity; his midnight visit to my house; his disappearance on that night, accompanied with signs of violence; my subsequent increase of wealth; and the seeming revelation of my waking dream ; and yet I am not guilty of this crime. If you will have patience to listen, I will tell you how far my guilt extended and where it stopped."

He then shows satisfactorily that he had nothing to do with the murder. The danger of capital conviction against innocent men seems to have painfully affected Griffin's mind. The impression was, perhaps, natural amidst the social circumstances of Ireland, where disturbance and discontent have been so permanent, and where the administration of law has been often so hasty, so partial, and so passionate ; where, as Lord Chancellor Redesdale averred, there was one law for the rich, and another for the poor. This state of things Griffin has illustrated in a story called "The Prophecy." "Tracy's Ambition," in "Tales of the Munster Festivals," is a powerful and impassioned narrative. It displays sharp insight into human nature and motives, and admirably exposes mean and base character and conduct. Family pride is a frequent topic with Griffin, and a peculiarly Irish form of it, in which a scoundrel glories in the contempt that his aristocratic relatives lavish on him. There is a character of this kind in "The Half-Sir," and another in "The Rivals." "Drink, my brother, drink," in the "Tales of the Jury-room," is a wild story of crime and passion, solemn, terrible, and pathetic.

Gerald Griffin was the author of three romances—"The Collegians," "The Duke of Monmouth," and "The Invasion." It is, however, "The Collegians" that has made Griffin most widely popular, and upon which it is likely that his fame will permanently rest.

This romance is founded on a real occurrence, the murder of a young girl, Ellen Hanlon, by her seducer, John Scanlan, a member of a respectable family, and his servant, Stephen Sullivan. The servant was the actual butcher, but it was at the imperative command of his master; and, in his confession before execution, he revealed an incident, a most affecting incident, which proved that humanity was not quite so dead in the servant as it was in the master. Scanlan sent Sullivan out in a boat with the girl to a desert place, some distance below the city of Limerick, where the Shannon is broad and drearily lonely. Sullivan carried with him a musket, a rope, and probably a stone. With the musket he was to batter his victim to death, and with the rope and stone to sink her corpse in the middle of the river. "The master remained u꞉ on the strand. After the interval of an hour, the boat returned, bearing back Ellen Hanlon unharmed. 'I thought I had made up my mind,' said the ruffian in his penitential declaration : 'I was just lifting the musket to dash her brains out; *but when I looked in her innocent face, I had not the heart to do it.*' This excuse made no impression on the merciless master." The master, having plied Sullivan with whiskey, sent him forth again; and this time the bloody work was finished. By a most surprising chain of circumstances, the guilty pair were connected with their crime; and Griffin, who so strongly objects to such kind of evidence, yet founds his story on it. The execution of Scanlan was attended with most painful and tragic circumstances. To the last moment, Scanlan denied his guilt; but, had there remained the slightest doubt, Sullivan's subsequent confession must have effectually removed it. The whole case is eloquently narrated in " Sheil's Sketches of the Irish Bar," published some years ago in New York, amply annotated by Dr. Shelton Mackenzie. Enough of the narrative to explain the story is given in an appendix to " The Collegians," in Sadlier's edition. I had nearly forgotten to mention that O'Connell was Scanlan's counsel. He says that he knocked up the principal witness against him. "But all would not do; there were proofs enough besides to convict him."

Of course, the real facts and personages are imaginatively colored in the romance. Hardress Cregan is a very modified John Scanlan, and Eily O'Connor is an idealized and purified representative of Ellen Hanlon. In Danny Mann, the wickedness of Sullivan is made more hideous by the addition of deformity. The rest of the many characters are original. As a dramatic tale of passion, we hardly know another which so quickly awakens interest, and which so intensely holds it to the end. This absorbing interest even the mechanical joinery of a playwright has not been able to weaken, in an adaptation of the story for the stage. The story has unity, action, movement—movement that, like fate, goes onward from the cheerful opening to the tragic close. The characters are numerous; and each, high or low, serious or comic, is a distinct individual. Hardress Cregan is very powerfully conceived, and the conception is carried out with consistency and force. High genius was required to make a man like Hardress Cregan, so inconsistent, preserve the unity of his character in the most contradictory of his inconsistencies. It was an extraordinary achievement to bring together in one individual qualities so opposite, and yet to make the union accordant with the facts of life and nature; high talents and tastes with low conduct; courage with meanness; generosity with selfishness; obstinate willfulness with feeble purpose;—a man having the elements of strong affections, and yet perverse, capricious, and unkind; having no real object but his own indulgence; devoted for one hour, inconstant the next; holding in jealous esteem the demands of honor, yet violating the simplest principles of honesty, truth, friendship, and humanity, until, at last, given over to a reprobate sense, dark with a self-blinded conscience in his moral life, he becomes villain enough to instigate his obedient slave to inflict cruel death on his loving and confiding victim; then he is cowardly enough basely to deny his share in the horrible consummation. In this powerfully-conceived character we see the havoc which passion, severed from the divine part of humanity, and moved by the sensual self, can work in the whole moral nature of an individual, and what misery and ruin it can bring on all that have any intimate relations with him. The utter wretchedness of Hardress Cregan's mind, as he approaches the crisis of his fate; his fitful, violent changes of mood and temper, amounting almost to paroxysms, especially in his later interviews with his mother and Ann Chute—show how well the author, both in action and suffering, knew the elements of tragedy that lie within the human heart. Danny Mann, the athletic, humpbacked servant, is as tragic a character as his master, and as powerfully drawn. The author is true to nature and art also in his female characters.

Ann Chute is a very brilliant creature ; but Eïy O'Connor rises into the very poetry of ideal girlhood ; a sweeter, a more beautiful, and more loveable feminine character, rendered imperfect by the imprudence of the heart, it never entered into the imagination of the poet to conceive. This character, and many others in the story, give evidence that the author was as able a master of the affections as of the passions. The Daly Family, both in their joys and sorrows, might be placed beside the "Primrose Family." They give occasion to very touching pictures of domestic life. The Cregan Family, however, consists of characters that are more individual, more striking, and more original. The comic characters are all very amusing in their humor, and very Irish. To point out the number of brilliant descriptions, and of impressive scenes scattered through the romance, would alone require a lecture longer than this. The scene of the dying huntsman, who, in giving the last "halloo" at the command of his drunken master, and, at the desire of his drunken guests, gasps forth his soul, is truly fearful, and borders on the horrible ; so is the chasing and cutting of Danny Mann by the intoxicated squires. But the author wished to illustrate the coarse manners of the time ; and for that purpose he puts back the period of the romance beyond the date of the real transaction on which it was founded. The closing interviews of Hardress with his mother are dismal and affecting, and the night scene with Danny Mann in prison is both solemn and terrible. One scene previously in the story, in which Hardress, drunk himself, makes Danny drunk also, when both are caught by Ann Chute in their maudlin frolics, has a Hogarthian force. He whom the interview of Eily with her uncle, the priest, shortly before her murder, will not melt to pity, would read all Shakespeare without a sigh, and must be poor indeed in moral as well as imaginative destitution.

No one can fail to admire the skill by which so extraordi-nary a variety of materials as there is in this romance is fused into a complete whole, and how every scene, character, description, and incident falls necessarily into the drama of the story—falls into it in the right time and place; and contributes each a needful share to the plot and to the catastrophe.

Still some critics might make objections ; they might adduce instances of melodramatic exaggeration ; but allow-ance must be made for Gerald Griffin's youth. I think that Ann Chute's saying to her lover, a few days before she is to be married to him, "What a dreadful death hanging must be!" is an instance of this kind. Though ignorant that Hardress, at the moment, was in mortal fear of such a death, the saying is coarse from a lady, and rather weakens the force of tragic impression. Many years ago, on first reading the romance, I thought the saying coarse ; and now I learn from the published correspondence in the biography, that Gerald's sister found fault with something unladylike in Ann Chute's character ; and I believe she must have had this expression in her mind. I could point out other incon-sistencies in Ann's character. I object to the catastrophe. I cannot agree that Hardress should get off with trans-portation, and respectably die of consumption at the end of the passage, while Danny Mann, the less guilty culprit, is left for the gallows. But Gerald says in a letter, "*If I hang him*, the public will never forgive me." I regard this as a mistake, except, perhaps, in reference to the public of senti-mental young ladies. John Scanlan was hanged in fact, and so should his representative, Hardress Cregan, have been hanged in fiction ; then poetical justice and practical justice would have corresponded. The real execution, moreover, of Scanlan was attended with strange and melancholy cir-cumstances that made it solemnly dramatic ; besides, the discrepancy between the fiction and the fact weakens the catastrophe and injures the illusion.

This extraordinary romance, so dramatic, so full of life, so crowded with characters — this romance, that opens the inmost chambers of the human heart, and sounds the depths of conscience and the passions—had been written, as I have mentioned, before the author had completed his twenty-fifth year. He began to print when he had only a volume and a half ready. The printers overtook him in the middle of the third volume. It was then a race from day to day between him and them to the end; and this hastily-written last moiety of the third volume is the finest portion of the book.

I have, in the course of this lecture, commended the moral spirit of Gerald Griffin's writings. My commendation is deserved, and with pleasure I declare it. How often has one to lament that he is compelled to admire grand intellectual power, which only lowers or disheartens him, darkens his spirit, or constrains his sympathies! A sure test, it has been often said, as to the good influence of a writer, is, that, when we lay aside his book, we feel better in ourselves, and we think better of others. This test, I believe, Gerald Griffin can safely stand.

DR. DOYLE.

JAMES WARREN DOYLE, the son of James Doyle, a respectable farmer near New Ross, in the County of Wexford, was born in the autumn of 1786. His father had died some weeks before his birth. His mother, Anne Warren, was a second wife. She was of Quaker descent, and a woman of determined moral firmness. A very characteristic anecdote is told of her. When she came near to the critical period when she must have medical attendance, but could not afford to have a physician from a distance, she walked some miles into town, took a cheap lodging, and put herself under the care of Dr. James Doyle, a man of considerable local eminence in his profession. This is a singular instance of sturdy independence, since the doctor was her own step-son, and the little stranger whom he introduced into the world was, accordingly, his half-brother. When Dr. Doyle was eleven years old, he witnessed the most terrific doings of the Irish rebellion in 1798. In Ross and around it that rebellion raged with its utmost fury. Having on one occasion strolled into fields where fighting came on, he narrowly escaped from being shot. He very early felt a vocation for the priesthood, and began the preparation for it. The teaching of childhood he had from his mother ; classical education he received in an Augustinian monastry, where he joined that order ; his academical and clerical training he obtained in the University of Coimbra, Portugal. Dr. Doyle, when about eighteen years of age, lost his mother, to whom he was infinitely indebted, to whom, in return, he was infinitely devoted. He seems, even in youth, to have had large intellectual tastes, and to have cultivated them by large and various reading. But he was not a mere bookworm; he was ready for action, when action was duty. On the invasion of Portugal by the French, young Doyle manfully shouldered his musket, and did such service faithfully as he was appointed to do. Sir Arthur Wellesley was cordial to him. "I was," says Dr. Doyle, "a sort of nondescript with the rank of captain, and an interpreter between the English and Portuguese armies. . . . . . I was present at the battles of Caldas, Rolica, and Vimiero; I was greatly exposed to the fire of the enemy, as I was obliged to keep going to and fro with orders and dispatches to the Portuguese general. He brought up General Anstruther's division, then returning from Sweden, within a comparatively short distance of Vimiero. They were in time to take their position in the field, and contributed to the success of that great day." But if young Doyle put on the soldier, he did not put off the saint. "Before and during the bloody engagements," he says, at Rolica, where the French lost fifteen hundred men, "I was intrenched behind a strong windmill, ball-proof, employed in giving spiritual assistance to a number of soldiers, who, knowing that I was in priest's orders, sought my aid."

Dr. Doyle returned to Ireland in 1808, to enter on the offices of teacher and of priest. He did not found the Roman Catholic College of Carlow, but he inspired it with new life, and gave it much of the power of his own character. He was Professor of Rhetoric. Notwithstanding his foreign education, and such a ludicrous pronunciation of English as used at first to make the students laugh, he yet imbued them with a manly taste. He overcame his own difficulties of expression, and cultivated for himself a style of uncommon clearness, flexibility, purity, and power. Afterwards he became, for a time, Professor of Theology. The severe duties of his professorship he most successfully discharged in connection with his labors as a priest. From these humble yet exalted functions he was called, in 1819, to be a bishop by the united voice of the clergy in the diocese, with the applauding consent of the Episcopacy in the kingdom, and with the unanimous approval of the authorities in Rome. He was then not three months beyond thirty years of age. He ruled his diocese with the force of a commanding and controlling mind, but also with the heart of a gentle, charitable, hospitable Christian pastor. Without neglecting in the least degree the greatest of his sacerdotal toils, he entered with abundant zeal into the politics which vitally concerned his country and his creed. A public writer of such special political ability as J. K. L. had not appeared since the days of Junius. Dr. Doyle died on the 15th of June, in the forty-eighth year of his age. As in the case of many other eminent men, all sorts of absurd stories were circulated regarding the state of mind in which he died. His political and polemical opponents would not let his remains be at peace. Some asserted that he died an infidel. Others, softening the fact, but not the scandal, reported that he refused the last rites of his Church. There were persons who sturdily maintained that he died a Protestant. Although there were more than a jury of eye-witnesses, male and female, lay and clerical, who knew the falsehood of these statements, and most solemnly denied their truth, zealots still continued to affirm them, and even to write bad and bulky pamphlets to prove them. But what will not zealots do for any creed or any cause? They are the blind, that will not see the light, shine it ever so clearly; they voluntarily make themselves blind, that they may not see the light; they are the deaf, that stuff their own ears to shut out hearing, and then insist that the sound of a trumpet is like the color of a rose. They have faith in nothing but their own illusions; they take their own narrow prejudices for universal and eternal facts; and when realities are asserted in contradiction to their prejudices, they *hate* the realities, and they *hate* those who assert them. They are in the universe, by their own passionate perverseness, infinite blunderers; as the ignorant confound the meanings of *shall* and *will*, zealots purposely reverse them, and, shouting defiance to everlasting truth, exclaim, "We *will* be drowned, and no veracity *shall* save us."

The matter of fact in the case before us is that the Rt. Rev. Dr. Doyle died simply as a Christian, and as a Roman Catholic bishop. He died in the creed in which he was educated, to which he had devoted his life and labors; which he had preached so eloquently; which he had so ably defended. He died surrounded by its ministers; he died with such faith and hope in God, in Jesus, in immortality, as any Christian feels to be the blessedness of the death-bed. There was in the nature of Dr. Doyle a strange combination of the Stoic and the Christian. When very near to death, he was asked by his Vicar-General if he did not wish to live longer. "About my death or recovery," said he, "I feel perfectly indifferent. I came into the world without any exercise of my own will, and it is only fitting that I should leave it in the same manner. I never knew any one who wished to live longer in order to do a great deal of good, who did not do a great deal of harm. All my hopes are in the mercies of God. Am I not as near them now as if I were to remain forty years longer on earth?"

If I were to use only a single word to indicate the predominating element in the character of Bishop Doyle, that word would be *strength*. Strength was the ruling quality of his inward and his outward life—strength of motive, strength of principle, strength of purpose. He always seemed to have a powerful conception of the reason and the right of whatever he did or proposed to do; and having this conception, his persistence and perseverance in giving it reality, or in sustaining the reality which involved it, were heroic and invincible. Once that his end was determined, he shrank from no labor, no sacrifice, no pain, suffering, loss, or danger, to reach it; but yet to reach it by worthy means. The strength of Dr. Doyle's character appears from whatever direction we consider it. It appears in his private and public life; it appears in his conduct as child, relative, friend, opponent; as pupil, student, teacher; as priest and prelate; as speaker and writer; as patriot and politician; and this integrity of moral force gave a most compact unity to the whole man. But moral force corresponded with an equal degree of intellectual force; and in such correspondence was the completeness of its power. There are men whose conscience is beyond suspicion, one might almost say beyond temptation, who yet, from want of mental balance, fail in moral wisdom, and do not rise to the higher order of virtues. The very source of their excellence is also, in a certain sense, the source of their weakness; so they become obstinate, or bigoted, or intolerant, or fanatical, or contentious, or meddlesome, or visionary. Prostrated under a mistaken sense of obligation, or puffed up with an overbearing zeal, they often only irritate when they mean to improve, and, with the best intentions, are most mischievous in their actions. A man of weak understanding may be a good man; but his goodness should be active humbly within the sphere of his capacity, in mind as in means. To be a great man as well as a good man, there must be a strong understanding; and this Dr. Doyle possessed. This, indeed, was his most prominent mental faculty.   Not deficient in imagination, in feeling, or in the sense of beauty, he was behind no man of his day in the vigor of his intellect.   The force which this, united with conscience, gave to his character—if not modified by human sympathy and softened by Christian graces—might have become stern and unrelenting rigor.   On occasions, Dr. Doyle approached the limit of a charitable severity.

No individual character consists of a single and simple principle ; but that I have stated the ruling one in the character of Dr. Doyle will, I think, be confirmed by such other qualities of his moral nature as my time will allow me to designate.   He was of undaunted courage—physical as well as moral.   I have already mentioned how manfully he shouldered his musket, under Wellington, when the French invaded Portugal.   He, an ecclesiastical student, was ready for strife, when duty told him that the cause was just.   Such examples as his are of great value.   They clear the clerical profession from the accusation of having refuge in more than a womanly security from danger; and one of the noblest lessons which our own sad war has taught us is written on the bloody graves to which our brave clergymen, of all creeds, have been sent, in their noble zeal for the discharge of their obligations as citizens and as priests.   This is as it should be.   The men who would inspire faith in another world must show us that they are without fear in this world.   We must revere those who would instruct us; and neither in respect to the present world nor the future can we listen with attention or edification to a craven.   How can we think that the man who trembles at the sound of a pistol believes in immortality?   How can we think that the man who quails before the danger of losing bodily life believes in the eternal reality of spiritual life?   It is well, therefore, even for the sake of moral influence, that our clergy should give the world assurance that they are men.

They have boldly given such assurance. I have myself
never assented to the doctrines of the Peace Society; I
have not scoffed or laughed at them; but, taking men as
they are, and as they are likely to be, I had no faith in
these doctrines. I have listened to preachers whose words
were soft and sweet—were like to those of Christian girlhood, meek and lowly—indeed, as opposite to war as milk
and honey are to gunpowder and cannon-shot. I have
lived to hear such voices shrill like the sounds of trumpets,
and their exhortations as calls to battle; to see priestly boldness as that of mighty captains; priestly death as that of
martyrs; and I have said to myself, "Well done, grand
souls! the stuff of manly greatness was in you, and saint-
hood was but the sanctification of heroism." Dr. Doyle
eloquently vindicated the profession of arms, and declared
that, had he not been called to a higher, arms would have
been his own profession. "From my earliest youth," he
says, "fear has been a feeling utterly unknown to me. I
know not what it is, and, unless from the knowledge one
gathers from common report, I know not what it is like."
Perhaps this explains his power as a polemic. And yet
he says, "I dislike controversy." This great courage of his
was displayed on several momentous occasions; as, for instance, in his several examinations before the High Court of
Parliament. To stand before the choice men of the British
Lords and Commons requires not only no ordinary intelligence, but no ordinary firmness. Very powerful men have
broken down in the trial, and utterly disappointed the
statesmen who summoned them as witnesses. On the contrary, Dr. Doyle did not tremble before the elect wisdom of
the British empire. He was calm and fearless in the midst
of most formidable opponents—for a great number of his
Parliamentary questioners took the position of antagonists.
Dr. Doyle in very important instances stood against O'Con-

nell. At what risk of popularity he did this, we learn from himself. Requested, in a special case, to resist O'Connell, "If I should do so," he replied, "the people of my own household would desert me." Nor did he shun the bodily danger which, even among portions of his own people, at one time seemed to threaten the most sacred personages. When not only landlords, land-jobbers, magistrates, constables, informers, tithe-proctors, process-servers, sheriffs, attorneys, and all such, were murdered, but even when priests themselves were assassinated, Dr. Doyle ventured into the most disturbed districts, and spoke to assemblies of fierce and reckless men, with bold and indignant eloquence. This courageous spirit Dr. Doyle evinced in speaking of Ireland itself. There are two conditions in civilized society in which national criticism, from within or from without, will not be tolerated. One is, when the country is young, strong, prosperous, full of energy, full of hope. Its fortune is the future, its possession is the immeasurable. Ideas take the place of experience. National criticism, in any form—such as satire, ridicule, caricature, or indignant expostulation—becomes a risk that the boldest will not undertake ; or which, if ventured on, soon drives the critics to silence or despair. The individual must join the chorus of the country, or modestly hold his peace. The other is, when the country is old; when it has lost its independence, and when its glory is in the past. The national affection is then in its traditions, and patriotism is more a sentiment of memory than of aspiration. Such a country has been Ireland. It is very sensitive. It holds closely, like a miser, all its hoarded wealth of national and proud recollections. Because impoverished in the present, it is all the more jealous of the past. And this treasure of national emotion is kept with the most watchful care in every genuinely Irish heart, from that of the laborer to that of the lord. It is difficult, therefore, to touch this sensibility, however innocently, without giving mortal offence. In the degree that the Irish have suffered pain, poverty, and historical humiliation, they bitterly resent even kindly strictures on their character or annals. Yet Dr. Doyle, in writing to a friend, says of Ireland : "Our origin and early possession of letters, and consequently of a certain degree of civilization, are, I think, points settled; but I cannot hide from myself that, though we possessed at certain periods a relative superiority over other countries, we never attained eminence as a nation." He then goes on to show how people with fewer advantages than the ancient Irish organized solid governments and secured their independence.

The strength of mind and of character which gives a man courage and candor saves him from being a bigot, and gives him a generous liberality of spirit. A zealous man is not necessarily a bigot. We have no right to complain of the scrupulousness, of the steadfastness, with which a man adheres to his creed, or of his devotion to the duties which it imposes, so long as he is faithful to social courtesies and to all natural and divine charities. It is his want of these, and not his belief, that makes him a bigot. The fact is, that, at least in this period of Christendom, bigotry is often more in the blood than in belief ; more a thing of temper than of theology. No man could be more firmly attached to his Church than was Dr. Doyle ; but this attachment interfered with no honorable affection, with no kindliness of humanity. Some of his most lovingly eloquent letters are to a lady who not only left the Roman Catholic religion, but became an enthusiastic opponent of it. She always had his friendship, and was ever welcome to his presence and to his house. "From my infancy," he says, "I never felt a dislike to any man on account of his religion. I have long had, among my most early and intimate friends, and still have, members of the Established Church and other Protestant communities, in whom I confide and whom I love as much as I do any people upon earth ; and if I had to choose a friend to whom I would confide my life or my honor, whether among people high in station or low, I should, at least among those high in station, prefer some of my Protestant friends to any others in the world." This was said, not in private correspondence or conversation, but before the assembled Commons of the British nation. Being told how ill an opinion the clergy of the Established Church had of him, he thus wrote : "They are mistaken. I hate their excessive Establishment ; . . . . . yet I respect them generally as a class of men, eminent many of them for their domestic virtues as well as for their literary acquirements." He condemned as forcibly as any man could, all temporal penalties and punishments in matters of religion. He gives up to reprobation all those who inflicted them and all those who would counsel their infliction, whether in Protestant or Roman Catholic States.

He was a strict man in all the relations of his authority. He was strict as a professor with his pupils. He was strict as a bishop with his priests. He forbade them to go to theatres, to attend races, to enter into field-sports, or to engage in secular employments or pursuits. He would not allow a priest to farm more than fourteen acres of land. He was jealous for the dignity of the priestly character even in externals. He was neat in his own dress, and he was anxious that his clergy should be so in theirs. He disliked a sloven or a clown in the priesthood. He used stimulants very slightly; he did not actually forbid them to priests, but he was extremely averse to the use of ardent spirits. When dying, a niece of his came to see him, and insisted that he should take some claret ; but the only bottle that was in the house was one which she herself had brought. He was a strict casuist. The Professor of Ethics in Maynooth maintained that an insolvent debtor, when legally discharged, was not morally bound, in future prosperity, to pay his creditors. Dr. Doyle opposed this doctrine in an able refutation, and showed that an honest debt was a perpetual obligation, from which no really honest man felt himself morally relieved, except by inability to pay it. But however strict the Bishop was with others, he was strictest of all with himself. He would accept no gifts. "They corrupt," he said, "the heart, abase the mind, and pervert the conscience." He was offered patronage for his friends by the Irish Government; but he would have none of it. "My kingdom," he replied, "is not of this world. I have no link to bind me to it." A lady had forced on him the present of a carriage, but only in a single instance did he ever enter it. "Whatever," he observes, "people may say of me, they shall never have it to say that I rode in my carriage." "I have not," he writes to a friend, "a coat to my back, not a shoe to my foot, and yet you talk of carriages. . . . . . Coach indeed! I have not even a horse; for my horse became broken-winded, and is now at cure— so that, with the exception of those animals found in cellars, my whole stock of four-footed creatures consists of a borrowed donkey, which, however, I do not ride." Bishop though he was, he writes to a friend, "I have been trying to make up the price of a new pair of shoes." He was happy through life in this honorable poverty. When a professor in Carlow College, in 1814, he writes to one of his family, "I have little to say; if good health, a good fireside, plenty of labor, plenty of money, and a good name be advantages, I enjoy them to the fullest extent." Yet his salary was at the utmost only £25 a year. His charity was unfailing, and his hospitality most generous—although, as a bishop, he was comparatively as poor as when he had been only a professor. He constantly kept a stock of bread and ale on hand for the refreshment of the poor. At Christmas he had oxen killed, and with beef he distributed clothing and blankets. Yet earnest preacher as Dr. Doyle was of personal beneficence, and high example as he was in the practice of it, he was, at the same time, the most strenuous advocate of a legal provision for the poor. Whether for good or evil, the poor-law system of Ireland is in a great measure owing to Dr. Doyle. Both good and evil belong to the system in Ireland, as to all human institutions everywhere ; but whether the good overbalances the evil in the poor-laws in Ireland I cannot venture to say; but the state of the country and of the poor seemed imperatively then to demand some method of legally providing for the destitute. And this was the general import of Dr. Doyle's arguments. Whatever vices or abuses have entered into the administration of the Irish poor-laws, the institution of them became inevitable. Owing to extensive absenteeism among the owners of Irish estates, and the inaccessibility to those who remained at home—for beggars were seldom allowed to enter even their outermost gates—the whole burden of pauperism was borne by the middle classes, and by classes themselves on the verge of pauperism, or even within it. It was right that property should not be left thus free ; if it did not do its duty voluntarily, it was right that it should be forced to do it. And yet it may be questioned whether the penalty it paid at last was not too stern. Lordly mansions became poor-houses, and some owners of such mansions were afterwards among the pauper inmates of them.

It was not Christmas alone that Dr. Doyle consecrated by special bounty to the poor ; he commemorated other festivals in the same manner. He was a cheerful giver, and a gentle one. To whomsoever he might be severe, he was to the destitute as meek in manner as he was merciful in action. He did not mock their poverty by insult or by rudeness; and whether blameless or otherwise, it was a claim to his respect as well as pity. He did not relieve with the hand and wound with the lips. He only desired to know that the want was real, and then he ministered to it to the extent of his means.

Nor was his compassion to the wants of the body alone; it extended still more deeply to the woes of the soul. Any soul burdened with grief, doubt, or sin had free access to him; its complaint was heard; such counsel or consolation as its case needed was given; and it did not matter whether the soul occupied the most lofty station in society, or the most lowly. When occupied by his episcopal duties, busy in the building of a cathedral, immersed in all sorts of controversies—when his pen was guiding the political opinions of millions, and his fame filled Europe—he was yet as laborious in the confessional as the humblest of his curates; nay, if a ragged beggar came to him specially, in distress of conscience, the Bishop as willingly gave him audience as he would in like case have given it to a mighty prince.

Strict man though he was, all the affections were powerful in his noble nature. He loved his kindred with all the tenderness of family instinct; he loved his friends with a generous and cordial confidence; he loved his enemies—if enemies he had—with Christian charity; he loved humanity with a fullness of regard which excluded no man from his pity or esteem; and he loved his country with the utmost passion of a patriot. Strict though the Bishop was, priests would sometimes "poke fun" at him. At a certain visitation, he rebuked a clergyman for irregularities in his parish. "I was much concerned," said he, "to observe, on this day, two of your parishioners fighting like a brace of bull-dogs." "My Lord," replied the priest, "the two men whom you observed boxing to-day were tailors from Carlow; and your

Lordship will admit that, if *you* could effect no reformation in their lives at Carlow, it is unreasonable to expect that I could do so here, where they are merely birds of passage." "Never did any Christian pastor," writes Thackeray, in his Irish Sketch-Book, referring to Dr. Doyle, "merit the affection of his flock more than that great and high-minded man. He was the best champion the Catholic Church and cause ever had in Ireland—in learning, and admirable kindness, and virtue, the best example to the clergy of his religion; and if the country is now filled with schools, where the humblest peasant in it can have the benefit of a liberal and wholesome education, it owes this great boon mainly to his noble exertions and to the noble spirit which they awakened."

I cannot discuss at much length the genius of Dr. Doyle. The most powerful faculty in it was his vigorous understanding. All the other faculties were in subordination to this. Intellect ruled his mind with as rigorous a discipline as he himself ruled his diocese. He was not speculative, soaring, or imaginative; he was mostly on the solid ground, close to his subject; and in public affairs he was always more the statesman than the philosopher. He was a great logician; but logic was his servant, not his lord. The art had become so natural to him, was so identical with the action of his thought, that, as a good speaker or writer does with the rules of grammar, being in full possession of the spirit, he threw away the forms. It was the same with rhetoric. He had thoroughly studied it, as the art of expression; but when he had gained power in the *spirit* of expression, he cared nothing for the technicalities. Perhaps no writer was ever more free from stiffness or mannerism than Dr. Doyle. This freedom is to be obtained, not only by ability, but by an instinct for the right use of words, trained by exercise and experience. It is also aided by wide conversation with men, with real life, and with history. Best of all, it is cultivated by having interest that heartily engage the mind, and become the stimulants of action. Then language is used unconsciously; it is a medium through which thought passes on to its end, without stopping to examine curiously the nature of the way. A tailor is not at ease in his clothes, because his attention is always occupied in making clothes. A dancing-master—the instructor of others in graceful movement—is usually himself, away from his lessons, awkward and ungainly, because his attention dwells on modes of movement. A professional elocutionist, who teaches others to speak and read—and teaches them successfully—is seldom himself a good speaker or reader, because his attention is absorbed in the processes of speaking and reading. And we know of learned authors on the English language who themselves write execrable English. This, too, may be because their attention is fixed on the construction of the language, instead of their energies being engaged in the use of it, in literatue or life. Dr. Doyle spoke and wrote freely and forcibly, because his attention was not on speaking or writing, but on the *objects* which he hoped by speaking and writing to accomplish. He was a great master of statement and of argument—clear and strong in both. He was always practical and to the point. So little was he given to all that was extraneous to his topic, in embellishment, sentiment, or thought, that, Irishman though he was to the utmost, his style seemed to have been formed rather by the severest culture of England than by the impulsive culture of his own country. He was not, in the poetic sense, imaginative; but he had passion and conviction which raised his thinking into eloquence—often indignant, often persuasive, often pathetic. He had fancy which could sharpen his thinking into wit; he had, when morally provoked, an energy of scorn that turned his thinking into barbs of sarcasm, which he hurled with such directness that they never missed their aim, and with such force that, though the wounds they inflicted might possibly be healed, they could never be forgotten. His intellect was aided by an enormous memory. "My memory," said Dr. Doyle to a friend, "is singularly tenacious. I never read an able argument, from the earliest period of my life to this hour, that is not distinctly inscribed on the tablet of my mind; and I protest I think, that, were it necessary, I could take my oath of the precise page whereon any remarkable theological opinion is recorded." This is like Niebuhr, who thought that his health was on the decline when his memory required the slightest effort; for the normal state of that memory seemed to be rather the intuition of a present consciousness than the recalling of a past consciousness, so easy was its action.

Able as Dr. Doyle was in his writings, his greatest mental triumphs were before the Houses of Parliament. In 1825 he was examined before committees of the Commons and of the Lords, in relation to the question of Catholic Emancipation. In 1830 he was examined before a committee of the Commons, in relation to a legal provision for the poor. In 1832 he was examined before committees of the Commons and of the Lords, in relation to the question of tithes. His answers in the first examination would form a folio of divinity; in the second, a body of social science; and in the third, a treatise on Church History and Ecclesiastical Antiquities. The questions put to him in the second examination amounted to 468, and his replies often extended to disquisitions. In the first examination, he was warned by a friend that it would be entirely theological, the questions being prepared by the ablest divines from Oxford and Cambridge. The friend hoped that he was supplied with such works for consultation as would enable him to go safely through this ordeal. The Bishop assured his friend that he brought no

book with him but his Breviary. It was as his friend foretold it would be, a comprehensive, searching, polemical,
theological examination. But the Doctor had, as we have
seen, a vast memory; he was not only a most learned priest,
but also a most learned lawyer; he had knowledge enough
to confute his questioners, and when he pleased he had art
enough to confound them. He was offered books in abundance, but he had little need of them, and he little used them.
He says himself of this examination: "I found it easier to
answer the bishops than the lords." His success delighted
his friends, and gained admiration from even his opponents.
Stanley, one of the most determined of these, paid the
highest tribute to the talents of Dr. Doyle. An eminent
peer declared that "Dr. Doyle as far surpassed O'Connell as
O'Connell surpassed other men." "Well, Duke," observed
another peer, who met Wellington as he was leaving the
committee-room, "are you examining Dr. Doyle?" "No,"
said his Grace, dryly, "Dr. Doyle is examining us." It has
been said that the impression of this examination on the
Duke's mind tended considerably towards his ultimate treatment of the Catholic question. "Who is there," says the
Morning Chronicle, "of the Established clergy, either of
England, Ireland, or Scotland, for instance, to compare with
Dr. Doyle? Compare his evidence before the Poor-Law
Committee with that of Dr. Chalmers, for instance, and the
superiority appears immense."

Dr. Doyle's power of labor was incredible; and yet his
readiness and versatility were equal to his power. He appeared before these committees day after day, and remained
before them several hours at a time. He had to be prepared to meet all sorts of questions, on all sorts of subjects,
and to answer them on the moment. He not only answered
them, but he answered them with a surplus wealth of knowledge. His mental treasury and his physical force seemed

alike inexhaustible, and at the close of each day's toil his strength seemed as unabated as it had been at the beginning. The members of the committee were arranged in the form of a horse-shoe. Dr. Doyle stood or sat within the hollow space. When excited, he arose, and often pursued a long and connected oration, which so chained the attention of his auditory that he was rarely interrupted.

His whole life was full of labor. He was not only strict in the duties of his office, but he enlarged those that were ordinary, and created others that were extraordinary. He was never without some public or patriotic demand that taxed his talents and his time. His fame made him a marked man for all sorts of attacks. He kept up a most extensive correspondence, political, ecclesiastical, and with his family and his friends. If we wonder that a man of such surprising abilities left no single great work, we must take these circumstances into account, and we must also remember the early age at which Dr. Doyle died. If the topics on which he wrote were temporary in duration, in the importance of consequences they had an everlasting interest. He so regarded and so treated them. But though the occasions which called forth his genius have passed away, not so his fame. That is immortal; and while Ireland cherishes love, gratitude, or admiration for the memory of those who have been devoted to her good, and have shed glory on her name, James Warren Doyle will be ranked among the brightest of her minds and among the greatest of her sons.

I shall not be able to expatiate on the times of Dr. Doyle with the fullness which I had originally intended. They were times full of agitations. I shall review some of the most prominent; such as the collective polemical exertions for Protestantizing the Catholics; the struggle of the Catholics for political emancipation; and, lastly, their opposition to tithes.

I do not impeach the motives of those who combined in the attempt to make Ireland a Protestant country. Christianity is essentially a proselytizing religion. It is not out of order that modifications of it have the same spirit, and of this spirit Protestantism has inherited an ample portion. Not only Churches, but every individual of strong and sincere convictions, should desire to make others partakers of them. But he must be amenable to all the laws of charity, courtesy, and reason, even when he believes that these convictions are needful to man's temporal and eternal welfare. No duty calls on him to be obtrusive or aggressive; to use arts which integrity does not sanction, even for this solemn purpose; he is not justified in abusing power for it, or in taking unfair advantage of opportunities, or in employing the influence of threats, promises, or favors. Not only does duty not require such endeavors, it indignantly forbids them. I will not say that policy excited this spiritual crusade against the Catholics; but if it succeeded, it would have admirably served policy. Some of the most active in the crusade were clergy of the Established Church. Now as this Church in Ireland was, and still indeed is, but the Church of a few, its claim to a national endowment, and a revenue paid by a vast majority who denied its doctrines and rejected its services, seemed, even to not a few of its own members, grossly unjust. But could this vast majority be converted to the Establishment, then, as the Church of the nation not only in name, but in reality, its claim would have a moral as well as a legal validity. If success came not, the failure arose from no want of zeal, energy, or perseverance. The apostleship included all orders of workers, lay and clerical, from peers and bishops to tract-distributers and Bible-readers; from the countess of the castle to the mistress of the village school. Some temporary results were obtained; a seed here and there seemed to take root;

it grew quickly, and as quickly withered. Where an abundant harvest had been hoped for, behold, all was barren.
The relapsed converts even mocked those whom they had
deceived, and laughed at the folly of their learned dupes.
How success could have been expected otherwise than by
miracle is to us a marvel. The Catholic Irish have intensely
the religious temperament, and they have been always ar-
dently attached to the Church of Rome. This attachment in
itself it would be inconceivably difficult to overcome. But
when we connect it with the circumstances and history of
the Catholic Irish, nothing in all the wildness of a dream
seems so unreal as those attempts to make them Protestants. The Irish are a people susceptible of the most vivid
impressions of the present, and have far-reaching and tenacious memories of the past. How would this present and
this past influence them towards Protestantism? The lands
which their forefathers owned, they saw Protestants living
on as lords, while they toiled on them as serfs—and, indeed,
rejoiced when they got leave to toil. The castles which
their ancestors held they saw monuments of humiliating
ruin, and in such of them as still retained their olden splendor, Protestants were the inhabitants. The grand cathe-
drals and abbeys, which had once beautified the country,
they saw given to the owls and to the bats; and the princely
incomes which had belonged to them they saw go into the
coffers of a Protestant hierarchy. They remembered that
the predecessors of the priests, from whom the preachers
sought to win them, had been hunted like wild beasts by
Protestant persecution. They remembered that the laws
which deprived them of all inheritance on their native soil,
of all right to property, that the laws which deprived their
ancestors of natural domestic rights, which deprived Catholic children of education, and encouraged them to violate
the most sacred of human instincts—they remembered that

all these were Protestant laws. Nay, more, the missionaries who expected the Catholic Irish to become Protestants acted—as far as the spirit of the age allowed—in the spirit of those laws. They held up the clergy of the people to unmitigated odium, and exhausted on them the whole vocabulary of denunciation and contempt. They rudely scorned all the beliefs and feelings which the people held as the most consecrated in the inmost sanctuaries of their religious affections. Beyond this, these missionaries were the most virulent opponents against the struggles of the people for the enjoyment of national and civic rights. They were zealous *for* the emancipation of the West Indian Negro, and equally zealous *against* the emancipation of the Irish Catholic; yet these were the men who thought that they had divinely assigned to them the duty, and the gifts, and the fitness to turn a rusty Irish Catholic into a brightly-plated Brummagem Protestant.

The part which Dr. Doyle took in these controversies was seldom purely theological. His polemics were usually incidental to his patriotism, and the defence of his Church was generally connected with that of the civil claims of its members. We shall select but one opponent with whom he powerfully grappled—we mean Archbishop Magee, author of a celebrated work on the Atonement. A few remarks on the Archbishop and his work may interest our readers. He was a native of Enniskillen, the son of a respectable but reduced merchant, and was born about 1764. He was educated at the expense of a wealthy relative. He entered Trinity College, Dublin, when he was only fifteen, and had for fellow-students Plunket and Thomas Addis Emmet. He was diligent in study and cheerful in temper; he loved the society of maidens, and the pursuit of mathematics; he had extraordinary skill in dancing and diaphantines. He obtained a fellowship, and, considering the enormous amount of learning and science demanded in the Dublin University in the candidate for such an office, the success of a young man in gaining it gave him deservedly very high distinction. He entered into orders, and, in spite of the law which enjoined celibacy on the fellows, and which he was sworn to observe, he married. In early life, he was a radical—a hater of England and an opponent of the Union. He was Irish of the Irish. Change of conviction, and with it change of colors, came in time. Poor and outcast Liberalism gave place to prosperous and exultant Toryism, and rebellious green bloomed into loyal orange. Magee became Dean of Cork, and, in due season, Archbishop of Dublin. Theological conversion, even with the greatest abilities, is seldom so favorable to ambition as political conversion. Kirwin, the most eloquent of preachers, of whom Grattan said, that "he awoke the slumbers of the Irish pulpit, and exhausted the oil of life in feeding the lamp of charity," changed his religion, and died in a wretched deanery. Magee changed his politics, and died in a wealthy archbishopric.

Such was the disputant with whom Dr. Doyle dared to enter the lists ; and here was the occasion. In a charge to his clergy, the Archbishop said : "My reverend brethren, we are hemmed in by two opposite descriptions of professing Christians—the one possessing a Church without what we call a Religion, and the other possessing a Religion without what we can call a Church." "And we, my reverend brethren," he might have added, "have a Church in Ireland without having what we can call a People ; but in compensation, my reverend brethren, though others feed the sheep, we shear them." The Church without a Religion was intended for the Roman Catholics; the Religion without a Church, for the Dissenters. Between these two the venerable Establishment, that was both a Church and a Religion suffered grievous persecution, and had to bear "heavy blows and great discouragements." The phrase here quoted from the Archbishop's charge, and the habit of using such phrases, caused him to be styled " the *antithetical Magee.*" Dr. Doyle took up his own side of the antithesis, and with such effect as must have taught the Archbishop the extreme danger of pointed sentences, which may be made to wound the author more deeply than those at whom they are aimed. A very favorite mode in those days, among Roman Catholic polemics, in dealing with their opponents of orthodox Protestant Churches, was to vindicate, on the grounds of individual conscience and of private interpretation, the religious claims of Unitarians. This mode of argument was often very annoying and perplexing to those against whom it was used. Dr. Doyle used it with stunning energy against Dr. Magee. "Are not Socinians," he wrote, "men of sound judgment? Have they not, according to your rule, a right —nay, are they not obliged—to follow the dictate of that judgment in preference to all authority on earth? And yet you exclude them from the kingdom of God because, in the exercise of their judgment, or in what you consider the discharge of their duty, they differ in opinion from yourself. Your opinion of them, if judged by your own principles, is unjust, uncharitable, and unreasonable."

Dr. Doyle went hand in hand with O'Connell during the last great struggle for Catholic Emancipation. His influence was very efficient in promoting O'Connell's election for Clare, which was the decisive blow that brought the Tory statesmen to their senses. The pen of Dr. Doyle was as powerful in its way as the tongue of O'Connell. Dr. Doyle had influence over classes which O'Connell did not reach. Dr. Doyle's writings were read by aristocratic and educated men of all parties—men who would not listen to O'Connell, and whom, if they would, O'Connell could not convince. O'Connell had the ears and hearts of the masses; Dr. Doyle had the attention and thoughts of the select.   He had many personal acquaintances among the most powerful and intellectual of the aristocratic politicians.   Dr. Doyle was himself by nature aristocratic ; O'Connell was democratic in temper, in talents, and by his training and experience among the people in their assembled multitudes.   Dr. Doyle's splendid evidence and eloquence before the leading men of the empire —lords, bishops, commons—gave authority to his words of counsel, of remonstrance, of history, of prophecy, which the words of an individual have rarely had in the concerns of mighty states.

I can only glance at the agitation against tithes, and a glance is all that is needed.

Tithes, even in the Church of England, have always been the most unpopular of legal imposts.   Yet a large mass of the English people belong to the Church, and among them are the wealthiest portion of the nation.   What must tithes have, then, been in Ireland, where the mass of the population are not only *not* of the Established Church, but thoroughly and passionately opposed to it, and where, moreover, the tithes weighed most heavily on the struggling and the poor!   I enter in no wise into the *rationale* or logic of the legal or the voluntary system of supporting religious institutions; I pass by all speculative arguments for tithes or against them.   I confine myself to broad and palpable facts.   On the face of the matter, it does seem unreasonable and unjust to force a man to pay for the administration of a religion which his conscience and conviction reject.   Even among Protestant sects, it appears hardly fair to make all the sects except one support that one.   But among Protestant sects there are only differences ; Roman Catholics are opposed to all forms of Protestantism, but of all forms of Protestantism in Ireland, the Church form was, perhaps, the most unpopular.   To it belonged the aristocracy, with which, rightly or wrongly, the Roman Catholic people associated conquest, plunder, confiscation, and oppression ; to it belonged a clergy whose creed they denied, whose incomes they were forced to pay, among whom they saw some of the most active and zealous denouncers of their own faith ; and, as I have said, the burden of this odious tax or tribute fell most heavily on the struggling and the poor. A collection of advertisements of tithe-auctions would open strange revelations of the strangest social condition ever made known in the whole existence of civilized humanity. In those auctions, the most wretched articles of the most wretchedly indigent were exposed to sale ; the only cow or donkey; the half-starved pig ; poultry; the solitary pot or platter ; the winter's stock of potatoes ; the bed-covering and wearing-apparel, down to the petticoat and the apron of Widow Gallaher. Lest this should be thought the exaggeration of burlesque, allow me to read from a volume before me a literal copy of one of these advertisements.

"To be soaled by Publick Cant in the town of Ballymore on the 15th Inst one Cowe, the property of Jas Scully one new bed & one gown the property of John Quinn seven hanks of yarn the property of Widow Scott one petty Coate & one apron the property of Widow Gallaher seized under & by virtue of a leasing warrant for tithe due the Rev John Ugher."

"If," says a statesman, "an established church is valuable because it provides for the religious wants of the poor, the Church of Ireland does the reverse of this ; it provides for the rich only, and compels the poor to pay." Now if tithes in their essential principle were so hateful to Irish Catholics that no amount of forbearance or prudence in collecting them could have rendered them tolerable, it is not easy to conceive the fearfulness of their grievance, when connected as they were with every possible abuse of administration. With the intervention of avaricious tithe-proctors, of unscrupulous appraisers, of lawyers, and of constables, the poor man often paid the fifth, instead of tenth, of his hard-earned property.

But it may be said that the clergy spent their incomes among the people. Not always. Sometimes the parson hardly ever visited the parish which paid him hundreds of pounds in yearly revenue. The present Archbishop of Cashel had been one of the most zealous of proselytizing orators. Besides other large benefices, he owned the richest parish in Cork, from which, it was estimated, he derived an income of two thousand pounds a year. The church at one time needed repairs, and the members of the congregation decided to tax themselves, and forego the legal claim for church-rates. The officers of the parish wrote to the rector for a subscription. He sent them five pounds. The officers sent the pittance back to him. This godly and evangelical divine never came near the parish, unless it happened to be within the range of an itinerating tour.

Dr. Doyle mentions the case of the rector of a rich living in the county of Kildare, who had never been there but once in all his life. Such a man was not singular, but representative of a class. Many of the clergy were magistrates, and many to their ecclesiastical office added that of land-agents. Tithes formed but one item of the Church wealth in Ireland. Besides these, there were bishop-lands, glebe-lands, and church-rates. The income of five hundred thousand acres of bishop-lands were estimated at one million dollars a year. A bishop's lease was but for twenty-one years, and the bishop accordingly could impose a heavy fine on the renewal of it. One see alone, as it appeared from parliamentary returns, possessed fifty-one thousand eight hundred and eighty acres; and it was shown that one bishop received fifty thousand pounds for the renewal of a single lease.* Add to all this, that the bishops have extensive patronage in the Church, and that they very generally use it for the benefit of their families and kindred. Many bishops die enormously wealthy, and this could not happen without the means of rapid accumulation, since a man seldom reaches the episcopacy until life has sobered into the gravity of years. Dr. Beresford, the late Archbishop of Armagh, was reputed to have left more than a million sterling. This was decent saving, although it was the gathering of forty thrifty years. Another Beresford went from a rich see to this vacant one, which was still richer. The clergy, in congratulating him on his promotion, spoke feelingly on the *apostolic simplicity* of his millionaire predecessor. In all that was secularly or sacredly gainful, the Beresfords were a most prosperous family; they had a mighty hunger for pelf and power, and good digestion waited upon ample appetite.

But the time came at last when the old tithe system must be no more. The decree had gone forth. The exhausted patience of the people could no further go. An individual here and there hesitated to pay; another challenged the legal claim. At last the spirit of resistance spread until it became universal. No active opposition was offered. The Catholics imitated the Quakers. They folded their arms; they moved no weapon; they used no word of threatening or sedition. They simply, by their manner, said, "You want to tax our goods to pay your Church; then come and take our goods to the amount of your tax." But that which was easy with an inconsiderable sect became terrific with a multitudinous nation. All Liberals sustained the movement, but O'Connell and Dr. Doyle were the soul and spirit of it. The mountain-sides were covered with people

* Edinburgh Review, November, 1824.

 Giles' Lectures.

who came to listen to orators who denounced the tithe system. Yet there was no violence. Property was seized, but there was no resistance. The property could not be sold in the localities wherein it was seized; so it was carried into adjacent cities, but in these also it could not be sold. Some property in this way was carried into Carlow, but twenty thousand men went in along with it. No person was bold enough to bid, and the property was returned to the owners. Some few cattle were seized in the County of Cork; but the authorities, despairing of finding a sale for them in the neighborhood, had them driven into the city. The largest open space was there appointed for the sale. On the morning destined for the auction there marched into the city some thirty thousand men from all sides of the county. They were young, healthy, strong, good-looking, and well dressed. They were unarmed; they had not even a *kippeen;* they were as sober as judges, and wore the gravest of faces. They came to *look on* at the auction, but there were none that dared to bid. Except the voice of the auctioneer, all was dumb show. These *lookers-on,* who came into the city in the most orderly manner, marshalled into divisions, brigades, regiments, and companies, keeping form and step with perfect regularity, left the city in the same admirable regularity. And what was most astonishing in those vast gatherings was the absence of intemperance and of disorder. This was really the most fearful element in them to the clergy of the Established Church. No tithes were to be paid; that was a decree which no Catholic disobeyed. No action for tithes could be enforced; the power of government seemed unequal to such enforcement. The government which could hold a discontented kingdom, could not compel the payment of a shilling to the parish rector.

I had desired to make some remarks on the vital and recuperative energy of the Irish race, which enables the people of that race to recover rapidly from the most disastrous circumstances, and to vindicate at home, and all the world over, their living power of mind and body. I can now add nothing but the expression of my heartfelt hope that the destinies of the Irish people may be brighter in the future than they have been in the past; more worthy of their merits as an intellectual, brave, generous, faithful race—a race that have always shown that they possess some of the best elements of genius and humanity—who are ever giving the world assurance that they have within them a worth and wealth of nature which time does not exhaust, and which misfortunes have not injured, but improved.

An able and eloquent biography of this able prelate, is by William John Fitzpatrick.

OLIVER GOLDSMITH.

Oliver Goldsmith was born November 10, 1728, in Pallas, County of Longford, Ireland. Other places contend for the honor of his birth, but this has the claim of authority. His father was a clergyman of numerous family, and of slender means, with no faculty of economy, and a strong desire for expenditure. It is needless to dwell minutely on a life so well known as his, or one that may so easily be known. His childhood had some eccentricities, and his college career was marked by a few rows and freaks; but with all his wildness, his writings show that the kind heart of his childhood continued fresh to the end, and that his college experience left him, at least, classical knowledge and classical tastes. Having been a medical student in Edinburgh and Leyden, then he became a penniless wanderer on the continent of Europe. After piping to peasants and spouting in convents, he returned to London, and there he began as a drudge to pedagogues, and ended as a drudge to publishers. The amount of desultory composition on every topic which, for years, he furnished to his employers, must excite our wonder; but that which most excites it is the general beauty which distinguishes these compositions, and the pittance by which they were recompensed. Herein, however, was the consolation of his privacy. He was just to his own powers; he gratified his own fine taste; labor was mitigated by an inward sense of dignity; and he was saved from that weight of lassitude which presses upon no hireling with so deadly an influence as upon the hireling of literature. At last, he toiled his way to fame ; but his expenditure outran his prosperity. Accustomed hitherto to small sums, moderate ones seemed exhaustless, and on this delusion of a poor man, unacquainted with money and the world, he acted.

Always thoughtless, he now became lavish ; he not only spent his money, but anticipated work ; he not only emptied his purse, but he drew extravagantly on his faculties. He was in arrears with his publishers for books not finished, even for books to be written. With much to pay, and nothing to receive, with difficulties pressing on the mental power which was required in its utmost vigor to remove them, his life was approaching to a crisis. A fever, rendered fatal by distress of mind, and by his own injudicious treatment, carried him off in the forty-sixth year of his age. Dr. Johnson, who did not often expose his sensibility, was extremely moved; and Edmund Burke burst into tears. It was computed that his debts, when he died, amounted to two thousand pounds, upon which Dr. Johnson exclaims, in a letter to Boswell, "Was poet ever so trusted before?" So loved, indeed, was Goldsmith, that the tradesmen to whom part of this was due murmured no complaint, put no stain upon his memory; but following departed genius with thoughts of charity, their affectionate observation was, that, if he had lived, he would have paid them all. Ay, if he had lived! if he had lived, he would have paid them all! and how much, too, would he have given to the world in addition to that obligation which the world never discharged! The greater part of the debt which encumbered the last days of his earthly existence was one for which booksellers held a mortgage upon his mind. To many of these men, his mind was a fountain of wealth ; and to us, it is a fountain of instruction and enjoyment. Cotemporaries gave Goldsmith a tomb ; his most venerable companion gave him an epitaph ; posterity have given him their hearts. Few can see the tomb ; few can understand the language of the epitaph ; but millions love his genius, and in the memory of their living affections they enshrine his name.

After all, his fate was not worse than others in his class. No man heard where, or cared how, Chatterton groaned away his soul ; so his heart broke in agony, and no Bristol trader inquired about the unhappy but inspired boy, who, perhaps, grew up beside his threshold. He knew nothing of the market or the stocks, and nobody listened to him, and nobody cared for him, and nobody heard him. He was alone ; his brother was not near him ; his sister knew not of the despair that gathered upon his sinking heart. He looked around him, and all was gloomy, all was dismal. He did not wait for starvation to do its worst, but ere it could come to wither and to kill him, from some process, easy as that of a bare bodkin, he sought his last and long quietus ; and where he sought, he found it.

The character of Goldsmith is one which does not tax analysis ; it is felt by instinct ; and that happy phrase, "good-natured," defines it with a singular accuracy. Goldsmith's good nature, though it exhausted his purse, did not exhaust itself. It was an unfailing well-spring ; it was ever pure and fresh, bubbling from a copious fountain of kindness, and refreshing life around him with streams of gayety, of fondness, and of pity. There was a benignity in him which gave his heart an interest in the humblest creature. Early in life, in writing home, he says, "If there be a favorite dog in the family, let me be remembered to him." His attachment to children was as strong as it was amiable. The younger Colman speaks in rapture of his acquaintance with Goldsmith, when in infant insolence he used to tweak the poet's nose ; and the poet, in return, played thimble-rig with the child. Nor was this merely deference to the son of a rich man and a critic. Goldsmith was an idol, also, to the children of the poor ; it was his common practice to. go among them with pockets full of gingerbread, and to set them dancing to the sound of his flute. His, in every scene, was a simple nature ; and he, around whom rustics pranced on the banks of the Loire, was the same around whom ragged innocents gabbled and rejoiced in the garrets of Old Bailey. Goldsmith's humanity to the poor, generally, was most courteous and most boun- tiful. His charity would often have been sublime, if the improvidence of his temper did not drive him to contriv- ances to supply it, which gave it an air of the ludicrous. One morning towards the close of his college course, a cousin and fellow-student of his knocked at the door of his chamber. No reply. He knocked again. Still no reply. He then broke it open. Goldsmith was in bed, literally in it, for he was stuck bodily into the feathers. Some poor woman had told him a tragical story ; he was out of money, so he brought her to the college, and gave her his blankets.

Let me take another instance from his later life—an instance which, as I think, is most characteristic of the author and the man. Suppose ourselves gazing into a hum- ble chamber, in the humblest part of London. A ragged bed is in one corner, a broken wash-stand is in another. A crazy table is placed near a small dusty window, and a man sits by this table on the only chair which the room contains. The stature of the man is short, and his face is pale ; his position has an air of thought, and his look, the glow of fancy. This man, whose forehead bulging out with senti- ments and ideas, so as to defy all rules of sculpture, is ugly ; but he is ugly only to those who cannot see light of the spirit

through the shrine of the countenance. To those who know
the touch of nature that makes all men akin, he is inexpres-
sibly dear; and they love to gaze on his homely portrait, as
if it were lovely as ever dawned upon a sculptor's dream.
The man is Oliver Goldsmith, and as we now describe him,
he is engaged in writing his Essay On the State of Polite
Learning in Europe. A knock at his lowly door arouses
him, and a visitor enters. The visitor is Bishop Percy, the
admirable collector of Reliques of Ancient English Poetry.
Goldsmith courteously gives the prelate his only chair, and
takes himself a seat upon the window-sill. They are engaged in an earnest conversation on bellelettres and the fine
arts, when a ragged but decent little girl comes into the
room, and with a respectful obeisance to Goldsmith, says,
"My mamma sends her compliments, Sir, and begs the favor
of you to lend her a pot of coals."

As Goldsmith's fortunes increased, so did his gifts; and
food was added to fuel. After he had entertained a large
party at breakfast, he distributed the fragments among a few
poor women whom he had kept waiting for the purpose. A
vulgar guest remarked, that he must be very rich to afford
such bounty. "It is not wealth, my dear Sir," said Goldsmith, "it is inclination; I have only to suppose that a few
more friends have been of the party, and then it amounts to
the same thing." He was, besides, always surrounded by a
circle of needy writers, whom he had not the firmness to
refuse, nor the prudence to discharge. He was also beset
by destitute countrymen, who found a ready way to his last
shilling through his compassion and his patriotism. To
such people, bounty was no virtue, but with Goldsmith, pity
gave ere charity began; and charity had always the start of
wisdom. Much as there was in such actions which implied
want of purpose and want of thought, there was goodness
too upon which no tone of distress ever fell in vain. "He

has been known," says Prior, the most genial of his biographers, "to quit his bed at night, and even when laboring under indisposition, in order to relieve the miserable; and when money was scarce, or to be procured with difficulty by borrowing, he has, nevertheless, shared it with such as presented any claims to charity.

"At an evening party of friends, he once threw down his cards, and rushed from the room, and when asked the cause, on his return, of such an abrupt retreat, 'I could not bear,' said he, 'to hear that unfortunate woman in the street, half singing, half sobbing; for such tones could only arise from the extremity of distress; her voice grated painfully on my ear, so that I could not rest until I had sent her away.' To the unfortunate, even to those made so by their own errors, he ever turned with the spirit of a good Samaritan; and when he had relieved them with his money, he pleaded for them with his pen. His word was ever for the feeble, the oppressed, and the unhappy; and passages of pathetic eloquence abound in his writings, which nothing could have inspired but the finest natural feeling. 'Who are those,' he exclaims, in the character of his Citizen of the World, 'who make the streets their couch, and find a short repose from wretchedness at the doors of the opulent? These are strangers, wanderers, orphans, whose circumstances are too humble to expect redress, and whose distresses are too great even for pity. Their wretchedness excites rather horror than compassion. Some are without the covering even of rags, and others emaciated with disease. The world has disclaimed them; society turns its back upon their distress, and has given them up to nakedness and hunger. . . . . Poor houseless creatures! the world will give you reproaches, but will not give you relief. The slightest misfortunes of the great, the most imaginary uneasiness of the rich, are aggravated with all the power of eloquence, and are held

up to engage our attention and sympathetic sorrow. The poor weep unheeded, persecuted by every species of petty tyranny, and every law which gives others a security becomes an enemy to them.'"

This generosity of temper, united with keen observation, enabled Goldsmith to pierce readily through the disguises of selfishness; so that, with his comic sagacity, and his genial perception of the ludicrous, no writer can give more amusing pictures than he does of sordid follies. Even in his very youth, we have the narrative of an adventure which promises all the thoughtful drollery that he afterwards exhibited. He had gone in a freak to Cork, mounted on a noble horse, and with thirty pounds in his pocket. It was not long ere he was returning, with merely five shillings, and mounted on an animal which he called Fiddle-back. He was, however, blithe and careless, for near to the city there was a college friend who had often pressed him to a visit. "We shall enjoy," he would say, "both the city and the country; and you shall command my stable and my purse."

Going towards his friend's house, he divided his five shillings with a destitute woman, and on his arrival, he found his friend an invalid; but so cordial was his reception, that remorse struck him for not having given the whole five shillings to his needy sister. He stated his case, and opened his heart to his friend. His friend walked to and fro, rubbed his hands, and Goldsmith attributed this to the force of his compassion, which required motion, and to the delicacy of his sentiments, which commanded silence. The hour was growing late, and Goldsmith's appetite had been long at craving point. "At length an old woman came into the room with two plates, one spoon, and a dirty cloth, which she laid upon the table. This appearance," says Goldsmith, "without increasing my spirits, did not diminish my appetite. My protectress soon returned with one bowl of sago, a small porringer of sour milk, a loaf of stale brown bread, and the heel of an old cheese. My friend," continues the poet, "apologized, that his illness obliged him to live on slops, and that better fare was not in the house; observing, at the same time, that a milk diet was certainly the most healthful. At eight o'clock he again recommended a regular life, declaring that, for his part, he would lie down with the lamb, and rise with the lark. My hunger was at this time so exceedingly sharp, that I wished for another slice of the loaf, but was obliged to go to bed without even that refreshment."

. Next morning Goldsmith spoke of his departure. "To be sure," said this munificent friend, "the longer you stay away from your mother, the more you will grieve her, and your other relatives; and possibly they are already afflicted at hearing of this foolish expedition you have made." Goldsmith, then reminding him of former good turns, tried to borrow a guinea from him. "Why look you, Mr. Goldsmith," said Solomon the younger, "I have paid you all you ever lent me, and this sickness of mine has left me bare of cash. But, I have bethought myself of a conveyance for you. Sell your horse, and I will furnish you with a much better one to ride on." I readily, said Goldsmith, grasped at this proposal, and begged to see the nag; on which he led me to his bedchamber, and from under the bed pulled out a stout oak stick. "Here," said he, "take this in your hand, and it will carry you to your mother's with more safety than such a horse as you ride." Goldsmith was about to lay it on his back, but a casual visitor coming in, his generous friend introduced him with eulogium and with enthusiasm. Both of them had an invitation to dinner; for which Goldsmith was quite prepared; and it seemed not less acceptable to the amiable invalid. At the close of the evening, the entertainer offered Goldsmith a bed, who then told his former host to go home and take care of his excellent horse, but that he would never enter his house again.

The objections against Goldsmith's benevolence of character, drawn from Boswell, are easily answered. Boswell did not like Goldsmith. He did not, and could not, do him justice. The position of Goldsmith near Johnson, was galling to Boswell. He was humiliated when Goldsmith was present; for, familiar as Boswell was with the great moralist, his relation to him was not like that of the poet, an equal and a brother. The conviction of such inferiority was intolerable to a man of Boswell's temper; and the sternness with which Johnson put to silence every effort of his to depreciate Goldsmith so sharpened his asperity, that occasionally it seemed half malignant. Whatever foibles belonged to Oliver Goldsmith, no one could be ignorant that the author of "The Traveler" was a man of genius; and the very dignity in which Johnson held the profession of letters, would never permit him, even if affection did not interfere, to treat Goldsmith with irreverence. If for a moment, in his turbulent dogmatism, he forgot the respect which was a brother's due, an immediate and complete apology expressed his contrition, and changed him from the superior to the suppliant.

It was a hard lot to Boswell, that, notwithstanding all his assiduity, Goldsmith maintained a communion with Johnson to which he could never dare. Boswell's situation was that of a petted favorite, a pleasant amanuensis, a lackey to the mind; but the place of Goldsmith was that of prince with prince. Goldsmith took little notice of Boswell, not from any special feeling, I apprehend, but because there was nothing in him that struck his fancy; and Boswell, who, like all favorites, was insolent, was mortally chagrined that one whom he would fain consider beneath him, should so quietly but so effectually show him that he was merely a subordinate. The impression of Goldsmith which Boswell's remarks tend to leave is, that he had not only a vanity which was disgusting, but an envy which was detestable. But Prior, who has sifted all the facts, exposes successfully the absurdity of the charges. Boswell himself was a man both vain and envious; and such a man is always the most likely to charge vanity and envy on another. Goldsmith unquestionably had vanity—a vanity which, added to a grotesque appearance and ungainly manners, became a ludicrous oddity, and, as in the case of every kind-hearted person of confiding simplicity and open speech, he was at the mercy of his critics. He had all the youthfulness of genius. Necessity compelled him to severe exertion. In the hours of relaxation he gambolled as a boy, and capered in every whim which his guileless and unsuspicious temper prompted. Much he said and did in sheer sportiveness, which Boswell has set down seriously, if not in malice; and much, therefore, which Boswell has written of Goldsmith, is worthy of as profound attention as the candid commentaries of Mrs. Trollope on domestic manners in America.

Goldsmith had vanity that was undisguised, but it had the association of goodness to save it from offending, and of genius to shield it from derision. Boswell, who ridicules the vanity of Goldsmith, had also a vanity of his own, but, sooth to say, it was of a very odd kind; it was the vanity of servitude, the vanity of voluntary abasement, the vanity that seemed paradoxically to combine the mean and the heroic; a meanness that first submitted to abuse, and a heroism that afterwards recorded it; a vanity which had strong resemblance to that ascribed by Dean Swift to "John," in "The Tale of the Tub;" the vanity, allow me to speak it in vernacular Saxon, the vanity of being kicked. I do not, however, deny that Boswell has left us a most fasci-

nating book, a book which he could not perhaps have written, had his mind been of an order more aspiring and more
independent.

I have confined my remarks chiefly to a distinctive quality
in the character of Goldsmith, universally conceded; but
his whole worth was by no means confined to this. No
gross vices are recorded against him; his general habits
appear to have been comparatively unstained; his general
tastes were simple; he was temperate almost to abstinence;
and excess he regarded with abhorrence. To speak thus
is to speak negatively, but these negatives, connected with
Goldsmith's position and his times, have a value that is
positive. But one virtue eminently positive, belongs to
Goldsmith, and that is, his exceeding literary purity; the
sacred independence with which he used his talents, and
the sacred purposes to which he applied them. Follies
were his, which gathered afflictions about his lot, which not
all his innocent hilarity could throw off. Carelessness
brought misfortunes upon him, which broke at last his
elastic capacity of endurance; but no destitution was ever
a temptation to his literary conscience; and no pressure
ever bent its rectitude. From the beginning, Goldsmith
eschewed patrons; he acted, from the first, on the manly
resolution of seeking support in the honest exertion of his
own powers. The Earl of Northumberland, going as Lord
Lieutenant of Ireland, offered him assistance; Goldsmith de-
clined for himself, but requested protection for his brother,
a worthy pastor and a worthy man. Sir John Hawkins
calls him a fool; but his own words show he was as wise as
he was conscientious: "I have," said he, "no dependence
on the promises of the great men. I look to the booksellers
for support; they are my best friends."

It is true, that Goldsmith could not always have an end
equal to his genius; but he never perjured his convictions,

nor bartered his soul. It is true, that his main object was often merely to do a certain quantity of work, and receive a certain sum of wages, and of this he sometimes complains with a sort of melancholy pleasantry. He says, in reference to his History of England, "I have been a good deal abused lately in the newspapers for betraying the liberty of the people. God knows, I had no thought for or against liberty in my head ; my whole aim being to make a book of a decent size, that, as Squire Richard says, would do no harm to nobody." But though Goldsmith had often to think more of sustenance than fame, he merely wrote rapidly, he did not write falsely. Living in an age when a name sold a book, and when patrons made a name, and when dedications earned patrons, Goldsmith passed over titles and gratified his affections. The first of his poems he inscribed to an indigent brother, and the others he inscribed to his immediate friends.

He was ever perplexed with debts and surrounded with difficulties. His heart always craving for money to give, and his supply always far behind his craving, yet he could reject propositions which men, who have secured a reputation for more austere virtue than Goldsmith, would have found elegant excuses for accepting. The British Cabinet, by a confidential agent, intimated a munificent remuneration for his pen. The poet occupied sordid chambers, and labored like a slave ; but here was his answer : "I can earn as much as will supply my wants without writing for any party; the assistance, therefore, which you offer is unnecessary to me."

Can you think of a much stronger temptation among earthly struggles, than the offer of a rich government to a poor writer? Judge Goldsmith, then, by the severity of his trial, and give him the credit of his victory. But he was honest with the public as he was with patrons. Needy though he was, he sought the suffrage of men only by means which tended to make them wiser, and to make them better; and of those compositions which multitudes seek, as much as they should shun them, and which it is as easy as it is dishonorable to produce, not one can be laid to the charge of Goldsmith. The spirit of his works is as chaste as their style is classical; and to him belongs the glory of having purified expression, when the phraseology even of women was coarse; and of having consecrated the novel to virtue, when the pen of fiction was dipped in the offscourings of passion.

I am compelled to pass from a brief review of Goldsmith's character, to an equally brief review of his writings. The writings of Goldsmith, if they had no other excellence, would be remarkable for their felicitous versatility. The author is successively presented to us as historian, essayist, dramatist, poet, and novelist. The few words I can say of Goldsmith, as a writer, will take the order which I have now indicated.

As a historian, Goldsmith accomplishes all at which he aims. He does not promise much, but he does more than he promises. He takes, it is true, facts which had been already collected, but he shapes them with an art that is all his own. He has the rare faculty of being brief without being dry; of being at once perspicuous and compressed, and of giving to the merest abridgment the interest of dramatic illusion. Dr. Johnson set a high value on Goldsmith, if not as a historian, at least as a narrator; and Dr. Johnson was a man whose critical austerity even friendship rarely softened. Dr. Johnson went so far as to place Goldsmith above Robertson. When we have taken into consideration Johnson's prejudices against Robertson for being a Scotchman and a Presbyterian, a worth will still remain in the opinion, which we must allow to Goldsmith. Robertson, Johnson represents as crushed under his own

weight ; or as like a man that packs gold in wool, the wool
taking more room than the gold. Goldsmith, he says, puts
into his book as much as his book will hold. No man, he
asserts, will read Robertson's cumbrous detail a second
time ; but Goldsmith's plain narrative will please again an
again. Johnson remarked of Goldsmith in one of his conversations, "He is now writing a Natural History, and he
will make it as entertaining as a Persian tale." With these
histories of Goldsmith we cannot dispense; a beautiful mixture of the agreeable and the useful, they are dear to us
with all their imperfections ; they are lessons for our childhood, and relaxation for our maturity. They have a permanent existence in our literature, and they deserve it. They
deserve it, not alone for their charms of expression, but for
qualities of higher worth ; for purity of sentiment, for honesty of purpose, for benevolence of heart, for the wisdom
of a liberal spirit, and the moderation of a humane temper.

As an essayist, Goldsmith ranks with the highest in our
language. With a keen observation of life and manners, he
unites delightful ease ; and he softens caustic sarcasm with
a pleasant humor. Amidst a varied experience, he preserved a simple heart ; and he drew human nature as he
found it, with the freedom of a satirist, but never with the
coldness of a cynic. The essays of Goldsmith are wise as
well as amusing, and display as much sagacity as variety.
They abound in impressive moral teachings, in apt examples, and in beautiful illustrations. Serious, when soberness
is wisdom, and gay when laughter is not folly ; they can
prompt the smile, they can also start the tear ; inspiration
comes with the occasion, in unexpected eloquence, and in
unbidden pathos.

To speak of Goldsmith as an essayist, is to suggest a
comparison of his merits with writers whose excellence in
didactic and humorous composition forms an elevated and

a severe standard. But Goldsmith will bear the comparison He has not, indeed, the undefinable grace of Addison; nor the solemn wisdom of Johnson. But neither has Addison his freshness, his hearty and broad ridicule, the cheerful comicry which will not be satisfied with an elegant simper, but must have the loud and open laugh. Johnson on the solemn themes of humanity maintains a melancholy grandeur; he sits in despondency and solitude; his general reflections on life and destiny are the deep sighings of a heart that seeks for hope, but has not found it; the pantings of a troubled soul alarmed by superstition, but wanting faith; they are lofty, but cheerless; they are eloquent, but monotonous; they have music, but it is the music of lamentation; they are the modulations of a dirge. Johnson knew well the dark abstractions which belong to our nature; but he did not understand the details of common existence as Goldsmith did. He could moralize, but he could not paint; he has spendid passages, but no pictures; he could philosophize, but he could not create. He has, therefore, left us no special individualities, to which our fancies can give local habitations; he has made no addition to that world of beings, whose population and whose history belong to imagination; he has given it no new inhabitant, none to walk beside the "Vicar of Wakefield" or "Sir Roger de Coverly." As for "Rasselas," he is a declamatory shadow; and cloud-formed as he is, the vapor does not long preserve a shape; for the outlines soon melt into the illimitable expanse of gloomy meditation.

After reading a paper in the "Rambler," or a chapter in "Rasselas," I take up Goldsmith's "Citizen of the World" with a new relish; and when I have perused some pages, I feel resuscitated from depression by its satire, its shrewdness, its pleasantry, and good sense. What a pungent impersonation of poverty and folly is Beau Tibbs, such an admirable combination of the dandy and the loafer. Johnson could have no more conceived of Beau Tibbs than he could have invented a dialect for little fishes. Goldsmith at one time told the critic, that if he gave little fishes language, that he would make little fishes speak like whales. So he would make Beau Tibbs speak like "The Last Man." But Goldsmith understood what little fishes should say, if they had the gift of speech ; it is no wonder, that he knew the proper phraseology of Beau Tibbs, who had that gift with a most miraculous fluency.

Beau Tibbs is a perfect character of the Jeremy Diddler school. Dressed in the finery of rag-fair, he talks of the balls and assemblies he attends. He has invitations to noblemen's feasts for a month to come ; yet he jumps at an offer to share a mug of porter ; he bets a thousand guineas, and in the same breath, it is "Dear Drybone, lend me half-a-crown for a minute or two." Once in company with his Chinese friend, the Citizen of the World, they are asked twenty pounds for a seat to see the coronation. The Chinese sage inquires whether a coronation will clothe, or feed, or fatten him. "Sir," replied the man, "you seem to be under a mistake ; all you can bring away is the pleasure of having it to say, that you saw the coronation." "Blast me," cries Tibbs, "if that be all, there is no need of paying for that, since I am resolved to have that pleasure, whether I am there or not."

Beau Tibbs, then, is a character, and so is the "Man in Black." Where will you find more originality? A most delightful compound is the "Man in Black ;" a rarity not to be met with often ; a true oddity, with the tongue of Timon and the heart of Uncle Toby. He proclaims war against pauperism, yet he cannot say "no" to a beggar. He ridicules generosity, yet would he share with the poor whatever he possessed. He glories in having become a niggard, as he wishes to be thought, and thus describes his conversion. Having told how he quitted the folly of liberality, "I now," said he, "pursued a course of uninterrupted frugality, seldom wanted a dinner, and was consequently invited to twenty. I soon began to get the character of a saving hunks, that had money, and insensibly I grew into esteem. Neighbors have asked my advice in the disposal of their daughters, and I have always taken care not to give any. I have contracted a friendship with an alderman only by observing, that if we take a farthing from a thousand pounds, it will be a thousand pounds no longer. I have been invited to a pawnbroker's table by pretending to hate gravy, and am now actually on a treaty of marriage with a rich widow, for only having observed that bread was rising. If ever I am asked a question, whether I know it or not, instead of answering it, I only smile, and look wise. If a charity is proposed, I go about with the hat, but put nothing in myself. If a wretch solicits my pity, I observe that the world is filled with impostors, and take a certain method of not being deceived by never relieving."

As a dramatist, Goldsmith is amusing; and if to excite laughter be, as Johnson asserts it is, the chief end of comedy, Goldsmith attains it. His plots, however, are extravagant, and his personages are oddities rather than characters. Goldsmith's plays want the contrivance which belongs to highest art; but they have all those ingenious accidents which are suitable for stage effect. They are, in fact, deficient in that insight which pertains only to great dramatic genius. "The Good-natured Man" is an agreeable satire on the follies of benevolence, and "She Stoops to Conquer," a laughable burlesque on a very improbable mistake. Croaker, in the one, is an effective caricature on men of groaning and long faces; and Tony Lumpkin, in the other, is a broad, grinning stereotype of a foolish mother's fool

These two comedies comprise all Goldsmith's theatrical writings. Both of them abound in drollery and strong touches of nature; but they do not give the author an exalted position among dramatists, and they do not promise that he could have reached it.

In referring to Goldsmith as a poet, I have no intention to commit the impertinence of formal criticism. I have an easy and a pleasant work. I have nothing to defend, and nothing to refute. I have only to call up simple recollections, which are endeared to us all by the unanimous experience of a common pleasure. Who has not read "The Traveler," and "The Deserted Village," and "The Hermit," and "Retaliation?" And who that has read them will forget, or not recall them, as among the sweetest melodies which his thoughts preserve? "The Traveler" has the most ambitious aim of Goldsmith's poetical compositions. The author, placed on a height of the Alps, muses and moralizes on the countries around him. His object, it appears, is to show the equality of happiness, which consists with diversities of circumstances and situations. The poem is, therefore, mainly didactic. Description and reflection are subservient to an ethical purpose, and this purpose is never left out of sight. The descriptive passages are all vivid, but some of them are imperfect. Italy, for instance, in its prominent aspects, is boldly sketched. We are transported to the midst of its mountains, woods, and temples; we are under its sunny skies, we are embosomed in its fruits and flowers, we breathe its fragrant air, and we are charmed by its matchless landscapes; but we miss the influence of its arts, and the solemn impression of its former grandeur. We are made to survey a nation in degeneracy and decay; but we are not relieved by the glow of Raffael, or excited by the might of the Colliseum.

The fact is, that Goldsmith, with a pure taste and a sweet

fancy, was not a man of varied culture, or of wide reflection. The general equality, the honest toil, the frugal habits, the domestic virtue, and the heroic patriotism of the Swiss, are eloquently commended. But of all countries on the European continent, France was the one of Goldsmith's affections, and his experience in that gay land is detailed with the partiality of a lover. The character of the Hollanders has the most severity; that of the English the most power. Whether Goldsmith's description of the English be considered true or false, none can deny the force of its expression:

> "Stern o'er each bosom, reason holds her state,
> With daring aims irregularly great;
> Pride in their port, defiance in their eye,
> I see the lords of human kind pass by;
> Intent on high designs, a thoughtful band,
> By forms unfashioned, fresh from nature's hand;
> Fierce in their native hardihood of soul,
> True to imagined right, above control;
> While e'en the peasant boasts these rights to scan,
> And learns to venerate himself as man."

"The Deserted Village" belongs to the heart, and the heart guards it from the profanation of analysis. It is a poem upon which the heart has long decided. Each of us might say, with the author of that Sweet Auburn which he has immortalized:

> "How often have I loitered o'er thy green,
> Where humble happiness endeared each scene!
> How often have I paused on every charm,
> The sheltered cot, the cultivated farm,
> The never-failing brook, the busy mill,
> The silent church, that topped the neighboring hill,
> The hawthorn bush, with seats beneath the shade
> For talking age and whispering lovers made."

The characters of this poem are our household friends, angels whom we love to entertain, yet not as strangers,—nor unawares. Their names were on our lips at school, and they will be pleasant to the grave. Who of us will not ever reverence the Village Pastor? Who of us have not been guests in his chimney corner, and listened with him to the aged beggar and the broken soldier?

> "The broken soldier kindly bade to stay,
>   Sat by the fire, and talked the night away;
>   Wept o'er his wounds, and tales of sorrow done,
>   Shouldered his crutch, and showed how fields were won."

We have all, too, followed this good man to the house of prayer, where he shone with unaffected grace, where the young loved him, and where the old admired; we have followed him to the house of mourning, where his steps were soft as mercy, and where his tones were filled with heaven:

> "Beside the bed, where parting life was laid,
>   And sorrow, guilt, and pain by turns dismayed,
>   The reverend champion stood; at his control
>   Despair and anguish fled the struggling soul;
>   Comfort came down, the trembling wretch to raise,
>   And his last faltering accents whispered praise."

Nor is the good old Schoolmaster less a favorite with us; for

> "He was kind, or if severe in aught,
>   The love he bore to learning was in fault;
>   The village wondered all, how much he knew,
>   'Twas certain he could write, and cipher too;
>   Lands he could measure, terms and tides presage,
>   And e'en the story ran that he could guage.
>   In arguing, too, the parson owned his skill,
>   For e'en though vanquished, he could argue still:
>   While words of learned length and thundering sound
>   Amazed the gazing rustics ranged around;
>   And still they gazed, and still the wonder grew
>   That one small head could carry all he knew."

Goldsmith deserves his popularity, for he loved the people; it was mankind he respected, and not office. In many ways he was not unlike Burns, but most like him in personal independence and popular sympathy. Burns, with all his impassioned aspiration, has nothing finer than this :

> " Hard fares the land to hastening ills a prey,
>   Where wealth accumulates, and men decay ;
>   Princes and lords may flourish or may fade—
>   A breath can make them, as a breath has made ;
>   But a bold peasantry, their country's pride,
>   When once destroyed, can never be supplied."

On Goldsmith's poetry the judgment of the literary and the laity seem unanimous ; both equally approve, and this is a rare consent. " The Traveler " and " The Deserted Village " are perfect in their kind ; and of his shorter productions, " The Hermit " is a masterpiece of tenderness, and " Retaliation " a masterpiece of sagacity.

Goldsmith as a novelist has based an undying reputation upon one brief tale. Nor is this tale, critically considered, without grave defects. Parts of the plot are improbable ; some of the incidents are even out of possibility, and much in each of the characters is inconsistent. " We cannot, for instance, conceive," Sir Walter Scott remarks, " how Sir William Thornhill should contrive to masquerade under the name of Burchell among his own tenantry, and upon his own estate ; and it is absolutely impossible to see how his nephew, the son doubtless of a younger brother (since Sir William inherited both title and property), should be nearly as old as the baronet himself. It may be added, that the character of Burchell, or Sir William Thornhill, is in itself extravagantly unnatural. A man of his benevolence would never have so long left his nephew in the possession of wealth, which he employed in the worst of purposes. Far less would he have permitted his scheme upon Olivia in a great measure to succeed, and that upon Sophia also to approach consummation ; for, in the first instance, he does not interfere at all, and in the second his intervention is accidental."

This is a criticism from the highest of novelists, upon one who was the kindest. It is not, however, a criticism advanced with the technicalities of art; it is one which simple nature indicates, and which, if simple readers could not readily discover, they will readily admit. In what then consists the charm, which striking blemishes are not able to dissolve? It consists in that most beautiful creation of English fiction, "The Primrose Family." In this fascinating group, there is a spell which rivets our attention, and fixes our affections, and we cannot throw it off. We are bound to the Primroses and their originality of innocence, by the purity of their domestic life, and by the strength of their domestic love. Each of the Primroses is a decided and distinct individual. The Vicar has become known to us as a daily neighbor; the good Vicar, at once so heroic and so childlike; so simple, and yet so wise; so strong in the energy of the true, so gentle in the meekness of the holy. Beside him, in evil times and good, we have his loyal dame, who thought people ought to hold up their heads; whose cunning plots were open to all eyes but her own; who was proud of her sagacity, proud of her station, proud of her children, but prouder than all of her husband. Then we have George, the sage-errant of the family. We have the girls, "a glory and a joy" within their home, each different in her loveliness; Olivia, with such gladness in her laughter; Sophia, with such sweetness in her smiles Moses, too, is a leading personage; Moses, half philosopher and half a fool, who, like his father, could talk of the ancients, and, like his mother, "knew what he was about." Even little Dick and Bill, the privileged prattlers of the circle, have their places in the story, and the story needs them. And did ever another story, in such compass, touch so many emotions, and touch them so deeply? We laugh at its breadth of humor, we repose over its quiet pictures, and in a moment we are startled into weeping by its pathos. When the Vicar discovers the absence of his Olivia, his beautiful child, and his beloved, the spotless dove that but lately nestled in his bosom, who is not stunned at his madness, and exalted as he passes from madness to submission? When, from this, we trace him through the fire that leaves him houseless, to the prison where his eldest son lies chained for death; where his family gather about him in mourning and in want; how sublime, in every position, in his conduct, and how cheering are his words! With what heavenly mercy does he seek his fallen daughter; with what fatherly pity does he receive and shield her!

Not tired in alleviating the affliction which has bruised the hopes of his own house, he bears consolation to the wicked with whom his own blameless lot is cast; he finds a brother in the assassin's cell, and in the felon's chains; for he finds in each a human being, and he wins him to repentance by the eloquence which evangelical sympathy alone inspires, and which evangelical sympathy alone can speak. His family companions, in his adversity, are transformed to his moral grandeur; his wife, chastened by suffering, lays aside her trifling, and shows herself a true-hearted woman. Even the rustic Moses, by his patient toil, not only earns the means of support for his imprisoned father, but for himself the meed of imperishable regard.

The humor of this tale is as delightful to cheer, as its wisdom is to instruct us. Nor does the wisdom lose force, but gains it in the humor by which it is relieved. The good Dr. Primrose seems himself aware, that people must smile at his zeal for "monogamy." Whiston had engraven on his wife's tomb, " that she was the only wife of William Whiston." "I wrote," says the Vicar, "a similar epitaph for my wife, though still living, in which I extolled her prudence, economy, and obedience, until death, and having got it copied fair, with an elegant frame, it was placed over the chimney-piece, where it answered several useful purposes. . . . It inspired her with a passion for fame, and constantly put her in mind of her end." Cousins to the fortieth degree claimed kindred, and had their claim allowed. Poor guests, well treated, make a happy company, and Dr. Primrose was, "by nature, an admirer of happy faces." When the guest was not desirable a second time, the Doctor says that he ever took care to lend him a riding coat, or a pair of boots, or sometimes a horse of small value; "and I always," observes the good Vicar, "had the satisfaction of finding that he never came back to return them." Travelers, too, would sometimes step in to taste Mrs. Primrose's gooseberry wine; "and I profess," says the Doctor, "on the veracity of a historian, that I never knew one of them find fault with it." The Doctor was as proud of his theory, as his spouse was of her gooseberry wine, and so lost a horse by his philosophical vanity.

"Are you, Sir," inquired Jenkins, "related to the great Dr. Primrose, that courageous monogamist, the bulwark of the Church ?"

"You behold, Sir, before you, that Dr. Primrose, whom you are pleased to call great ; you see here that unfortunate divine, who has so long, and it would ill become me to say, so successfully, struggled against the deuterogamy of the age."

"Thou glorious pillar of unshaken orthodoxy !" exclaims Jenkins.

Jenkins accepts the offer of his friendship; with his friendship he takes his horse, in return giving him a false note for payment. The wisdom of the Vicar was a notable climax to the sagacity of the son; and an empty check on

Farmer Flamborough, was an appropriate counterpart from the same hand which had furnished the gross of green spectacles. Moses was the oracle of his mother. Moses, she said, always knew what he was about. How proudly he traveled up to the door, after his horse-dealing speculation, with his deal box upon his shoulder; with what quietude of success he received the salutations of his father.

"Well Moses, my boy, what have you brought us from the fair?"

"Myself," cries Moses, with a sly look.

"Ah, Moses," cried my wife, "that we know, but where is the horse?"

"I have sold him," cried Moses, "for three pounds five shillings and two pence."

"Well done, my good boy," returned she, "I knew you would touch them off. Between ourselves, three pounds five shillings and two pence, is no bad day's work. Come, let us have it then."

"I have brought back no money," cried Moses, again; "I have laid it all out in a bargain, and here it is," pulling out a bundle from his breast; "here they are, a gross of green spectacles, with silver rims and shagreen cases."

George was a worthy member of the same family, who went to Holland to teach English, and did not reflect until he landed, that it was necessary to know Dutch. And quite in keeping with all, was the family picture, which was first ordered to be of a certain size, and was then found to be too large for the house. The Flamboroughs were drawn, seven of them, with seven oranges, "a thing quite out of taste, no variety in life, no composition in the world." We desired, says the Vicar, something in a brighter style, and then comes the detail.

"My wife," the Doctor observes, "desired to be represented as Venus, and the painter was desired not to be too frugal of his diamonds in her stomacher and hair. Her two little ones were to be Cupids by her side; while I, in my gown and bands, was to present her with my book on the Whistonian Controversy. Olivia would be drawn as an Amazon sitting on a bank of flowers, dressed in a green joseph, richly laced with gold, and a whip in her hand. Sophia was to be a shepherdess, with as many sheep as the painter would put in for nothing; and Moses was to be dressed out with a hat and white feather. Our taste so pleased the squire, that he insisted on being put in as one of the family, in the character of Alexander the Great, at Olivia's feet."

The character of Goldsmith is not of the most exalted kind, and though it is endeared to us from its simplicity, it does not command our highest admiration. It wanted self-denial; it therefore wanted the regulated foresight, the austere economy, by which lofty qualities are sustained and exercised. In virtues of the severe cast, that sacrifice is not the least, which, for the good of mankind, makes resignation of popular affections; and if we could perceive what great hearts have in this way endured, instead of esteeming them stoics, we would revere them as martyrs.

Goldsmith is one of those whom we cannot help liking, and whom we cannot criticise; yet he is one that should be praised with caution, if in our age there was much danger of his being imitated. We are too busy for meditative vagrancy; we are too practical for the delusions of scholarship; even with the felicitous genius of Oliver Goldsmith, the literary profession would now be an insecure basis for subsistence, and none at all for prodigality Extent of competition, the rigor of criticism, the difficulty of acting on an immensely reading public, repress the efforts of vanity; yet, except in a few instances, they do not compensate the efforts of power; the vain are driven to obscurity, but the powerful have little more than their fame. And though we possessed the abilities of Goldsmith, and were tempted to his follies, his life is before us for a memento, and his experience is sufficient for a warning. Yet is it agreeable to lay aside our prudence for a little, and enjoy with him, in fancy at least, the advantage of the hour; to participate in his thoughtless good nature, and to enter into his careless gayety; to sit with him in some lonely Swiss glen; or to listen to his flute among the peasantry of France; or to hear him debate logical puzzles in monastic Latin; to share the pride of his new purple coat, which Johnson would not praise, and which Boswell could not admire. More grateful still is the relief which we derive from the perusal of his works; for in these we have the beauty of his mind, and no shade upon its wisdom; the sweetness of humanity, and its dignity also.

We need the mental refreshment which writers like Goldsmith afford. Our active and our thoughtful powers are all on the stretch; and such, unless it has appropriate relaxations, is not a state of nature or a state of health. From the troubles of business, which absorb the attention or exhaust it; from the acclivities of society, which exemplify, in the same degree, the force of mechanism and the force of will; from the clamor of politics, from the asperity of religious discussions, we turn to philosophy and literature for less fatiguing or less disquieting interests. But our philosophy, when not dealing with matter, is one which, in seeking the limits of reason, carries it ever into the infinite and obscure; our literature is one which, in its genuine forms, has equal intensity of passion and intensity of expression; which, in its spurious forms, mistakes extravagance for the one, and bombast for the other. Our genuine literature is the production of natural causes, and has its peculiar excellence. But from the excitement of our present literature, whether genuine or spurious, it is a pleasant change to take up the tranquil pages of Goldsmith ; to feel the sunny glow of his thoughts upon our hearts, and on our fancies the gentle music of his words. In laying down his writings, we are tempted to exclaim, "O that the author of 'The Deserted Village' had written more poetry! O that the author of 'The Vicar of Wakefield' had written more novels!"

THE CHRISTIAN IDEA IN CATHOLIC ART AND IN PROTESTANT CULTURE.

MY present subject, "The Christian Idea in Catholic Art and in Protestant Culture," has a theological appearance in the title ; but there is no theological intention in either its conception or its discussion. I had a desire to take the subject in a broader view, and to speak on "Mediæval Art and Modern Culture ;" but this scope was too extensive for the limits of a single essay, also for the limits of my power As my object is to indicate certain social and æsthetic tendencies in modern Christendom, the more specific designation includes the general idea, and is closer to my purpose. There are in modern Christendom, independently of polemics and theology, a Catholic tendency and a Protestant tendency, that is emotional and artistic—this, rationalistic and intellectual. If these do not always blend together, they very thoroughly modify and influence each other. The Catholic element is acted on by the Protestant ; the Protestant is acted on by the Catholic. Neither is what it would be without the other ; and Christian society is not the same with both as it would be with only one of them. By going back towards their sources, we learn to discriminate each tendency in its methods, agencies, and instruments. But in carrying such tendencies as these back to their simple condition, they connect themselves more and more directly with religion. In religion it is, however, that we find the origin of whatever gives force and expression to man's highest mental nature. In this we find the elementary roots of all man's subsequent and complicated growth; and there is nothing that we in the highest sense call civilized which has not primitively been deemed sacred. So, when civilized life is most radically analyzed, its most vital principles are found in the depths of the religious life.

One of the most instructive sentiments is the religious. After the first affections and wants, it is the earliest that man feels—whether we regard man in the life of the individual or in the life of history. Nay, these affections and wants help, through their own experience, to unfold the religious sentiment. They suggest to the soul the mysteries which surround it in universal being, and they stir within the soul the sense of its infinite relations to these mysteries. Thought, conscience, passion, weakness, desire, in revealing man to himself, reveal the universe to him also; and there is that which is neither himself nor the universe included in the revelation. The infinite unknown the soul does not fail to seek for. Grossness, ignorance, terror, mistake, may darken the search, and hinder full discovery, but still there is the inward craving in the soul which only the absolute and the perfect can satisfy. This craving is in the pang of grief, it is in the throb of joy—in the longings of hope, in the lamentations of disappointment; and no sin, no crime, can utterly stifle or destroy it. Such cravings leave within it the conviction that life is surrounded by a potency which is measureless and invisible. Out of this consciousness comes worship. Worship is, therefore, man's first ideal utterance, and art is one medium of it. Art is born out of worship; the altar is before the throne, and a temple precedes a theatre. The gods have statues before heroes have them; and hymns are older than battle-chants. This is no matter of convention or of culture—no transient condition of social order·

it belongs to the original and everlasting inspiration of the soul. So it is now, as it was at the beginning. Revolutions in civilization have made in this no change. Now, in the multiplications of mechanism, man in his religious nature has the same order that he had before the invention of the shuttle or the plough; for the soul is ever nearer to eternity than it is to time—nearer to infinity than it is to place—nearer to God than it is to man. The stars above are closer to mind than the bounds of parish; the immortal with the mind more intimate than yesterday; "and God is all in all." God is with the soul everywhere and always. Socrates and Plato, even Moses and Paul, are afar off, and at distant intervals. Thus that which is most transcendent in nature and relation is often to feeling the nearest and the simplest. The child conceives of heaven, but of the political state he has no idea. He knows of duty, but not of citizenship; and the authority of his father never suggests to him the authority of the magistrate. Religion, and not government, is the first ideal instinct of humanity, and this instinct is shaped into art before other instincts are spiritualized into law. We are, however, concerned with religious art only as it is connected with the Christian Idea. The dawn of Christian Art was as lowly as Christianity itself. Christianity was born in a stable, and the art to which Christ's religion gave birth was cradled in dens and caves. The origin of art in the Western Church is traced to the catacombs of Rome; and it is only in the Western Church that Christian art ascended to triumphant eminence. These catacombs of Rome, as all know, consist of hollow passages, which extend for miles in the vicinity of the Eternal City. They were caverns made by the quarrying out of stone. The origin of them lies beyond all history and all tradition in the remotest antiquity. Accessible portions of these excavations had been used even by pagan Romans as places of sepulture;

and at the opening of the Christian era portions of them were still worked for the materials of building. The toils-men so employed were, it is supposed, among the first Roman converts to Christianity, and they belonged to the most destitute classes of the community. They were famil-iar with those sunless and dreary labyrinths; and when the storm of persecution sorely raged, they knew where to find shelter for themselves, and where to provide it for others. The catacombs, accordingly, became the resort of multitudes who were exposed to danger. When the danger had passed away, the catacombs became sanctuaries, hal-lowed with memories of those who had suffered for the truth, and were held in reverence as consecrated by the sanctity of such blessed memories. There it was that Christian art had its birth and its beginning. It did not arise from taste; for those poor converts were the rudest of the rude. It did not arise from luxury, for these were the children of want—predestinated heirs of poverty—naked, shivering orphans, whom a proud and lust-ful city scorned and oppressed. As little as did Christian art in this its unconscious origin arise from any innate sense of beauty, from any impulse to ideal forms, any craving after what is fair to the eye, and what is eupho·nious to the ear, ancient Romans, at best, wanted native sensibilities for art, and those were ancient Romans of the most uncultivated order. But as their hearts prompted, they traced on the walls of these prisons and burial places signs of faith, and words of hope, of prayer, of lamentation, and of triumph. The earlier figures are most distorted and unshapely. The inscriptions evince the baldest ignorance of spelling, phrase, and grammar. What prompted those lowly men and women to daub these uncouth images and to scrawl these barbarian words? They were so prompted by the urgency of feelings, which, to those untaught records and delineations, gave a glory that no merely civilized genius can give to its most magnificent creations—a splendor of holy and heavenly lustre which shone divinely to the eye of faith. These delineations belonged to the movements of the soul—deeper than any earthly desire—deeper than taste— deeper than any longing for the beautiful. They came from the innermost recesses of the heart—and from the depths of love, and faith, and hope. They came not forth at the bidding of imagination or of sense, but in answer to yearning instincts of the spiritual, inward, and immortal life.

Household affection traces images of kindred; holy admiration delineates the forms of martyrs; pious meditation draws pictured scenes from Scripture; and that desire of the soul to indicate ideas which shun expression, or which transcend it, has here in all directions inscribed its emblems in mystic mark and in sacramental emblem. In these dismal caverns, I repeat, which to early Roman Christians were at once dwellings, tombs, and temples, we have the germs of Christian art, the source of its power, and the reason of its existence. For what is the source of its power? Faith —faith in the invisible and the deathless; hope that grows out of faith; and love, that is the life of all. In such spiritual principles we find the interpretation of every image and superscription which this imprisoned Christianity left behind. Ever there is a meaning in them of affection, homage, or aspiration, that is not born of the blood, that does not belong unto the world, and that looks beyond the boundary of time. This interpretation of Christian art in its origin gives also the reasons of its existence. It was intended to perpetuate the knowledge of the good, and to do them reverence; it was intended to recall the wonders and the worthies of the past; it was intended to shadow or suggest the mysterious and the infinite. Christian art is therefore, in its general conditions, commemorative, representative, or symbolic. All these conditions are essentially included in the struggling but soul-felt manipulations of the catacombs. We find in them the elements of commemorative art, in pictures of departed relatives and of slaughtered saints; of representative art, in various scenes from the Old and New Testament; of symbolic art, in manifold devisings, of which the sacred import is Christian salvation and eternity. And so, if at first Christian preaching was not in the world's wisdom, as little was Christian art in the splendor of man's invention or in the cunning of his skill. And yet, from these dark vaults, from the effigies scraped upon their walls, from hymns that died away in their infinitude of desolation, there gradually came forth a spirit of art which, in architecture, sculpture, painting, and music, became the wonder and the spell of nations.

As we advance into the Middle Ages, we observe the Christian idea unfolding itself in art of imposing majesty and of exceeding beauty. First, naturally in architecture. The architecture which ultimately prevailed in the sacred buildings of Western Europe was that which we call the Gothic. I enter into no discussion on its name, its origin, its varieties, and its transitions. The distinctive spirit which pervades all its forms, is what we have to consider. That, I would say, was the spirit of mystery and of aspiration. A Gothic cathedral seemed an epitome of creation. In its vastness it was a sacramental image of the universe; in its diversity it resembled nature, and in its unity it suggested God. But it suggested man too. It was the work of man's hands, shaping the solemn visions of his soul into embodied adoration. It was therefore the grandest symbol of union between the divine and human which imagination ever conceived, which art ever molded; and it was in being symbolic of such union, that it had its Christian peculiarity. The mold of its structure was a perpetual commemoration of Christ's sufferings, and a sublime publication of his glory. Its ground plan in the figure of a cross was emblematic of Calvary. Its pinnacles, which tapered through the clouds and vanished into light, pointed to those heavens to which the crucified had ascended. Here is the mystery of death and sorrow. And that mystery is intensified in the sufferings of Christ; hence is the aspiration of life and hope, as it is exalted in the victory of Christ.

In yet other ways mystery and aspiration are suggested in the sacred structures of Gothic architecture. I particularly refer to structures of ancient and majestic greatness. The mere bulk of one of those seems at the same time to overpower the mind, and yet to lift it up to heaven. The mere personal presence of a human being seems lost in its mighty space; but while the body is dwarfed, the soul is magnified. As we look and wonder, the thought ever comes that man it was who conceived, consolidated, upreared those monuments of immensity; and the spirit of his immortal being seems to throb in every stone. Here, then, is the mystery of man in his lowliness and his grandeur, in his dust and dignity, touching earth and heaven—feeble as an insect, and mighty as an angel. Again, if we look through a vast cathedral in its many and dim-lit passages, our sight, " in wandering mazes lost," finds no end and no beginning. Then does the thought occur to us, that, if we cannot with the eye take in the windings of a church, how infinitely less can we with the mind discover all the ways of God. Who, we ask ourselves, can find out the Almighty to perfection? Such knowledge is too wonderful for us. "We cannot attain unto it." It is as high as heaven, what can we do? Deeper than hell, what can we know? The measure thereof is longer than the earth and broader than the sea. We feel that we are as nothing when we try to fathom God's counsels, to conceive of all the methods of his wisdom amidst the infinites of the universe, or the secrecies of his providence. It is all mystery and immensity. And while the cathedral gives us in one aspect a sense of sacred mystery, in another it gives us an impression of the boundless. Its awful spaces of naves and aisles carry our thoughts away into the amplitude of God's dominion. Its bold and lofty arches lift them up to the battlements of his throne. The mere gloom of a silent cathedral has power in it. In the stillness of its spacious obscurity, solemn voices awaken in the heart that have impressive meanings for the soul. When we behold these structures in their solidity, as looking onward to centuries, or as having survived centuries, they draw us into communion with the mysteries of duration, and, pacing within them, reading the inscriptions that recall the memory of the dead, we turn from what has perished in the past to that which is eternal with everlasting life. And when we gaze upward and outside to their dizzy elevation, to their pinnacles, which grow beneath from massive towers into points invisible towards the stars, we mount with them, stage by stage, until we, like them, lose ourselves in the skies. We rest not in the sentiment which these structures inspire; we think also of the sentiment by which they were created—of that inward and living faith whence they arose, and to which they bore witness. The Egyptians had temples of astonishing magnitude and of ponderous design. But spirituality the Egyptians had none. The great ideas which filled the Egyptian mind, that mind endeavored to actualize in outward vastness and solidity. The result was, that in the work of Egyptian art, matter and form are not vivified by spirit, but spirit is buried in bulk. Sculptured blocks, quarried temples, heavy pyramids, do not arouse the soul; they despondently oppress it. They give no sense of motion; they indicate a duration, not of life, but of stability. In truth, stability was the Egyptian's only idea of duration. Continuance in being was to him associated with compactness, and nonentity with dissolution. Accordingly, his art was most directed to cause things to hold together. When the breath was out of the body, he made a mummy of it. For the same reason he gave supreme attention in his buildings to all the means of massive consolidation. His mummies have been as lasting as his buildings, and his buildings have been as inanimate as his mummies. They are all of them but signs and sacraments of death. Death was in them from the first, death has ever brooded over them, and death is all that they suggest. The Egyptian mind had, in its way, a sense of mystery, but it had no sense of aspiration. The mystery was all darkness, with no light beyond; and the mystery implied in its sacred edifices is not one of mind, of thought, of awe, but one of cunning, of concealment, and of fraud. Now, the Christian cathedral gains in force of life as it gains in majesty of size; it is mystic with the mystery of the soul, and it is durable as the symbol of eternity. It has compass and firmness on the earth, but then it is graceful in beauty as it rises. In the last particular, as well as in its expanse of measure and its depth of shadow, it is in contrast with the Grecian temple. The Grecian temple is of an exquisite simplicity—a most lovely and fair creation. It is within the grasp of a single view, and satisfies at once the senses and the mind. It lies low along the earth, and calls forth no ideas but those which the earth can answer. It was not so with the Christian cathedral. To the multitudes which it gathered into its courts, it shadowed forth things which the senses could not apprehend, and it points to an existence far away above the earth. Must not faith and hope in this unseen existence have been concerned in the creation of the Christian cathedral? Was it not the soul, reaching to its sublimest strivings, which placed turret above tower and spire above turret, until the cross, over all, seemed to melt away into immortal light. I love with the strength of early love the sacred structures of the Middle Ages. I speak of them, not with the knowledge of science, but with the feelings of memory. Ireland, the country of my birth and of my youth, is covered with the ruins of olden sanctuaries, and in their sombre silence many an hour of my early life was passed. The rustic parish church, the pontifical cathedral, though all unroofed, were even in their desolation lovely; and more days than I can now remember they were my lonely shelter from the sun of summer noontide. Then, in such visions as under the spells of hoary Time the young imagination dreams, I have built these ruins up again—flung out the sound of matin chimes upon the morning air—awakened once more, at sunset, the vesper hymn—called from the sleeping dust prelates, priests, choristers, congregations — bade the long procession move — caused the lofty altar to blaze with light—listened to the chanted Mass—heard the swelling response of surpliced singers, and thrilled with the reverberation of the mighty organ. Even now, in hours of idle musing, the dream comes back, and the form of a pine-tree, projected on the sunshine of Maine, or of New Hampshire, or of Massachusetts, can still cheat me for a moment to believe it the shadow of an ancient spire. Such temples, though silent, had a language of deep meaning; silent to the ear, their language was to the soul. They told me of the power, the earnestness of faith. They told me of men in other days, strong in conviction, patient in hope, and persevering in believing work. They told me of the ancient dead. They told me how generations have come and passed away like the changes of a dream—how centuries are less than seconds on the horologe of the universe. They proclaimed eternity in the presence of the tomb, and announced immortality on the ashes of the grave.

Sculpture is the natural associate of architecture. Christian sculpture was at first principally monumental. The figure was carved flat upon the tomb, and was merely an effigy of the dead. But as inspiration advanced into life, skill advanced into power ; then the figure was raised. At length it was wholly severed from the tomb ; and, from being a dead body, it became a living soul. At this point, the figure was fully under the control of the plastic imagination, and might be molded as Christian art should desire or design. Sculpture has not, however, answered to the Christian spirit. Christian art has not used it much. Sculpture was better fitted for pagan art—better fitted to image forth the strength and the beauty which the Greeks deified and adored, than the spiritual purity which Christian art labors to express. The Greeks, too, giving special value to the body, had enthusiasm for the art which idealized it ; and those who had genius to idealize the body, had all opportunities of seeing it to perfection in Grecian discipline and in Grecian games. When Grecian genius, therefore, failed in the power of creative originality, sculpture, as a living force, seemed to be exhausted. Not only must a new impulse have a new invention, a new idea must have a new art. Christianity demanded a medium more subtile than sculpture, and more delicate, less palpable, and of greater variety. This it found in painting—an art which made the surface tell to the soul what the solid could not, the secrets of the heart in the tintings of the cheek, and the visions of thought in the lights of the eye. Christian art in painting brought the holy into unison with the beautiful, and made it seem a new revelation to the world. It raised loveliness above the region of desire, and crowned it with the lustre of an eternal sanctity. Sacred painting has done an immortal good—if in nothing else, in showing how grand, how sublime, how godlike may be the face of man, how

angelic the face of woman, in the imagination of a noble soul.
But, more particularly than any, music is a religious art; for,
beyond any, it belongs to the infinite. It excludes all that
is logical and restrictive—all that is combative and contro-
versial. In the undefined and the undefinable above, it is
purely in its element. Without bound or body, it belongs
only to emotion, and is truly the spirit of movement and of
soul. In union with Christian inspiration it is that music
has most revealed its mystic power—shown that there is a
spirit of soul which has its only revelation in a spirit of
sound. The organ is hardly less a creation of Christian
genius than is the cathedral itself; and if the cathedral
would be bare without statues and paintings, without the
organ it would be dumb. Each of these arts separately
grand, all of them answer in excellent harmony united. A
cathedral amplifies the soul; a noble statue calms it; glorious pictures illumine it; sublime music inspires it; and thus,
by the majesty of the temple, the embodied eloquence of its
sculptures, the saintly beauty of its paintings, the divine
harmonies, the subtile rapture of its music, the consecrated
genius of a thousand years ministers to the life of a moment,
and makes the life of that moment seem in its power an
image of eternity. Thus art, in the fourfold manifestation
to which we usually confine it—namely, architecture, sculpture, painting, music—become, according to the manner
of Catholicism, in some sense a sacramental ministration
of the Christian idea. How this came to be so we can only
learn in the past of Christendom. Classic civilization had
influence on one side, the Hebrew ritual had influence on the
other, and no long time was required to multiply liturgic ceremonies, and to heighten external pomp, when Christianity
had become the religion of the Roman empire. Something,
too, must be ascribed to the necessity of circumstances.
Early Christianity could not have been to any extent a

religion that could be learned or felt, as now, from books;
nor could it have been to many in any way, a religion of
documents.   In a great degree it must have been a religion
of tradition.   Apostolic epistles were indeed among the
churches, narrations also of Christ's ministry and sufferings,
but the mass of believers must have had most of their knowledge by transmitted report and by public instruction.   As
this would hardly be enough to give permanent nurture to
emotion to keep faith alive and zeal in action, symbolic
rites, delineation of sacred persons and events, and the imposing awe of grand and consecrated edifices would be
demanded for an effectual ministry to the general religious
feeling of the era.   When the Scriptures were gathered into
a collective unity, when the canon had been determined, and
the sanction of ecclesiastical authority stamped upon it,
manuscripts were yet few, and readers were not many.   The
Scriptures were, indeed, studied; they were abundantly
quoted in the writings of the ancient Fathers, in those also
of the Mediæval theologians; but religious inspiration was
still of necessity imparted to the people by means of oral
teaching and visible impression.   These remarks are sufficiently ample to account for the relation which I have been
tracing between the Christian Idea and Catholic Art.

But in course of time another instrumentality came into
action in a merely mechanical invention.   We hear of late
years much glorification of machinery and mechanism.   Of
themselves, they prove nothing but the growth of human
want; and the nature of the progress that they indicate
must be determined by the nature of the want for which
they provide, or in which they originate.   Wonder, in our
day, is in constant excitement at the never-ceasing applications of science to the uses of life.   Like life itself, they
are of all gradations, from the trifling and the minute to the
magnificent and the sublime.   Yet in all this infinite diver-

sification of thought, cunning, and contrivance, you will find that, primarily, the uses which they mostly serve are those of physical desire or of social convenience—those of need, of comfort, and of luxury—those of interchange, of intercourse, and of vanity. The uses to which mechanical inventions minister are seldom directly intellectual or spiritual ; they seldom originate in wants of the soul, and seldom in their influence do they act upon such wants. But immediately out of such wants came the invention of printing ; and on such wants most profoundly is the agency of its influence. Judged, therefore, by the noble need from which it sprung, and the order of desire that it gratifies, among all the many inventions which the uneasy brain of man has sought out, printing may claim to be of a special dignity. It may not, indeed, improve the quality of writings, but it gives them infinity in quantity. Like the miracle of the prophet which made a single cake and a cruise of oil afford sustenance to a household for many days, the press makes the same ideas the mental nutriment of millions ; and for all generations, it immortalizes such as are worthy to live.

The Book, the great instrument of modern culture, was born of the press. The Manuscript had only a secret life— a life with no large or open atmosphere—a life which did not breathe fully, and had no power of liberty or of expression. The Manuscript belonged to the scholar and the priest ; the Book became the property of mankind. The Christian idea in Protestant culture made the sacred Book its only authority, and found in that alone the divine source of all which most ennobles and most sanctifies existence.

I propose to dwell on some relations of this principle to Art and Culture.

Protestant culture began in resistance to ecclesiastical unity of power. The tendency of it, therefore, was to dissociate the Christian idea from mystic symbol and outward type. It appealed from usage and tradition to individual judgment and direct interpretation of the written word. The tendency was first of all unfavorable to grand ecclesiastical architecture. The book had become the stronger rival of the building—not the sacred book merely of the sacred building, but the secular book also of the secular building. Victor Hugo makes his monk, Claude Frolls, say, in the fifteenth century, in Paris, as he points with one hand to a printed book, and with the other to the Cathedral of Notre Dame, "This will kill that." Printing had recently been invented. The letter was to take the place of the symbol; the book was gradually to subvert the building. Printing, as Victor Hugo generalizes the statement, was to kill architecture. Printing interfered with architecture in general. But Protestant culture, with the Bible for its centre, was necessarily fatal to church architecture in particular. The book did in this case certainly kill the building. First, it deprived the building of spiritual import; and a religious building without spiritual import, is void of life; it becomes mere space, bulk, and form, with only an æsthetic value. The sacred building is indeed by Protestantism consecrated to worship, but it is no longer in itself a thing of worship. It is made for people to assemble in and pray, but it is no longer in its own silent majesty a mighty and perpetual act of prayer.

The building, while yet the book was not among the people, was not only significant, but also, with its history, its traditions, its legends, its pictures, monuments, and statues, had excitement for the intellect, and was in its way a teacher. But when the book prevailed, the building lost its inspiration, lost its function of suggestive ministry to belief, and feeling was at an end. So, soon as the authority of the book supersedes the authority of the Church, the book kills the building, which has in that authority the very life and reason of its being. This influence is altogether independent of that polemic and destructive temper with which the Christian idea in Protestant culture was at first associated. Such temper belongs to every great spiritual as well as every great social revolution. The early Christians, when they had power, spared neither the buildings nor the books of pagans. To earnest and devout minds, the creation of pagan genius seemed all the offspring of impurest wickedness ; and so, by means of Christian zeal, pagan literature as well as pagan art suffered calamitous devastation. The teaching of the Reformers, especially that of Calvin, aroused at first a similar antagonism against Catholic art. Calvin was a man of logical and stern intellect. Void of sensibility, barren of imagination, he never arose to the rapture of passionate emotion —never had glimpses of the poet's heaven in the vision of ideal beauty. Luther was a man of different spirit. He was a man of sensitive and impassioned nature—rich in imagination, large in his capacities of life, large in his capacities of engagement. Such a man has always a living interest in art. He had that sense of the grand to which architecture ministers. He loved painting, and was in music an enthusiast. Though he renounced the authority of the Roman Church, he did not cast off all his historical sympathies. He burned with no iconoclastic fierceness. He still maintained a Ritual, and was favorable to a moderate pomp in worship. None the less, the influence of his doctrine was unfavorable to religious architecture. It may indeed be said, that art had already reached the utmost vigor of its creative spirit, and would henceforth, independently of any theological influence, have entered, as it did enter, on deterioration and decline. But the conservative spirit of sentiment and of memory cherishes what art has already accomplished, when the creative spirit of genius, with its fertile invention, with its grace and force of execution, is no longer active. Of this conservative spirit early Protestantism had none ; and though later Protestantism has, in some degree, returned to it, early Protestantism was, in general, its determined opponent. The line of tradition was broken. The continuity of feeling which flows with the sentiment of one age into the life of another, which carries the unfinished purpose of one generation to that which next succeeds it — this continuity was interrupted, vital supply failed, then set in decline and death. Old buildings were not repaired ; buildings in progress were not completed ; completed buildings were void of use or object ; invention was no longer demanded, and originality expired.

Thus, secondly, "the book kills the building," because it subverts the conditions which create and sustain the building. A great edifice is not only a great unity—it is also the result and the creation of a great unity. A mighty religious edifice presupposes unity as a necessary condition to its existence. It requires unity of combination ; unity of combination requires unity of purpose ; unity of purpose requires unity of sentiment ; unity of sentiment requires unity of doctrine ; unity of doctrine requires unity of belief, at least it requires unity of assent. Now, in all these particulars, Protestant culture leads not to unity, but to division. Such must be the case, since the centre of it is individual judgment and private interpretation. The book here must kill the building—since it must break up that unity in which alone the building can originate, or by which it can be sustained. To erect a cathedral demanded the contributions of generations. But Protestant culture unfolds itself variously from age to age. A cathedral stood in the midst of a province, and had space to hold the multitudes which crowded to its worship. But wherever there is actual mental freedom in religion, Protestantism produces in every community a variety of theological opinions, and each opinion has its own organization. It can gather its members only from limited space, and it has occasion rarely for any but a moderate edifice. Protestantism breaks up unity of district and dogma. It broke up Western Christendom into religious nationalities; it broke up the nationalities into sects; the sects it still continues to divide and modify. We can easily see that such a tendency can admit of no church architecture; which needs a perfect unity of sentiment for its inspiration, and the sublimity of vast dimensions for its power.

Hence, thirdly, "the book kills the building," because it takes away its uses. The Christian idea in Protestant culture insists on simplicity of worship, and gives emphatic importance to the sermon. The Christian idea, therefore, in Protestant culture demands a building not so much for ritual as for mental purposes. A Protestant temple is not intended for magnificent ceremonial pomps. It wants no lengthened aisles for great processions, no chapels for separate services, no deep retreats for the confessional; it wants no mystic gloom to contrast with the illuminations of lamps and tapers, with the brilliant decoration of the altars, or with the sparkling and splendid vestments of the priesthood; but it *does* want a construction which will enable every one to hear the preacher and to see him. The conditions of a good building, as laid down by Sir Henry Wotton, are, "commodity, firmness, delight." To these we may add two general rules prescribed by the late Mr. Pugin, the greatest modern master of ecclesiastical architecture: "First, there should be no features about a building which are not necessary for convenience, construction, or propriety; second, all ornament should consist of enrichment of the essential construction of the building." Let Protestantism be true to

these rules, then it will be true to itself, and it will be true to
nature.   But it cannot be true to them in the use of Gothic
structure, without considerable adaptation.   An order of
architecture we often observe in modern churches which
should not be called the Gothic, but the grotesque.   Now it
is wall and buttress, run to seed in spire; then it is a dismal
vault, crowded with thick and stunted pillars; here it is a
gaudy nondescript, about which one is uncertain whether it
was originally intended for worship or the opera.   Sometimes it seems like the realization of a drowsy dream, and
again it has the perplexed confusion of a delirious vision.
Used wisely, Gothic architecture has the inspiration of mystic genius, and, as associated with venerable memories, it is a
fitting and suggestive form for a Christian temple.   But in
architecture for worship there should, above all things, be
truthfulness.   No pretence should be there—no deception—
no vanity.   A sacred building ought itself to be a sacrament
of veracity, of rectitude, of integrity; it ought to be so in
structure, in material, in ornament.   It should symbolize
throughout a sincere and right spirit; otherwise it can have
no beauty, and least of all the beauty of holiness.   One
ought not to enter through a portico of shabby splendor to
hear the levities of the world censured; one ought not to
have their boards made counterfeits for solid marble, when
he is to listen to denunciations against hypocrisy.   The
house of prayer should be built, as it should be entered, in
a spirit of truth and a spirit of worship.   The humblest
substance will take the shape of beauty, but if not, it is better to have unsightly honesty than seemly falsehood.   The
spirit of beauty is indeed divine as well as the spirit of
truth, because both are equally from God; but if semblance
is put for fact, then the form of beauty, like the form of
truth, is a lie.   We might use abstract arguments for pictures and statues in churches—but to what purpose?   We

might ask, why should an illustrated church be evil, and an illustrated Bible be excellent? Why should a statue or a picture which has the beauty of *meaning* be wrong, and carving and coloring, which have only the beauty of ornament be right? If we commemorate by art the worker, the statesman, the patriot, the magistrate, why should we not the prophet, the apostle, the martyr? If the soldier has his statue, why should not the saint? If the battle-field may be delineated, to how much better purpose may be " The Last Supper?" And if art may thus minister to civic virtue in secular places, why should it not minister to religious sentiment in sacred places? But, I repeat, to what end are such questions? When feeling desires such applications of genius in religion, it will have them; but while feeling is against them, no mere reasoning avails. Protestantism is not, however, without pious artistic genius. The magnificent Thorwalsden devoted some of his sublimest sculptures to the Protestant sanctuary; and Ruskin, alike profound in reverence, in feeling, and in knowledge, is not only a most original critic on art in general, but a most eloquent writer on sacred art in particular, and he brings to his grand vocation the harmonized endowment of the poet, the thinker, the orator, and the Christian. The masterpieces which the genius of early times consecrated to the altar, the genius of no other times will probably ever equal. But the popular and diffusive spirit of the new civilization does not allow their loveliness to be in vain. By prints and copies, it sheds some light of their beauty throughout the world. We are also to consider that the genius which had once worked mainly for the sanctuary has gone abroad into common life, and gives itself more widely to the varied interests of humanity. One art there is centred in primitive emotion that is always young, always pure—which belongs to no age, and is confined to no creed. That art is Music. Of all arts, music is the most sympathetic and the most human; it is also the most incorruptible, the most divine; and because thus at once sensuous and spiritual, it is universal and immortal.

Æsthetic genius, which the Church almost entirely monopolized, had done its greatest works before the Protestant idea had come into distinct form; and that idea only noticeably marked a general movement of which the Reformation was a special portion. The European mind had in many directions begun to question tradition and authority, to loosen itself from the visible and emotional, to give itself to the promptings of doubt, and to the searchings of the inquiring intellect. The invention of printing intensified this tendency. The Reformation, aided by the agency of printing, still further intensified it, and for a period gave it the concentration of a theological controversy, and the compass of a social revolution—the tendency of which, Protestantism was at first the most decisive form. Protestant culture has ever since assumed to express and to direct. · The aim of this culture is inward, individual, intellectual, practical. As it withdrew the mind from external ministries, it directed attention to forces that are spiritual. As faith was not to rely on ecclesiastical authority, but in the written word, that every one should be able to read the written word, became, according to Protestant logic, almost a necessary condition of religious or moral life. Protestantism was bound, therefore, by its own first and most essential principle to provide universally for such requisite ability. But in this, as in all that is human, fact will not bear close comparison with theory; and in spite of theory, there may be found within the dominion and history of Protestantism dense masses of popular ignorance, and gross neglect of popular instruction. Still, to the degree that Protestant culture is active and has effect, it tends to diffuse intelligence and develop individuality. Individuality of character abounds in English literature, especially in comedy and humor. This is partly an element of race ; but under Protestant culture, it seems to have attained a marvellous diversity. Individuality of opinion is constantly seen not only in ceaseless conflicts of thought, but in oddity, obstinacy, dogmatism, and stubborn personality, which, though they may have been born of the blood, have been nurtured by the brain. Protestant culture tends to endless diversity. In the speculative sphere, there is no end to its philosophical systems, nor, in the theological, to its religious sects. Above all, Protestant culture is hardly ever mystic, or thoughtless of the real. Idea, it insists, must pass into deed, science into the uses of life, and skill into productive labor. Faith is everything in the Protestant doctrine ; work is everything in Protestant practice.

I have here traced two tendencies of humanity within the sphere of Christendom — the æsthetic and emotional in Catholic art ; in Protestant culture, the intellectual and the practical. The Catholic idea and the Protestant idea can never, in religion, be theologically reconciled ; yet, in social civilization, the influence of both come together, intercommune, interpenetrate, and mutually receive and give power. The Catholic idea allies itself with grace and deepens into sentiment ; the Protestant idea allies itself with intellect, with will, and becomes realized in knowledge and activity. I, looking tolerantly on both, can see in Catholicity and Protestantism that which neither, from a polemic aspect, can see in the other. I can see deep spiritual suggestiveness in what is called the materialism of Catholicity. I can see grand and entrancing imagery in what is called the bare intellectuality of Protestantism. I can well understand the power which a ritual and traditional Christianity can exercise over the soul as well as over the fancy and the heart. I can profoundly feel how the poor man can be lifted up

by the cathedral dome, that seems an image of the sky—
how the music that fills its majestic spaces may draw him
from the grosser world, and make his bosom heave with
a sense of heaven. I can well conceive how the dullest
man can carry away affecting impressions from the services
of a pictured and illuminated altar ; and how, in the toils
of the day, in the visions of the night, his mind may call
back those sights and sounds—hold communion through
them with invisible perfection, and gain from the religious
inspiration that may brighten and consecrate his life. I
know that sense, imagination, feeling belong to our nature,
and that therefore they must belong to religion. I see that
all creation is rich with glorious phenomena that arouse,
delight, and satisfy the spirit through the senses. If the
heart is not in despair, if the blood is not perturbed, the eye
cannot open but to look on beauty, the ear cannot listen but
to hear music, and thought cannot be awake but to be alive
to the infinite power with which it is encompassed. The
ministeries of religion may surely be made consonant with
the ministeries of nature, and those sacred arts may be
employed in the service of religion which typify, in their
inspired devisings, the sublimest and the loveliest works of
God.

On the other side, I can behold a solitary Protestant, as
he leans over the Bible, translating the letter into vision,
and presenting to the inward eye such images of wonder
and of glory as artists may indeed have conceived, but
which art has never executed. He sees not only the patriarch asleep with the sky for his canopy and the wilderness
for his bed, but he enters into the patriarch's dreams, gazes
into the open heavens, beholds the angels that ascend and
descend by the ladder, which, resting upon the earth,
reaches up to the throne of God. He looks upon the
majesty of ancient Egypt ; he witnesses the tragedies of

its guilt and of its punishment. He stands on the border of the Red Sea; he sees a passage opened between two walls of water, which gives outlet to the hosts of Israel; he sees these walls rush together in a roaring crash over the hosts of Egypt. He wanders through the desert with emancipated people, marvels at the pillar of cloud by day and the pillar of fire by night; is awe-struck at the darkness of Mount Sinai, and quakes in the presence of its terrors. Then arise to his view the pictured history and life of the Hebrew nation : the wars of David—the power of Solomon—the glories of Jerusalem—the successive scenes in the awful drama of tragic prophecies and their tragic fulfillment. The New Testament crowds his brain with ideals of sanctity and of beauty, as the Old Testament crowds it with those of sublimity and might. At last this imagination is lost in the mystic trance of the Apocalypse, that, with its stupendous and terrific imagery, embraces all duration, all space, all power, all existence, all destiny. Has not this man, too, a pictorial ministry—a medium through which his fancy is kindled into light, and opened to all that divinest light reveals? Has he not also a grand cathedral, magnificent in its riches and its pomp, with altars mountains high, and lights in suns and stars, and priesthoods as old as time, and liturgies of inspiration chanted for all humanity? If this man can make the letter live, has he not that in the book before him which can call into exercise all within him that is most primitively and deeply, as well as spiritually and sublimely, artistic?

And here, in conclusion, is the very principle which gives to all art its power. The essence of art is in our own intuition and our instinct—and so it is that we ever live more in art than we do in science. Human life, in all that is spontaneous, is, in its way, an artistic activity. Man is by his nature an artist : first, for the necessary and the useful;

secondly, for the pleasurable and the ideal; afterwards for both united, as occasion demands or prompts. By art man struggles out of savage need into civilized comfort; exerts inventive skill, for subsistence and protection; unfolds imagination for the joy of beauty. The life of art is inward, and it is infinite. It is inevitable to the consciousness of our own life; and through our sense of art in nature we apprehend the life of God. It is by pictures in the mind that we recall the past. How busy imagination is in painting—and how every faculty keeps her at work, especially memory and passion! How rapidly she changes her representations! How she brings the scenes of youth, the dreams of love, and all the drama of deeds and feelings! It is by pictures in the mind that we conceive of the distant as well as of the past, of the possible and the ideal. Thus what chambers of imagery our minds become, as we read history, travels, romance, poetry. It is by our sense of art, I have said, we apprehend in nature the life of God. In science we have the laws of God in nature; but it is in our sense of art that we feel his life in the infinite grandeur and beauty of the universe. How wonderful this grandeur, and how exhaustless this beauty! Think on the the pomp of heaven, and on the glory of this rounded earth —on earth and heaven, ever moving in communion, and at every point, through every season, through every second, presenting pictures which fill all space with splendor!—in which we might reverently say, that God's imagination comes into vision, and shows itself to sight. The sun himself, enthroned afar off though he is in the midst of the worlds, is a most excellent likeness-taker. As he shines equally on the just and on the unjust, so does he impartially paint the homely and the fair, the youthful and the aged. With strictest rectitude, he paints them as they are. The poor he does not disfigure, and the rich he does not flatter.

And nature lives to the sense of art as well through the ear
as through the eye ; gives it music in the ocean, in the torrent, in the air, in the voices of life ; and nature in all
whether to the eye or to the ear, gives by this sense of
art a sense also of the divine. There is then a spirit of art
which is·primitively and transcendently religious ; and if
there was no temple built with hands, souls that could rise
into exalted worship would find a temple for God in the
hollow sky, and pictures for the temple in all that the sun
illumes, in all that the firmament displays ; and priesthood
in all pure hearts, and liturgies in all worthy aspirations
and anthems, choruses and hymns in the sea, in the winds,
in the young raven's cry, in the breathing of a mother's
love, in the whispers of a mother's prayer.

THE COST OF WAR.

My subject is, The Cost of War.

War is a matter of great diversity in human history. I would like to discuss it in its variety of forms, principles, changes, characteristics, and conditions. Such a discussion would open a wide field of interesting contemplation, and one not less sad than interesting—a field indeed glorious with sublime heroism and achievement, but also dark with wickedness and woe. It is a field that we have here no time to survey. Such a survey would embrace the whole course of public strife, from the first battles with clubs to the later battles which tax the utmost resources of human intellect and human prowess. And we should have also to enter into a moral analysis, and discuss the distinctions between wars that are justifiable and those which are not— wars which are aggressive and those which are defensive— wars which are those of conquest, political intrigue, of national vanity, and those which are wars for national security, national preservation, for the assertion and maintenance of right and liberty—those wars which are deliberately and unscrupulously planned, and those which suddenly arise and become inevitable in some unforeseen complications of international concerns. My purpose is not thus comprehensive, and yet what I propose to say on my subject will apply to all wars, the best even as well as the worst. I desire to confine my attention to that which is essential to war, to that which is inseparable from its existence. But while I count the cost, I would have men, when duty demands, bravely pay it to the utmost.

I. One cost of war is that of hostility. Peace must be broken. Parties who had been friendly, or who, at least, had been tolerant to each other, must take opposite sides, and enter on a work of mutual injury. War is outward, inward, universal contest. It is not on the battle-field alone that men at war with one another come into collision, but at almost every point of life. Where they used to join in the grand commerce and comities of the world, they meet to fight; and land and sea, which used to be common to them all for intercourse and pleasure, for travel and for traffic, are now beset with danger and destruction. They will not buy of one another, they will not sell to one another, and the third party who would deal with both will have, by turns, both for his enemies. The have no longer together a common object or a common interest. They can unite in no august plans of principles or of actions—can have no interchange of congregated courtesies— can have no joyous multitudes reciprocally paying or returning visits—can have no combined associations for the promotion of science, of art, of agriculture—can have in union no Crystal Palace. In these respects, modern wars differ from those of ancient Greece, and from those of the Middle Ages; for the wars of ancient Greece did not interfere with the sacred games, and the wars of the Middle Ages had temporary cessation during the truce of God. But the men and times in those instances were different from our men and times; and as the sooner wars are concluded the better, it is perhaps an advantage that they should as little as possible be prolonged.

The hostile relations into which war throws men are not confined to open and palpable ones. Hostility penetrates to their inmost consciousness. It enters into their thoughts, their feelings, their opinions, their passions ; head, heart, and conscience share in it ; it saturates not alone the social and the physical man, but the intellectual, the moral, the spiritual man. Men opposed to each other in war cannot think or feel of each other as they do in peace ; they cannot justly estimate each other, and they can hardly pray for each other. From the fullness of the mind the mouth speaks, so men in these relations seldom speak well or truly of each other. Nor is it thus with those alone who practically fight in the quarrel, or who politically govern it, but with whole nations and communities ; and often the disposition grows into fierceness in proportion to its distance from the centre of the contest. Those who actually engage in the contest may learn to respect, even to admire each other ; those who politically govern it are generally, by the nature of their position, kept free from personal excitements ; they are either calm in the elevation of their views, or they are cool in the sagacity of cunning or ambition. The fire is hottest among the passions of the many, and it is such passions that supply the energies by which the contest is sustained. In these passions is the motive power, and without that motive power, the best intellects to guide, the best instruments to execute, would be inert and in vain. Let the fire go out which boils popular feeling into steam, then the best-contrived machineries of war will soon be stopped. A state of war is, upon the whole, a condition of public anger ; and individuals or classes share in it according to their temperaments, habits, or education. The anger may be righteous or not, may be noble or otherwise, may have been aroused by the most enlightened sentiments or by the blindest passions, but none the less, for the time being, it is anger. A wise man can be angry as well as a fool ; and though there may be wisdom in the wise man's anger, and only folly in the fool's, both are in a condition of excitement. A just man may be terrible in his wrath, and in his wrath he may not forget justice ; but he is not the calm, just man until his wrath has ceased. Now, we know that the best man cannot look upon cause or person while thus moved as he did while he was yet tranquil ; and however fitting the movement may be, we must not confound it with mental and moral conditions entirely different. These remarks are true of nations and communities ; they are, while in a state of war, in a state of anger, and this anger, as shown in the aggregate of popular feelings, has generally a strong mixture in it of hatred, scorn, and contempt. Take the case of the English and French throughout the Bonapartean wars. Napoleon was not only hated by the English masses with the deepest hatred, he was abused with the grossest ribaldry, and mocked in every manner in which the most scoffing caricatures and lampoons could mock him. The higher literature, though in a different way, was of the same spirit. Would Colonel Napier have dared to write of Napoleon, for even educated Englishmen, while the war was going on, as he wrote of him afterwards, when the war was over? Then, among most Englishmen who had not made the trial, it was an accepted maxim, that one Johnny Bull was equal to three Johnny Crapeaus, and there was no phrase or attitude of contempt too scurrilous or despicable in which to represent Johnny Crapeau. The French paid all this back in their own fashion, and did not spare Wellington, the Prince Regent, or the whole nation of Johnny Bulls.

Such, in general, is hostility as we observe it in national wars. In civil war it is in every way intensified, and in degree to the nearness of relationship which had before existed between the parties. The more they had lived a common life in language, religion, intelligence, education, and wealth

—the more they had possessed in common of social and civil equality, of political knowledge, of military means and skill, the more determined is their strife, and the greater are the numbers involved in it.

II. A second cost of war consists in the demands which it makes on wealth, and, at the same time, the injuries which it does to wealth. Armies must be collected, and they must, in general, be taken from the working population. Laborers are drawn away, and yet those who leave, as well as those who remain, must have support. The soldier, particularly, must be cared for, and that not stingily. It was a prime maxim of Napoleon, "that an army should always be in a condition to fight," but so it cannot be if soldiers are neglected. If unsheltered, ill clothed, and ill fed, they become sick, spiritless, and feeble. If soldiers are to fight like men, they need in all respects the treatment of men, and this morally as well as physically; "for character," Sir William Napier observes, "is half the strength of an army." Money has been called the sinew of war, but it is as much also the sinew of peace; and it is from this sinew of peace that the sinew of war must derive its strength. Money has been growing in modern times more and more towards being the only medium of exchangeable value, and likewise of nearly all the duties and charities that minister succor to the needy or the helpless. Formerly, a man shared his roof with the stranger or the homeless; now he sends him to the village inn or to the town establishment, and charges the expense to the poor-tax of which he regularly pays his assessment. A man once shared with the needy, as he went along through life, his house, his food, his clothes, his labor, his personal compassion; and thus people, at least people of middling or humble means, met most of the demands made on their practical sympathies. Now, I repeat, they pay the poor-tax. If rich and generous, besides paying their taxes, they found or endow institutions, while living, or, when dying, leave them legacies. And this is all done with money, or what is equivalent to money. In accordance with the habits of the age, whether we pay or give, we do so not in kind, but in coin; and thus also an army must be supported. And this is in accordance with the humanity of the age, as well as with its habits; for the humanity of the age will not allow an army to live by plunder or exactions. In some cases the defeated are made to pay the expenses of the war; but this, whether right or wrong, is not always possible. England has in two instances compelled the Chinese to do so; but in the Continental wars against Napoleon, she had not only to pay her own armies, but also to subsidize those of her allies. But if the conquered paid for every war, war is not the less a charge on the aggregate wealth of the world. War must be paid for, and, whatever comes in the end, each party must pay its own expenses for the time being. How is that to be done? Simply, with money. Whence is that to be procured? In a war of emergency, and one in which a whole people are concerned, conscientiously, earnestly, and passionately, the government will be largely aided by contributions, and to some extent by gratuitous service. But such aids can at best be but temporary; and if the war endures, it must be systematically sustained by regular pay and a standing army. How is this army to have sustenance and wages? Public and private generosity has done all that it can or will. The answer now will be—the means must come from taxes. But a large army and a long war soon, in the richest countries, exhaust the taxes. After a while, the direst exigence, the utmost coercion or persuasion, can make the people yield no more. The pressure will bear even more heavily where wealth has not been hoarded, but is the product of present and continuous labor. The army and the war, in either case, press on the energies which supply taxation; and while the demands become more numerous and exacting, the means to meet them become fewer and more impoverished. Labor is cramped; commerce is plundered or imprisoned; business is bankrupt or embarrassed, men stand idle in the market-place, and women sit listlessly at home; but the war must be honorably sustained, the army must be honorably paid and sufficiently supplied. How is this to be done? The present must be mortgaged to the future, the taxes must be aided by a loan, and the credit of to-morrow must be accountable for the borrowings of to-day. This is a dangerous remedy; but when the case is urgent, the remedy must be accepted. Doctors, in the crisis of a desperate disease, will administer medicines which in other circumstances would be deadly, but they take care that the doses shall as soon as possible be discontinued; then they apply themselves to relieve the patient from the after-effects of the drug, and to strengthen his constitution. This would be also a good method for political doctors to follow who are forced, in critical times, to pursue a daring course of treatment of alarming symptoms in the political body. Such a crisis comes when the public expenditure exceeds the public revenue. A public debt is then the remedy; and with a prudent foresight to its steady payment, and within a reasonable period, it is often the easiest and the best remedy. If one generation bequeaths benefits to its successor, that successor must willingly accept some burdens with the benefits. In nations where war is chronic, this debt sometimes becomes so huge as to be beyond the hope of any final disbursement. But the yoke does not press alike on all, for then all would combine to break it. The toilsman, who should have the least of it to bear, it often goads to madness. It is a load most grievous to bear in the best times, but in bad times it crushes its bearer body and soul. When the industrious may justly complain, there is profound cause for social anxiety. There is darkness in their discomfort, and there is danger in their discontent. It is the solemn duty of rulers to take heed how they deal with the earnings and energies of workers. It is at a terrible peril that they consume the wealth which exists already, and sign away for ever large portions of that which is yet to be created. I find the following statement in newspapers as to the money cost of a few great wars. The war preceding the Treaty of Ryswick, in 1697, cost $130,000,000. The Spanish war of 1739, settled for at Aix-la-Chapelle, cost $270,000,000. The war of the Spanish Succession cost $311,000,000. The Treaty of Paris, in 1763, ended a bloody struggle which cost $560,000,000. The war of American Independence cost England and this country $930,000,000. The war of ten years, which is known as "the French Revolution of 1793," cost $230,000,000. The war against the first Napoleon, which began in 1803 and ended in 1815, cost the extraordinary amount of $5,800,000,000. The Crimean War cost $84,000,000. The last Italian war, not including the hostilities between Victor Emmanuel, Garibaldi, Bomba, etc., cost $45,000,000. The last war in India cost England $38,000,000.

But the largest regular cost of war is, after, all but a fraction compared with the damage which it is to wealth and to every kind of human property. The amount of wealth which it hinders from being produced, the amount of wealth which it hinders from being distributed, is, of course, not calculable, but that it must be vast is certain. To this must be added the loss which all wealth suffers by the positive destructiveness of war. The havoc which war has committed on land and sea, even within the limits of public law, there is no human imagination great enough to estimate. Could all the treasures which war has buried in the depths of ocean or otherwise destroyed, be restored, there would be enough, it is probable, to enrich the world for many generations. The money loss, however, of what war has destroyed is of small account. It is better that, in this matter, every era should look to its own needs, and tax its own energies to meet them. But war has destroyed treasures which can never be restored. It has swept away the records of nations. It has cooked the victuals of its camps by the blaze of books which man in his noblest genius and wisdom had written. It would roll up ball-cartridges in the lost manuscripts of Livy, if it found them, and even if it knew them when it found them. It has cast down and defaced the most wondrous works of sculptured beauty, such as imagination dreams but once, and never dreams again. It has turned into wreck, or ground into ruins, structures at which all beholders wondered, and which, in exciting wonder, made the beholders greater. And war has done this in all ages, and throughout the earth—in Heathendom and in Christendom. War has dilapidated some of the most beautiful monuments of Christian genius; and even Christian Rome has been sacked more than once by Christian depredators. The insane and wanton spirit of mischief in war is often uncontrollable. The destructiveness of war is bad enough within its legalized limits; but to such limits it can never be restricted. When the passions of armies are in their hottest rage, it is not in the power of the most humane or the most commanding authority to stop or stay the conflagration, moral or material, which they enkindle or extend. The British armies have not been the worst. The Duke of Wellington had a stern control over his troops, and was, withal, a leader that hated cruelty or license ; yet, in spite of him and the rest of the officers, the British forces, in the capture of Badajoz, did such devilish deeds as must have made the historian blush for his nature while he gave account of them, and which account will be read by civilized men, for all time, with pain and shame. Atrocities as bad as those of Badajoz are not singular events in the history of British armies. They are common in the histories of all armies—not alone in pagan and Mohammedan armies, but also in Christian armies; and in these, not alone with men of unsparing hearts for commanders, but also in Christian armies led by men of as much clemency as courage. Under certain conditions, such evils are almost inevitable; and though the temper of war has progressively become more humanized, it is yet doubtful whether these evils can ever be entirely eradicated. War is by its very purpose destructive; it will always be destructive beyond allowed usages; and in states of phrenzied excitement, it will carry destructiveness to the extremes of cruelty and inhumanity Then, horrible moral depravity accompanies the desire to destroy and spoil. Could villages, towns, cities, districts, be shown to us in one awful vision, of all time, as war deals with them — as ravaged, sacked, burned, devastated—it would seem as if hell were opened with its anarchy of flames and ruin, and as if heaven were darkened with the smoke of the bottomless pit.

III. A third cost of war is loss of life.

On this point there is no occasion for any very extended remarks. It is obvious enough in itself, and it is of such magnitude as not to be reducible to definite statement. Any attempt to present to the mind's conception the measure of mortality by war, must be vague and feeble; it can amount to little more than the intangible calculations of conjectural statistics, or the generalities of interjectional rhetoric. The function of war is to fight, and to fight with every human energy; "to imitate," as Shakespeare teaches, "the action of the tiger; to stiffen the sinews, summon up the blood; to disguise fair nature with hard-favored rage; to hold hard the breath, and bend up every spirit to his full height." Thus the function of war is to fight, and to fight with all

the strength which mind or muscle can supply. The purpose of fighting is to kill, and to kill as rapidly and as numerously as possible—not merely to fell an enemy in every
blow, and deal a blow in every second, but to sweep enemies
away by hundreds, by thousands, by a continued tempest
of missiles and fire, in which time ceases to be noted, while
Death rides upon the whirlwind and directs the storm. To
kill is the office and the object of war ; to kill in open strife
is its direct intention. Yet death in war, by battle or by
siege, forms the least part of war's mortality. This fact a
single instance will distinctly and comprehensively illustrate.
The instance goes to show that neglect and other contingen-
cies are more fatal causes of mortality in war than the most
deadly conflict. Neglect may be corrected, but many silent
exterminators of life are associated with war which defy all
experience, and which no skill can baffle. Here is the
instance to which I referred, and I take it from the pages
of an English Review. "Napoleon," the Reviewer observes,
"bestowed much thought on the preservation of his army
in the intervals between fighting. But even Napoleon lost
more men out of action than in it. The Russian campaign
of 1812 was a signal instance of this ; for though he fought
the bloodiest battle on record since the use of gunpowder,
the killed and wounded make but little show in the whole-
sale destruction which mismanagement brought upon "The
Grand Army." The Reviewer then proves from authentic
documents the following facts. "The invading army which
crossed the Niemen numbered 302,000 men and 104,000
horses. The great battle of Borodino was fought on the
way to Moscow. In this battle the killed and wounded
were, on the side of Russia, 30 generals, 1,600 officers, and
42,000 men ; on the side of France, 40 generals, 1,800
officers, and 52,000 men. The cold began on November 7th,
but three days before the cold began—namely, on the 4th

of November—there remained of the mighty host that had crossed the Niemen but 55,000 men and 12,000 horses ; 247,000 men had perished or become ineffective in 133 days. Of the remaining 55,000 men, 40,000 returned to France, showing how few men were lost in that masterly retreat, either by the severity of the winter or the harrassing attacks of the enemy. Even if three-fourths of the wounded had died, and allowing for those killed in minor actions and operations, it would follow that nearly 200,000 men perished by insufficient commissariat, by want of forethought. Here is an instance under the greatest of generals, that it is not the enemy, however numerous or skillful, who effect the destruction of armies. It is fatigue, exposure, want of food, want of shelter, want of clothing, want of sanitary prevention."

Here is a still later authority on the general destructiveness of life in war in a single army during two years. We have these statistics of the sickness and mortality in the French Army in the Crimean War. Dr. G. Scrive, Surgeon-General of the French Army in the Crimea, in his final report said, that the Crimean War lasted, without any intermission, summer and winter, for twenty-four months. The total number of French troops sent to the East at different times amounted to 309,268 men, of whom 200,000 entered the ambulances and hospitals to receive medical aid —50,000 for wounds, and 150,000 for diseases of various kinds. The total mortality was 69,229, or 22½ per cent. Of these, 16,320 died of wounds, and nearly 53,000 from diseases—more than three times as many by diseases as from wounds. Of ordinary wounds, 2,185 ; gunshot wounds, 22,891 ; frost-bitten, 3,472 ; typhus fever, 3,840 ; cholera, 3,196 ; scurvy, 17,576 ; feverish, 63,124 ; venereal, 241 ; itch, 124. The mortality from scurvy was fearful ; also from frost-bites. If such was the case with the French, who, 1 believe, suffered least, what must it have been with the English, the Turks, the Sardinians, and the Russians. How terrible must have been the united total of want, pain, disease, and death.

Fear of death is a natural instinct, which man shares with every animal that has any distinct consciousness of life. To have it impeaches no man's courage; to acknowledge the feeling is to the credit of a man's honor, and the acknowledgment bears witness to his regard for truth. Men who became afterwards the boldest and ablest captains, had the feeling while war was yet new to them; and when many victories had crowned their glory, they did not shrink from confessing the weakness of their early inexperience. If I remember rightly, Frederick the Great was not, in the beginning of the Seven Years' War, the daring soldier which he subsequently became.

An anecdote told to Coleridge by an eminent officer of the British Navy of Sir Alexander Ball, shows that a casual lapse may not be cowardice, and should not be severely treated.

"When Sir Alexander was Lieutenant Ball," this gentleman related, "he was the officer whom I accompanied in my first boat expedition, being then a midshipman, and only in my fourteenth year. As we were rowing up to the vessel which we were to attack, amid a discharge of musketry, I was overpowered by fear, my knees trembled under me, and I seemed on the point of fainting away. Lieutenant Ball, who saw the condition I was in, placed himself close beside me, and still keeping his countenance directed towards the enemy, took hold of my hand, and, pressing it in the most friendly manner, said, in a low voice, 'Courage, my dear boy! Don't be afraid of yourself! You will recover in a minute or so. I was just the same when I first went out in this way.' Sir, added the officer, it was as if

an angel had put a new soul into me. With the feeling that
I was not yet dishonored, the whole burden of agony was
removed ; and from that moment I was as fearless and forward as the oldest of the boat's crew, and, on our return,
the lieutenant spoke highly of me to the captain. I am
scarcely less convinced of my own being than that I should
have been what I tremble to think of, if, instead of his
humane encouragement, he had at that moment scoffed,
threatened, or reviled."—*Coleridge's Works*, Vol. II., p. 489
(Harper's Edition).

This natural emotion is counteracted by other tendencies
—by pride of manfulness, by ambition, by a sense of honor,
by a sense of duty, and, beyond all, by habit. Hardness of
nerve is not courage. Stupid indifference to death is not
courage ; mindless disregard of life is not courage. He is
most truly a brave man who is not blind to the reality of
danger, but who is yet cool in the clear view of it. Nelson
was such a man. In the midst of the fiery tempest at
Copenhagen, he had occasion to write to the authorities
of the place. He neatly folded and superscribed the letter,
refused the offer of a wafer, but sealed it elegantly with
wax, and did all as tranquilly as if he was in his library at
home—proving thus to those on shore with whom he corresponded that he was in neither flurry nor confusion.
History has no record of a braver man than Nelson. He
was brave in all modes of bravery, and with all the qualities
which render bravery sublime—which cause it to give to
character and actions a glory that excites enthusiasm for
ever, and that affects the imagination and the heart like
poetry and music. Nelson was equally great in the courage
of deliberation and of defiance, in the passion for combat,
and in the genius of command ; yet, with all this impetuosity and hardihood, Nelson was of a delicate constitution
and of a womanly sensibility. Perhaps no other man ever

united so much tenderness with so much indomitable force
and purpose. Sensibility does not lessen courage, but
beautify it, and the feelings of the man exalt the courage
of the hero. We might add many names to that of Nelson,
of men who, though not equal to him in warlike fame,
resembled him in temperament—such as Chevalier Bayard,
Sir Philip Sydney, Sir John Moore, and General Wolfe.

I have merely hinted at the immensity of death amidst
which war has reveled throughout all time, and throughout
the world. I will also merely hint at terrible varieties of
pain with which war inflicts death. These are as many, as
changeable, and as novel as if they were contrived by the
untiring ingenuity of diabolical invention. War lays hold
on the best mechanical genius, and gives to it wealth and
reputation, according to its success in devising the means
of human slaughter. The conical bullet has been much
commended, because, when well directed, its course is sure,
and the wound it then makes terrible, deep, and mortal.
And so with all other contrivances that are the best adapted
to their murderous purpose. I will not be specific in these
matters, and bring to mental vision what works of death
war can do with any weapon; I will not traverse scenes of
contest, and survey them just when fights have closed, to
look on the heaps of the slain or listen to the groans of the
dying; I will not pace over bloody decks, and gaze upon
shapeless fragments that shortly before had been living
bodies, comely, strong, and full of prowess; I will not contemplate the ghastly spectacles of the hospital or the cockpit; I will leave all this to imaginations stronger than my
own, that may find interest in such musings. If there are
some who desire hints more literal, I advise them to read
Sir Charles Bell's "Letter from Waterloo;" the account of
the Russian Campaign, by Baron Larry, or, perhaps better
still, that very eminent man's treatise on Military Surgery.

I do not wonder at the reticence of men who have had experience in actual war, or at the sobriety of their words when questioned on it. Wellington disliked to speak of his battles, and often promptly put down attempts which tended to give conversation a direction towards them. When he did speak of war, he spoke briefly, solemnly, suggestively. "Next to a defeat," said he, "a victory is the greatest of calamities." That declaration is more honorable to him than a hundred trophies.

An intelligent soldier has a just sense of danger, and by no means despises it. He enters the field with a firm step and a serious face; he feels that the next moment may be his last, and he does not trifle with the thought. The experienced veteran would call the man a coward or a fool who would treat such circumstances with a mock bravado. At the approach of a general engagement most minds are serious, and this mood continues until it is lost in the ardor of the fight. So I have learned from the reading of many military memoirs, and from conversation with men who had known war in all its varieties on land or sea, and these men always referred to war with thoughtfulness and gravity. But from these sources of inquiry I also learned that in war an army often longs heartily for battle—at times from sheer desire for excitement, at times from impatience or suspense. There are occasions when a soldier sighs for battle as the sick sigh for the morning. When fatigued and starved—when wornout with marches and counter-marches—when his spirits have lost all cheerfulness, and his will all resolution—when his hope decays, and his head is weary with watching, then he will hail the prospect of a battle with wishful expectations, because it gives him the promise of deliverance by victory or death. The fear of death is, therefore, never that which unmans the soldier; this is done by the evils and vexations which irritate his temper, undermine his health, and which, having consumed the vigor of his life, leave only the dregs behind. Let this vigor be not exhausted, then the soldier goes to battle strong in heart and hand, and if death there strikes him instantly down, it is while he glows with the extacy of impetuous action and with the passion of high excitement. It was probably of such a death Robert Burns was thinking when he wrote:

> "Thou grim king of terrors, thou life's gloomy foe!
>   Go, frighten the coward and slave;
> Go, teach them to tremble, fell tyrant! but know,
>   No terrors hast thou for the brave."

IV. The only other cost of war to which I will allude consists in the amount of misery and affliction, passing all comprehension, of which it ever has been and ever must be the source. To begin at the centre. The sufferings of armies themselves are not all comprised in bodily pain or physical discomfort. There is the mortification of defeat. Think you how this often pierces the heart of a brave man more sharply than the sword. The royal Saul, of strong, passionate, and courageous temper, wounded in body and hopeless in soul, sooner than become prisoner to the Philistines, gave himself the mortal blow. Numbers of brave men, have thus chosen the refuge of suicide, or sought voluntary death at the close of hope, amidst the throng of their enemies. And we well believe that this mortification is not confined to leaders, but is shared almost to madness by the common ranks. The mere suspicion of being blamed, drove the intrepid Villeneuve to do as Saul and others had done; and we have all read how whole regiments, under the sting of censure, have, in order to prove their valor, and to relieve their mental suffering, rushed into the most devouring danger. There is also the disgrace of flight, and the complicated hardships and humiliations to which it subjects the conquered and pursued. There are the tediums and troubles of captivity; and not the least painful among the griefs that soldiers feel, is home-sickness, which among some armies has often been as fatal as a pestilence. I speak not of the demoralization incident to armies within themselves, or of that which they spread around them, for the very nature of the topic forbids me to dwell on it. I merely say, that if there are those who think that large bodies of men can be brought together as armies are, without any intensification of the common vices, they have not read history or human nature as I have. I would desire, for the credit of man, and for the good of the world, it were otherwise; but if it is *not* otherwise, I would not blind my imagination to the fact, or indulge my imagination in an idle dream. The fact may perhaps be mitigated, and for this end it is the duty of society to use all possible means; but when society has done its utmost, it may have lessened the evil—it will not have cured it. Regular armies, in peace and under the strictest discipline, are not, at best, the purest class of men; but the very license of armies in peace, would be virtue in the armies of war. I speak not of the wrongs which such armies commit on the residents of countries through which they pass, or in which they may hold temporary sojourn, often without attack or provocation. I simply suggest that, in the best conditions, injuries are done and woes inflicted of which history or law takes no account, and of which heaven alone is the witness and the avenger.

As we go out from the centre, we find in diversified ramifications, that war spreads miseries and afflictions to the remotest bounds that are in any way related to it. Into homes near it and afar off, war carries anxiety, difficulty, struggle with reduced means, and the bareness of positive destitution. Into these homes war, of course, introduces likewise the mental troubles, domestic uneasiness, all the various vexations that belong to disturbed or impoverished households. And it works sadly thus throughout society It reduces the rich man to bankruptcy ; it drives the poor man to desperation ; scarcely an individual, high or humble, within the reach of its influence, who does not have a share in its calamity. To some it may bring worldly success, and the elation of mind which accompanies good fortune ; but while war may exalt one, it pulls down a thousand, and for every heart that it spares, it wounds or bruises myriads. From the *heart*, however, it is that it exacts its keenest cost. *There* it has more than a Shylock-spirit, for it does not merely cut nearest the heart, but it cuts the very heart itself. If it drenches in blood the places of its fighting, it waters with tears the secret retirements of life. When the battle is over and the dead are buried, many are they who listen for the news, and ask with fear for tidings of the loved. Many are they who ask in vain, or who will never hear tidings but such as make the day seem dismal and the night unblessed. 'Many are they who thenceforth become changed for ever, who accept their affliction with wordless tears, who utter no complaint, but keep to themselves the holy mystery of their hidden grief.

When a body of the British army was, some years ago, cut off in the mountain-passes of Northern India, the news of the catastrophe cast a deathly gloom through the habitations of the British islands, from the palace to the hut. What, then, must have been the mourning of the land for those whom the insurgent Sepoys massacred ? Under all the choruses of exultant Italy, what low or silent anguish must have been in thousands of saddened homes all over Europe occasioned by Solferino and the groups of murderous battles connected with it ? Waterloo, twice twenty years before, filled the private life of Europe with even a deeper anguish, for it closed the bloody strifes of half a century— closed the excitement of war in the lassitude of peace, and gave leisure to the bereaved, not only to pine over recent loss, but to count up successive losses in melancholy retrospection. If, on one side, there was the loud rejoicing of victory, and, on the other, indignant despondency for defeat, thousands on both sides were so smitten in those affections wherein all men are kindred as to be equal in the common humanity of natural sorrow. There are wounds given by war otherwise than by the sword—wounds that are deep, and that do not close when war has ceased—wounds that are long in healing, and in some cases that are never healed, but that though apparently grown well, are only dried up, always ready to break out again, and to bleed afresh. When thus looking steadily and earnestly on the many and dread realities of war, one has moods of feeling when he is almost ready to lament its presence or its prospect in the passionate and pathetic words of the prophet : "Let mine eyes run down with tears night and day, and let them not cease."

But with all these costs, war must be accepted. First, as a matter of fact. Man seems so constituted that he must fight, and decide by battle all his greatest controversies. Why this should be so, it is hard to say, but so it is, and, in spite of logic or philosophy, so it will probably remain. Human nature it is scarcely to be expected will ever become so radically changed as to dispense entirely with war. The war-spirit may be modified, it may be restrained, but, while man is a being of affections and passions, as well as of intellect and conscience, the war-spirit will live in him. The movements of his blood will often direct the movements of his brain, and he will rather strike than reason, or he will hold that, in certain crises of affairs, blows are the only fitting arguments. This method is so rude, and apparently so inconsequent, that the hope never dies entirely away which looks forward to some other more reasonable mode

of settling national or ultimate political controversies.
There are intervals every now and then when long-con-
tinued peace and prudent negotiation strengthen the hope
in good men's souls that the time is approaching when war
shall be no more. But while the sky is all serene, and
people fondly dream that the millennial morning has
dawned, a speck of cloud dims the brightness, ere long
the whole horizon is thick with darkness, and the tempest
of mortal strife howls all around us. Then we look again
more deeply into human nature, and we come to the painful
conclusion that it is no further from the disposition for war
than it ever had been. We also discover that the long-
continued peace, and the prudent negotiation which had
encouraged hope, were owing to any other causes than
unwillingness for war. But bad as war is, I cannot see with
this constitution of man, and the general state of the world,
how it is to be entirely avoided. When two parties assert
contradictory claims, and there is no supreme authority to
which they will submit, the only trial which then seems
possible is a trial of strength. This appears irrational,
yet it is not so, for it is the last reason, not of kings only,
but of peoples likewise, and it is, moreover, the last alternative. If all men and nations lived according to the moral
reason, or according to the spirit of Christianity, which is
the perfection of moral reason, there could be no war.
But the best live thus only very partially ; and while they
do so, we must, as best we can, strike the balance with our
infirmities, and, wisely as we are able, take our choice of
evils. It is better that men should even be rash than
craven ; it is better that they should take the risks of war
than be zealous for peace in a mercenary love of gain or a
dastard love of life. If men will not strive after the perfection of Christian virtue, which is holiness, it is desirable
that they should not fall below the dignity of pagan virtue,

which was courage. The very word *virtue* is Roman, and the import of it is manhood. War may indeed often be a great crime, and the cause of great crimes ; it is often but the sanguinary sophistry of godless pride or of covetous injustice ; and yet, in whatever states native military passions have been wanting, grown feeble, or died out, we do not find instead of them grand or generous virtues, but mean and selfish vices.

But, secondly, war must not merely be accepted as a matter of fact—it must often be endured, undertaken, and conducted as a duty. The combative instincts and passions must be its immediate agencies, but the great jury of civilized men will in the long run, under heaven, decide the right. Through many tribulations, some great questions have been already decided. War becomes a duty in many cases that cannot be defined. But there are cases in which no man can be indifferent—cases in which every man, unless he is coward or traitor, must take a side. There may be mistakes as to the merits of a cause, but there should be none as to the position of a citizen. It is well that this should be so. It is well that loyalty to institutions, that love to country and the state, should be proved in the face of death. If these, the supreme affections of the world, can be vindicated only by war, why, then, war is inevitable, and its necessity becomes a virtue. But warfare should not be hatred. It may strike a human brother down, but the slayer must not rejoice in his brother's fall. The slayer may take his brother's life, but he must not take it with the malice of murder in the stroke that kills him. Neither should warfare be ever regarded as a contest of mere animal forces. In physical fight, as in all struggles, *mind* should vindicate its dignity ; even then, as always, *mind* should illumine and lift up the body ;

and only where *mind* rules, is contempt of danger worthy the name of courage. There alone is the highest con- sciousness of life—there alone is a deliberate estimate of the cost in losing it. The true and complete man learns equally to think, to do, and to die.

POPULAR WIT AND HUMOR; ESPECIALLY IN SCOTLAND.

ARE wit and humor necessaries of life, or are they merely luxuries? Suppose a mental tariff, which should exclude from charge of duty whatever was not of prime necessity,—would wit and humor in such case be taxable commodities?

leave these questions for critical political economists to solve. For myself, I am not inquisitive, but enjoy "good sayings" as I do "good things," and I am not too curious to speculate about or to analyze them. A certain gentleman of the olden time, concerning whom many people talk, whose writings a few people read, has left it on record, that "The man that hath no music in himself .... is fit for treasons, stratagems, and spoils." Now, with all due deference to "the immortal Williams," the saying would be still more true of the man that hath no laughter in his heart. And for this we have even authority from "the immortal Williams" himself, or rather from the immortal Cæsar :—

> "Let me," he says, "have men about me that are fat;
>   Sleek-headed men, and such as sleep o' nights :
>   Yond' Cassius has a lean and hungry look ;
>   He thinks too much : such men are dangerous.
>   .   .   .   .   .   He reads much ;
>   He is a great observer, and he looks
>   Quite through the deeds of men. He loves no plays;
>   .   .   .   .   .   he hears no music :
>   Seldom he smiles ; and smiles in such a sort,
>   As if he mocked himself, and scorned his spirit,
>   That could be moved to smile at anything."

The vulgar proverb, "Laugh and grow fat," has thus, it seems, ancient and sublime corroboration. Then will men not fear or shun you, but love and court you. You will grow in favor as you grow in size, and according to your bulk so will be deemed your benignity. You will become fat because you laugh, and you will laugh because you become fat. You will be doubly a benefactor, to yourself and to your friends ; you will have laughter in your self, and be the cause of it in others. Sometimes they will laugh *with* you ; sometimes they will laugh *at* you. But what signifies the means if the end is gained? If we had little wit, says the good Dr. Primrose, we had plenty of laughter.

This is no cynical philosophy ; and Heaven forbid that such a philosophy should ever be ours. On this matter there are two classes of cynics—the "unco gude" and the ultra-polite. We will not, with Sterne, say that gravity is a mask for the concealment of hypocrisy, but we do think, that to cultivate gravity for its own sake is grim and solemn folly. We do not blame men who, by natural temperament, are habitually serious, or who are made so by weighty duties, by many cares, or by a sad experience. Pitiable and pitiful is that levity which can easily escape from the honest tasks of life, or that elasticity which no grief or sympathy can press down or burden. For such characters we have no respect, and, if better feelings did not restrain us, we should hold them simply in contempt. That disposition alone is nobly joyous which is also profoundly earnest ; for imagination and sensibility are but poor without intellect and conscience. Imagination and sensibility are the faculties which are the most directly productive of wit and humor ; but void of moral feeling, wit is only keen indecency or pungent malice ; void of thought, humor is merely vulgar grimace or swaggering buffoonery ; it is the presence of moral feeling in both that gives them worth and dignity of mind, innocency and gladness of heart.

The brightest life has gloomy hours ; the best life has remorseful hours ; the most happy life has painful ones— and every life should have solemn ones ; and this is in the order of Providence and nature. Every year, in climates the most fit for man, has its winter. For a time the skies are dark, the air is cold, the earth is barren, the trees are naked, and all the cheerful beauty of the world seems to have disappeared. But out of this comes soon again the budding spring, and the annual new birth of animated being—the glory of summer, with its splendor, rapture, strength, and song ; the maturity of autumn, with its gorgeous coloring and its gracious plenty. But the "unco gude" would have nothing in the year of man's life save winter. Man must be always sad of face, of frosty manner and of doleful speech ; he must not caper, or dance, or joke he must not tell stories or sing songs—or if he does sing, it must be a psalm, at least something like a psalm ; he must not go to opera or play, and a concert is but barely tole- rated ; he may work as hard as he can six days out of seven, but the seventh must not be a day of free, healthful, and grateful rest ; it must be one of hard routine and ritual servitude ; in short, human existence must be at once a penance and a toil, wearing by turns the sackcloth of a sin- ner and the garment of a slave ; regarding the earth only as a place of bondage for the living and a place of burial for the dead ; looking to the heavens only as the roof of a work- house or the dome of a sepulchre.

Next in error to these are the ultra-polite. As the "unco gude" would destroy the freedom and spontaneity of life by spiritual formality, the "ultra-polite" would destroy them by conventional formality. They are creatures of class and clique, of clothing and etiquette, who, by much toil and hard training, succeed in giving up to their "set" all that was meant for their souls, and who allow fashion and manners to spoil the grace of nature and to burlesque the work of God. In other days all this was done gravely ; in our day it is done grotesquely. It is hard to say what there is between them to choose. The grave, perhaps, can be more deeply vicious than the absurd ; it is certainly less amusing.

Tradition reports Lord Chesterfield to have been a man of genuine elegance. His own manners, then, must have been very different from his theory, or his elegance must have cost him dearly. Why, a straight-waistcoat would be a loose and easy dressing-gown compared with the attainment or practice of it. A good deal of it might be summed up in the direction, "When in company, except in extreme necessity, don't laugh, smile, or show your teeth." Now, we can not only tolerate these vulgarisms—we rejoice in them ; we like to be where they are found, and found abundantly. We not only allow people to show their teeth, but, for every purpose except to bite, they may show them as often as they wish; if the teeth are handsome, we share the owners' pleasure ; if they are ugly, we admire their courage. We can not merely tolerate a smile, we delight in a grin—the broader the better; we are even willing ourselves to grin, moderately or immoderately, and we ask for no gingerbread in payment. We would hinder no man of his laugh, and a man who lovingly laughs at another man's jokes makes good his title, we hold, to laugh at his own joke. Would you give none of the game to the dog which catches it? Would you muzzle the ox which treadeth out the corn? According to Chesterfield, a gentleman must not open a conversation with allusions to the weather. Then we humbly inquire how conversations ever would be opened—ay, or mouths either, except for eating or drinking. General society would be one great order of La Trappe. A gentleman, according to the same authority, must be brief and infrequent in relating anecdotes and stories, because otherwise he would betray a want of imagination. A good rule, but a bad reason ; for in general society there is no lack more plentiful than a lack of imagination—as the very fewest and shortest anecdotes or stories soon make evident. A man should be brief in his relation, in order not to annoy his neighbor, who is impatient to hear his own talk ; and a man should not intrude on the company too often, since every one else loves the sound of his own voice as much as he does. Lord Chesterfield would not allow a gentleman to play the flute, because playing the flute distorts the countenance ; but a gentleman may fight a duel, and with an honorable conscience blow the soul out of his brother's body, or risk the blowing out of his own soul—may risk even worse than this for both. A gentleman, his Lordship maintains, should not play the fiddle, because playing the fiddle involves ungraceful gesture ; a gentleman must avoid a fiddle-bow, but, without impeachment of his elegance, he may draw a long bow. A gentleman may be unjust, but he must not be rude ; he may hate, but he must not be uncourteous ; and the more enmity there is in his heart, the more elegance there must be in his bearing towards the object of it. We trust that the actual behavior of Lord Chesterfield was more natural than his code of manners, and that his real character and conduct were the opposite to his code of morals.

There is sometimes a rustic gravity—the result partly of religious training, and partly of social training—which often becomes an occasion of humorous incident. The reserve thus nurtured makes any strong outward demonstration of enthusiasm appear unseemly, not only as a violation of serious-mindedness, but as a breach of decent manners. A certain habitual shyness, withal, belongs to this reserve, which imposes silence when the heart would cry aloud. This becomes to those who in presence address the public an embarrassment, an ,uncertainty, and a discouragement. When the great Mrs. Siddons first acted Lady Macbeth in Edinburgh, it was to an audience that seemed moveless and dumb. She was in despair. She went more zealously to work, and studied some special passages which she thought *must* arouse them, and gave the passages with electric passion. For a moment all was as still as usual, until an old man arose in the pit, and shouted, "*It's nae bad, that!*" The silence was broken, applause came in thunders, and ever since no national theatre has been more noisy than the Scottish.

When popular lectures began in New England, the quiet of the audience was a sore test to the speaker, and especially if from the other side of the Atlantic. A person not long from England was invited to lecture in a country village. Should he succeed, he hoped that lecturing might afford him a useful sphere of employment. He began his lecture. He allowed ten minutes for gaining attention ; but twenty minutes passed away, and still no sign of recognition ; at twenty-five minutes he was despondent, and at half an hour he was desperate. Ignorant of New England manners, and knowing that any speaking at all noticeable was soon in Old England cheered, or at the worst hissed, "Well," thought he, "lecturing is not to be my destiny; I can't say *my* occupation's gone, for it never is to come." The audience moved out at the close as if they were going from a house of mourning—a chief mourner indeed was the poor, woe-stricken, disappointed lecturer. All his best got-up thunder turned out to be but a blank cartridge. The lecturer walked with a gentleman who was to be his host. The host had thoughts, it would seem, too deep for words ; the guest, alas! had thoughts too deep for tears : both went along in serious meditation, but not in fancy free. At length the host said, with a gravity of tone which befitted the occasion, "What a splendid lecture you gave us!" the guest was then indeed speechless, for he became almost choked with gratified astonishment. As if the popular habit was not sufficiently strong, and the hearers might possibly be surprised into an ill-behaved murmur, the president usually, before the lecture began, requested them to avoid demonstration, and to observe an orderly quietude. Ungrateful that we are, and always discontented with possesion, we would now willingly call back some of that tranquil decorum which brought into the lecture-room the sober attention of the church, and yet had its side of humorous consciousness. Many a face was farcial in its drum-tight rigidity, and much fun, drollery, and frolic were hidden away in laughing corners of the heart ; not a little, too, of satire and criticism. It was amusing to observe the gradations with which a stoic presiding officer—the pattern and fugleman to the meeting, of immutable propriety—gave way to comic influences which he could not resist. The face would be at first like that of a judge passing sentence of death, then relaxed into wrinkles, then approaching to the placid, then cognate to the pleasant, then a twinkle in the eye, then a twitching of the lip, then facial longitude losing itself in facial latitude, and at last an explosive laugh. But this was rare.

In late years we have changed all this, and much of it for the better. Variety is the spice of life ; wit and humor are the salt of it. We cannot sustain physical life pleasantly without spice, or at all without salt ; neither can we sustain mental and social life without wit and humor, which are not only its salt, but also the most pungent of the spices which season its variety.

Wit and humor seems to have given a keen relish to

Dean Ramsay; as we see by the keen relish, which he has of them, as they appear in the life of the Scottish people. He has evidently much enjoyed them, and he does not spoil his enjoyment by reasoning on it. What is wit, what is humor, and what is the difference between them, are questions that he leaves to take care of themselves, or to metaphysicians, who know everthing in the abstract and nothing in the concrete, everything in general and nothing in particular. The fact is, that wit and humor, being matters of feeling as well as of intellect, evade strict definition, and whatever does, evades logic. Logic, in any direction, goes a short way with life, and shortest way of all in the direction of sport and mirth. We feel what humor is, but we cannot define it. We feel what wit is, but we cannot define it. We sometimes feel when wit is not humor, and humor is not wit, and there are times when we cannot tell the one from the other — at least we cannot tell the difference between them.. Sterne has a fine piece of ridicule on Locke's distinction between wit and judgment, and his idea that where there is much judgment there must be little wit, and little judgment where there is much wit. Sterne compares wit and judgment to two knobs on the back of a chair, where each answers to each, and where one for harmony needs the other. We would use this illustration in reference to wit and humor. They often seem as like as the knobs on the chair ; often you can only distinguish them, as you do the knobs, by the mere difference of position ; and frequently, as the knobs cannot do, wit and humor so run into one another as to be undistinguishable and inseparable. There is, however, one point of difference which often separates them ; it is this : wit is always *conscious* and personal, it is an intentional exercise of mind in the agent of it ; humor on the contrary may be unconscious and impersonal, may be merely casual, incidental, and entirely undesigned. Thus, for instance, a man may be an occasion for humor, or an instrument of it, when he has not in himself the least faculty for it or the least sense of it. Again, a man may be in humorous relations to persons, places, objects, or circumstances, and be so most unwittingly. These are facts of every-day occurence. A man who is a humorist in character, as distinct from one who is a humorist consciously and by comic talent, is a man that is seldom aware of the humor which he embodies, acts, speaks, and lives; like Monsieur Jourdin's writing prose, this man performs comedy all his life, and does not know it; and badly indeed could comedy do without him. So far is this kind of humorist from knowing his own oddity or eccentricity, that he considers himself a model of regularity and order; and so far is he from thinking his character a ludicrous one, that he esteems it in the highest degree commanding and dignified. It is this very ignorance of what he is, and the contrast to others between what he is and what he deems himself, that are the comic conditions of his character.

We might dilate more at large on the general subject of wit and humor: we might consider them in relation to the individual, to society, to nations; also in relation to times, civilizations, customs, fashions: we might inquire under what conditions wit and humor most abound; under what conditions they are best or worst; what is their moral and intellectual value: we might distinguish wit and humor, as they are unwritten among the people, or as they become written and pass into letters: we might ask, and try to answer the question, why English literature should be so rich, and the mass of the English people so poor, in wit and humor. We might further inquire, why grave nations, like the Spanish and the Scotch, should have so far excelled in humor brilliant nations, like the Italians and the French;

or, perhaps, why the Irish and Arabians, in some departments of the comic, have so excelled them all. But we must decline such inquiries, and turn to the more attractive matter of our author.

Dean Ramsay entitles his work, "Reminiscences of Scottish Life and character;" but they are nearly all on the humorous side. A cheerful, cordial, and humane spirit must the man have had, to have gathered and garnered from the Past, such a goodly store of pleasant memories. What a companion he would be in the twilight of a summer's evening, or by the winter's evening fire, or in a quiet rural journey! If Scottish life and character were such as we see it in the genial vision of Dean Ramsay, Scotland must have been a delightful place to live in. The vision makes us think of a northwestern paradise, and inclines us to oelieve that Smollett's Lishmahago, after all, was not so extravagant as we used to deem him in his patriotic idolatry.

The serious portion of the Scotch have always endeavored, ethically and legally, to enforce a sterner outward keeping of the Christian Sunday than it could ever have been possible to enforce, even of the Jewish Sabbath. This tendency often led to ludicrous results. A traveling artist, in a Sunday stroll, asked a Scotch peasant to tell him something of a ruin that he was passing in his walk. "It's no the day," said he, "to be speering sic things." This brings to mind an incident which was related to us in our boyhood. We had a friend who studied medicine in Edinburgh. Visiting a hospital on a Sunday morning, in company with his class and the professor, he came to a certain patient. It was feared that the patient was in danger of lockjaw, and, to test his condition, the professor desired him to whistle. "The Lord forbid," said the patient, "that I should do so on God's blessed Sabbath."

"On the first introduction of Tractarianism into Scotland, the full choir service had been established in an Episcopal church, where a noble family had adopted those views, and carried them out regardless of expense. The lady who had been instrumental in getting up these musical services was very anxious that a favorite female servant of the family, a Presbyterian of the old school, should have an opportunity of hearing them; accordingly, she very kindly took her down to church in the carriage, and, on returning, asked her what she thought of the music, etc. 'Ou, it's varra bonny, varra bonny; but oh, my lady, it's an awfu' way of spending the Sabbath.'" This puts us in mind of a Scotch old lady whom we heard of twenty years ago, in Newburgh, N. Y. She belonged to the Presbyterian Church there, and was very liberal in its support. Music was common in most churches by that day. The Newburgh Presbyterians decided to introduce it into theirs. But how would the Scotch lady take it? She was a Jenny Geddes in her way, and intensified by exile in all her prejudices. So the choir determined to be cautious. They merely introduced a bass-viol at first, which they supposed would be lost to the old lady's deafness in the mass of the harmony. But for the slightest sound of horse-hair and catgut in meeting the old lady had the ear of a hare. She called immediately on the minister. "Sae," said she, "ye hae got a fiddle in the kirk!" "O, madam," he said, deprecatingly, "only an instrument to regulate the voices." "Weel, weel," she replied, "ye may fiddle yersels to the deil, gin it pleeses ye, but ye shana fiddle me alang wi' ye,"—and she angrily darted out of the room. The fiddle or the lady must go, and the fiddle went.

"The following dialogue," writes the author, "between Mr. M—— of Glasgow and an old Highland acquaintance, will illustrate the contrast between the severity of judgment passed upon treating the Sabbath with levity and the lighter censure attached to indulgence in whiskey. Mr. M—— begins : 'Donald, what brought you here ?' 'Ou, weel, sir, it waas a bad place yon ; they were baad folk—but they're a God-fearin' set o' folk here !' 'Well, Donald,' said Mr. M——, 'I'm glad to hear it.' 'Ou, ay, sir, deed are they; and I'll gie you an instance o't. Last Sabbath, just as the kirk was skalin', there was a drover chield frae Dumfries comin' along the road whustlin', an' lookin' *as happy* as if it was ta muddle o' the week ; weel, sir, oor laads is a God-fearin' set o' laads, an' they were just coomin' oot o' the kirk —od, they yokit upon him, an' a'most killed him !' Mr. M—— inquired whether the assaulters might not have been drunk ? 'Weel, weel, sir,' said Donald, 'I'll no say but they might be.' 'Depend upon it,' said Mr. M——, 'it's a bad thing, whiskey.' 'Weel, weel, sir,' replied Donald, 'I'll no say but it *may*,' adding, in a very decided tone, 'speeciallie *baad* whuskey !' "

We once heard of an old Irishwoman who was quite as good a special pleader as this exemplary Scotchman. In order to make our anecdote intelligible, we must explain an Irish provincial phrase. When one, at least formerly, said in Ireland, "Surely, I have *earned* you," it was to claim the dearest title to your regard. It was to say, that the highest price had been paid for you, and the last sacrifice suffered for you. So the young wife, who had lost all for her careless husband, would say, "Ah ! Shamas darling, don't you know —how I *earned* you?" Or the old mother would say to her profligate son, " Paudtheen dear, think of me, and think of how I *earned* you, mavourneen !" Now the venerable matron with whom our anecdote is concerned had, on the anniversary of the patron saint, indulged in strong potations too devoutly deep, and was on the next morning sadly sick with qualms and headache ; then groaned she out in the martyrdom of her misery, "*Och, my sweet Saint Patrick, if it isn't I that did'nt earn you last night?*" Here is a piece of unconscious humor. A benovelent lady in one of her visits asked a poor woman if she ever went to church? "Ou, ay," she replied, "there's a man ca'd Chalmers preaches here, and I whiles gang-in and hear him just to encourage him, puir body!" We heard in Scotland a story in connection with the Doctor's name, almost as good as this. The great preacher was once during his sermon annoyed by some dogs in the church. He stopped, and ordered them to be turned out. When service was over, one old woman said to another, "An' how did ye like the Doctor the day?" "Ach, but he was gran'!" she replied. "Did ye understaun' him?" inquired her companion. "The Lord forbid," she answered, "that I should hae sic presumption; but wasn't he bonnie on thae dogs?"

In the religious element of Scottish humor we see the keen moral sense of the people, and this is often felt in the sarcastic rebuke which their sayings often administer to levity or impiety. A young man, going from home, was making a great fuss about his preparing to leave, and the putting up of his habiliments. His old aunt was much annoyed at all this bustle, and stopped him by the somewhat contemptuous question, "Whaur's this you're gaun, Robby, that ye mak sic a grand wark about yer claes?" The young man lost temper, and pettishly replied, "I'm going to the devil." "'Deed Robby, then," was the quiet answer, "ye needna be sae nice, he'll juist tak ye as ye are." We quote another saying full as good. A man was fiercely denouncing the doctrine of original sin. "Mr. H." said a neighbor to him, "it seems to me that you needna fash yoursel' about *original* sin, for to my certain knowledge you have as much *akwal* (actual) sin as will do your business." If these and other sayings evince sharpness and sagacity, we find many

sayings that evince simple-mindedness. We give an instance.
A man and his wife fell on a Sunday evening into a critical
dispute. The wife said she thought David (King David)
hadna taen much pains when he *metred* the Psalms ; on
which the husband " flew into a passion at her ignorance,
and reminded her that it was George Buchanan who *metred*
the Psalms."

The chapter on the old Scottish domestic servant is more
pathetic than comic. It is very interesting. But the old-
time domestic—loyal, odd, vexatious, affectionate, impudent,
trust-worthy, presuming, care-taking, reverential, disrespectful, wilful, stubborn, daring of speech to criticise master
and mistress to the face, bold of word or blow for their
honor behind their back, within doors loose of tongue to
censure faults, without doors close of lip to hide them—such
a domestic was not peculiar to Scotland ; every country has
nad him or her, and no country in more perfection than
Ireland. In that country, in our youth, we knew a very
complete specimen of the "genus" Caleb Balderstone. His
name was Paddy—and truer Paddy of his nation or his
class never existed. His master was suddenly deprived
of an ample revenue, and at once cast down from the
height of prosperity to the depth of poverty. It was that
worst kind of poverty which we call genteel poverty.
Paddy was as thorny as a thistle, and his motto might well
have been, " Nemo me impune lacessit." But to the family
after their misfortune he was soft and gentle as a rose. An
old gentleman and his three or four young daughters, with
Paddy, made the household. They had dismissed the other
servants, but Paddy they could not get rid of. To the master
to whom when rich he had been saucy, he was humble when
poor. The young ladies he loved with more than a father's
love, honored with more than a knight's courtesy, and
nothing was more a grief to him than that these ladies

should soil their hands or profane themselves with kitchen-work. Any drudgery taken from him he considered as taken unrightfully; the deprivation was an insult or a wrong. It was the only matter, within doors, which made him angry or made him scold. But outside he was all brag or battle. He had a hard cause to defend, a hard fight to maintain; he would insist that his master had a princely income, when he asked a pound of butter on credit; and he was ready to knock any one down who hinted a suspicion about his pantry or cellar, when the family often dined on potatoes and salt. The house was encircled by a high stone wall, and the entrance to it was by a single gate. This gate Paddy kept bolted against bailiffs and executions. It was impossible to outwit his cunning or to outwatch his vigilance. He was so fierce in his temper to intruders, that even sheriffs' officers became affraid of him. The family were restored to their former opulence; Paddy, of course, shared in it, and in a good old age he died honored and lamented. This is no romance. For the credit of human nature we are glad to say it is merely matter-of-fact reality.

The author, at some length, dwells on old Scottish conviviality. This is not a very pleasant part of the book, and could not in our day be of any book. Such habits may, it is true, have been connected with much in custom and character that was hospitable, genial, and mirthful, but the better side is so counterbalanced by the worse, that the generation of a more temperate age can see in these olden convivialities little but their grossness and excess, and these they only regard with revulsion and disgust.

In the chapter on Scottish wit and humor as arising out of the Scottish language—including Scottish proverbs, besides many excellent etymological and critical observations—we find several instances of the quaintest drollery and the slyest humor. In an examination of the magistrates

of Edinburgh before the House of Peers, concerning the
Porteous mob in 1736, the Duke of Newcastle asked the
Provost with what kind of shot the town guard, commanded
by Porteous, had loaded their muskets. " Ou," he replied,
"juist sic as ane shutes dukes and sic like fools wi'."   This
was at first thought an insult to the House, till the Duke
of Argyle explained that it meant to describe the shot used
for *ducks and water-fowl.* John Clerk, an eminent Scotch
lawyer, in pleading before the House of Lords in the case
of a dispute about a mill-stream, pronounced the word
water as if written *watter.* "Mr. Clerk," said the Chancellor, " do you spell water in Scotland with two t's ?"   Clerk,
a little nettled at this hit at his national tongue, answered,
" Na, my lord, we dinna spell watter " (making the word as
short as he could) " wi' twa t's ; but we spell mainners "
(making the word as long as he could) " wi' twa n's."   We
heard another story of John Clerk, as characteristic as
this of his sarcastic boldness.   He was arguing a case before
the House of Lords, and spoke in the broadest Scotch.   A
conceited young peer interrupted him, and said, " Really,
Mr. Clerk, I cannot understand you."   Clerk retorted, " I
dinna ken if yer Lordship can understaun' me, but I ken
ony mon of common sense could."

As we are on wit and humor that arise out of forms of
language, we shall put a few instances that we find in the
book under this head.   A child, reading the Scripture passage where the words occur, " He took Paul's girdle," said
with much confidence, " I ken what he took that for ;" and
being asked to explain, replied at once, " To bake's bannocks on "—"girdle" being, in the North, the name for
the iron plate hung over the fire for making oat-cakes
or bannocks.   The actual word, however, is *griddle,* and in
Ireland it is always so pronounced.   The Scotch word is a
corruption, and hence the child's mistake.   But there is a

New England story, founded on a similar mistake, that has
in it a much more audacious humor. We heard it once
inimitably told by a man venerable for talent, goodness,
and piety, as brilliant in wit as distinguished in worth.
We fear that we spoil it in our repetition. A youth in
Connecticut was reading the Bible on Saturday evening in
the family circle—the elderly parents at the ends of the
table, children and domestics occupying intermediate places.
All, of course, were reverently attentive. The boy was
reading the twenty-sixth chapter of Exodus, in which descriptions are given for constructing certain portions of
the tabernacle. Words are constantly occurring in such
portions of the Scriptures that would stagger a scholar.
What wonder that a young boy should blunder? So, when
the lad came to verse fourteen, instead of reading, "Thou
shalt make a covering for the tent of ram's skins dyed red,
and a covering above of *badgers'* skins," he read in the last
clause, "and a covering above of *beggars'* skins." "Stop
there, now, my son," said the patriarch; "let us meditate
on that. See what blessed times we live in, and what good
things the Gospel has done for us. When a man becomes
poor among us we provide for him, we furnish him with
shelter, food, clothes, and all other necessaries and comforts;
we care for him, and we console him; we visit him in his
afflictions; we cheer him in his age, and in his death we
honor him. But you observe in them ere old Jewish barbarian times, if a man got down in the world, it was only
pull off his hide and put it on a tabernacle." As we are in
this region of association, we quote a story from our author
that belongs to it. "A lad had come for examination previous to his receiving his first communion. The pastor,
knowing that his young friend was not very profound in
his theology, and not wishing to discourage him,..... began
by what he thought a safe question, and what would give

him confidence. So he took the Old Testament, and asked him, in reference to the Mosaic law, how many commandments there were. After a little thought, he put his answer into the modest form of a supposition, and replied cautiously, 'Aiblins [perhaps] a hunner.' The clergyman was angry, and for that time dismissed him. On returning home, he met a friend on his way to the manse, and learning that he, too, was going to the minister for examination, shrewdly asked him, 'Weel, what will ye say noo if the minister speers hoo mony commandments there are?' 'Say! I shall say *ten* to be sure.' To which the other rejoined with great triumph, 'TEN! Try ye him wi' ten! I tried him wi' a hunner, and he wasna satisfied.'"

The author adduces some very ludicrous mistakes made by strangers in Scotland, who assumed to be adepts in the national tongue. But he gives no illustration more absurd than one which we ourselves heard of in Scotland. A conceited young Englishman was dining at a ducal residence there, and was boasting to the company of his familiarity with the Scottish language. He was sitting by the daughter of the house, a witty and most beautiful girl. As the ladies retired from the dining-room the youth was alert to open the door; the maiden, slowly passing him, said, with an arch smile, "*My canty callant, come prie my mou !*" and thus turned what might have been his privilege into his punishment; for she simply said, "My gay young fellow, come taste my mouth "—that is—"Kiss me ;" and the gay young fellow looked very like—a fool.

The section on "Proverbs" we have not touched, for we felt that it would require to itself an entire article, and deserve it. The Scottish proverbs, as given by our author, are a treasury of originality, shrewdness, sagacity, and humor. They have all a strong savor of nationality; many are peculiar to the characteristics of the language and the people, and to those which have been adopted from other nations, or which are common to all nations, the Scottish mind has given its own marked impression.

Dean Ramsay has a chapter "On Scottish Stories of Wit and Humor." We cannot see why the Dean has this special chapter, since nearly the whole book consist of such stories. We have already selected some of these stories ; we will select two or three more. The author tells of an old sick beggar-woman, "who drank six bottles of beer and half a bottle of whiskey, then fell asleep for forty-eight hours, at the end of which time she awoke quite recovered!" This beats Lover's Irishman, who also on a certain occasion slept *forty-eight* hours. He mistook a ship bound to Bengal for one bound to Fingal, got into it, and slept forty-eight hours in the hold. When discovered and questioned, nothing surprised the captain so much as the length of his sleep. "Why," said the captain, "I never heard of any one who could sleep forty-eight hours at a stretch." " *Och, yer Honor,*" observed the passenger, "*ye see, whin we Irishmin shleeps, we pays attintion to it.*"

Dean Ramsay ascribes the legend of the roast goose, the the goose with one leg, to a waggish old cook in Scotland. He admits, however, that a parallel story is in " The Decameron," but fancies that, as there was a coincidence of vocation between the Venetian Chichibio and the Scottish John Frazer, there may have been also a coincidence of invention. The Dean's version of the story is rather bald. We have often heard a more dramatic version among the Irish peasantry, and they knew as little of Boccaccio or the Decameron as John Frazer did. The legend is probably of Oriental origin, and may have come down in several independent traditions. The Irish peasantry always connected it with Dean Swift, as they did, not only all that was mirthful, but much that was marvellous. A part of our chilhood was spent near the ruin of a castle as old as the Anglo-Norman invasion; but many of the people believed that Dean Swift had once dwelt in it, and therein studied and practised the black art. His mythic servant was always called "John," and in the many wit-combats between the master and the man, John was always the victor. And here is the Irish legend of the goose. It was wet, wintry weather. The Dean and John were traveling together on horseback. They stopped over night at an inn. The next morning John brought the Dean's boots to him thick covered with dry mud. "Why didn't you clane my boots, you thief?" said the Dean. "Becase, it wouldn't bo of any use," said John; "wouldn't they be as dirty as iver to-morrow?" "That's thrue," said the Dean; "faix, John, you're a janius, and the world will hear of you, so it will." The Dean quietly put on his boots, and gave secret orders that John should have no breakfast. When they set out on their journey, John had a long and melancholy face. "What ails you, John?" asked the Dean. "I have had no breakfast, yer riverence," answered John. "What's the use of having breakfast," said the Dean; "you'll want it as badly to-morrow." "Och, Master agra, but the ould boy could'nt hold a rush-light to you!" They rode quietly along, John a little behind his master, and his master reading what the people would consider a volume of devotion. A gentleman meeting them passes the Dean, but says to John, "Who's that?" "Who's that?" returns John. "Don't you know? That's the great Dean of St. Patrick's—England's pride and Ireland's glory!" "Where may ye be going?" inquired the gentleman. "We're going to heaven," answered John. "Is this the way to heaven?" asked the gentleman. "It is," answered John; "Master's prayin' and I'm fastin', and if that isn't the way to heaven, I'd like to know which is." At the close of the day they

came again to an inn. The Dean ordered a roast goose for
dinner. John, when the goose was done, served it up to
his master void of a leg, which he had torn off in the ravenous impatience of his hunger. " Where's the other leg of
the goose ?" said the Dean. " Did yer riverence iver know
a goose to have two legs, and spicially in winter ?" retorted
John. " Well, I had forgotten," observed the Dean. The
next morning they rode along, and, as the weather was
frosty, the geese along the road stood each upon a single
leg. " Didn't I tell yer riverence," said John, " geese
niver has but one leg, spicially in winter ?" " Whew !"
shouted the Dean, and cracked his whip. The geese, of
course, scampered off, and showed plainly that they belonged to the biped genus. " What do you say to *that*,
John," cried the Dean ; and with exultant mockery went
on, " Geese niver has but one leg, spicially in winter."
" Och, yer riverence," exclaimed John, " why didn't you
shout, ' Whew !' last night, and crack your whip then ?
Who knows but the goose would have had two legs ?"

That is a capital instance of sly humor and vindictive
patriotism which the author quotes from Lockhart's Life
of Scott. Sir Walter met a quack practising medicine in
a small country town south of the Border, whom he had
formerly known as a blacksmith and a horse-doctor. The
fellow was dispensing immoderate doses of " laudomy and
calomel," but excused himself by saying, " It would be
lang before they made up for Flodden." Something like
this was the spirit of an Irish schoolmaster. He had been
deeply involved in the rebellion of 1798, fled for his life,
and suffered unutterable wretchedness in an obscure hid-
ing-place of London. Being a good classical scholar, he
after a while obtained employment as an assistant in a
school, and subsequently made a fortune as the head of a
great academy. He was one day boasting of his wealth to

a compatriot—"And how do you think," said he, "I made it? *Well, I made it by the blessing of God, and flogging the sons of Irish Tories.*"

There are three public characters of whom our author makes a good deal—"the Parish Idiot," "the Town Betheral" (or Beadle), and "the Parish Clergyman." We must omit comment on the "Betheral." The character is too locally Scottish to be made briefly intelligible, and we have no space for explanatory quotation. If we bring " the Parish Idiot" and " the Parish Clergyman" into juxtaposition, it is with no feeling of disrespect to the clergyman, and with no idea that between the two characters there is the least possibly analogy. In fact, the order of relation is not ours, it is the Dean's own, and the Dean has no want of reverence for his cloth. We begin with the Parish Idiot, or, rather, the harmless, half-witted, chartered simpleton of the district. The mental and moral traits of this character are well discriminated by Dean Ramsay, and, as is proper in such a case, with " a humorous sadness,"—with " smiles that might as well be tears." One trait of this character was diligence in attending church, and a desire to be near the pulpit. One Sunday, in a Scottish kirk, the minister, on entering, found the parish idiot, Tam, actually *in* the pulpit. " Come down, sir, immediately," was the peremptory and indignant call of the clergyman ; and, on Tam being unmoved, it was repeated with still greater energy. " Na, na," replied Tam, looking down, " juist ye come up 'wi' me. This is a perverse generation, and, faith, they need us baith." This reply evinces another trait which was often found in this character, namely, an occasional power of sarcasm, and a keen sense of the ludicrous. " Jamie Frazer was sitting in the front gallery of the kirk, wide awake, when many of the congregation were slumbering round him. The clergyman endeavored to awaken the attention of his hearers by stating the fact, saying, "You see, Jamie Frazer, the idiot, does not fall asleep, as many of you are doing." "An' I had na been an idiot," cried out Jamie, "I wad ha' been sleeping too." Jamie may have felt as did a certain friend of ours about preaching. We asked him if he ever went to sleep at the sermon? "No," said he, "but I often wish I could." We once, when listening to a very silly sermon, heard a gentleman behind us whisper to another: "The preacher thinks we are little children." "No," said another, "he thinks we are little idiots." But such idiots as Jamie Frazer would not easily have been imposed on. Great readiness of reply is attributed also to this order of character. "Daft Will Speir" was a privileged hunter in the Eglingtoun grounds. He was discovered by the Earl, one day, taking a near cut, and crossing a fence in the demesne. The Earl called out, "Come back, sir, that's not the road." "Do ye ken," said Will, "whaur I'm gaun?" "No," replied his Lordship. "Well, hoo do ye ken whether this be the road or no?" Another trait in the half-witted character is a dislike to work. "John," said the minister to daft Jock Gray, the supposed original of Davie Gellatley, "you are an idle fellow; you might herd a few cows." "Me herd!" replied Jock, "I dinna ken corn frae garse." This was as good as what an able-bodied beggar said to a nobleman, who reproached him for asking alms. "Ah, but your Lordship would pity me, did you only know how lazy I am." One more trait, not illustrated in this book, sometimes belongs to the half-witted, and that is, a wonderful faculty of calculation. We once witnessed a case in which a seeming idiot astonished the most brilliant arithmeticians and algebraists. Their pens, as compared with his brain, were as the weaver's shuttle to the lightning's flash.

His rapidity and power of combining and analyzing numbers was almost a thing incredible. It was inquired, "What method he used?" He said that he did not count by *tens*, but by *twelves*. This curiously agrees with what Walker —once a Professor of Trinity College, Dublin—maintains in his "Philosophy of Arithmetic," that *twelves* in calculations would have been insuperably superior to *tens*.

Ireland had its local simpleton as well as Scotland; and, as in Scotland, between him and the people there was much the same set of feelings and relations. We will ourselves preserve for history the memory of a local simpleton, whom we will call Johnny Grimes. There was a tragic element in his story and his character. Johnny was not only born with his natural faculties, but to a good worldly inheritance. But in childhood he became an orphan, and a diabolical uncle ruined him in his intellect and robbed him of his property. Johnny was in mortal fear of a.gun— and to suggest that a wall near which he stood was unsteady, put him into.agonies of horror. He was good and gentle; when otherwise, it was owing to thoughtless or rude tormentors. He belonged to a numerous kindred of wealthy farmers; every door was open to him; as he willed he wandered, and with whom that pleased him for the time he lived. He had most of the traits which we have already ascribed to his class. The Scottish idiot was a thorough Presbyterian; Johnny was as earnest a Catholic. The Scottish idiot would be near the pulpit, Johnny would be near the altar—and it was sometimes difficult to prevent him from being *on* it. He was very imitative, and would even copy the priest's gestures. There was one old woman in the congregation who was a sad torment to him. She was one of those suspected pietists, who in ordinary phrase are called devotees, but whom the Irish more contemptuously call *voteens*. There was no end to her groanings, her grimaces, her genuflections, and the beating of her breast. Johnny admired her, and wished to out-do her; but after a while gave up the struggle in despair. This woman's name was Moll Byrne; and when Johnny was asked what progress he made in his pious contest, " Well," said he, " I gave one thump, I gave two thumps, I gave a hundred—but ould Nebuchadnezzar couldn't keep thumping with Moll Byrne." Johnny was fond of tea, a rare rustic luxury at that time. An ambitious young beauty gave him quite a feast of tea, cakes, etc., that in public he should call her *Miss* Murphy. The next time Johnny met her, in her finest, at a dance, he went up to her, and exclaimed, in his loudest tones, " Och, good luck to you, Biddy; don't you remember the fine meal of bread and cake and tea you gave me to call you *Miss* Murph." Johnny had the aversion of his class to work, and whenever his entertainers wished to get rid of him, they had only to request of him the smallest task; then Johnny was off, without any formal ceremony of taking leave.

We are sorry that we must soon close. We have not half exhausted our author's treasury, or our own. We regret that we cannot expand upon the parish minister. We must refer our readers to Dean Ramsay's book. The Dean speaks of the difference between the olden clergy and the present, in humor and free speech. The change is partly owing to a change of sentiment, and not a little to a change of costume. A man might safely joke from under a wig, who, wearing his own hair, would be forced to caution; a gold-headed cane and a clerical hat were strong safeguards against obtrusive liberties. The clergy of the present day are prim and proper; but what else can they be, when look alone distinguishes them from others, or the white cravat, which they share in common with well-dressed waiters?

The racy speech in old-time ministers must have been

very pleasant. " Maister Dunlop," said two wags in Dumfries, to a minister of this kind, " dae ye hear the news?" " What news?" " O, the Deil's dead." " Is he," said Mr. Dunlop, " then I maun pray for twa faitherless bairns." We are glad to see that quaint comment on a verse in the Psalms made historical, which we had always regarded as mythical.   It was, it seems, a Mr. Shirra of Kirkcaldy who remarked, when reading out of the 116 Psalm, " I said in my haste, all men are liars,"—" Indeed, Dauvid, an ye had been i' this parish, ye might hae said it at your leesure."   The *naïveté* and simplicity of those old-time clergy were not less remarkable than their freedom of speech and manner.   To Mr. Ramsay's stories we will ourselves add two.   A Highland preacher was told that many of his congregation complained of his sermons as being too long. The old man was indignant.   On the next Sunday he took occasion to allude to the complaint.   " And sae," said he, " ye think my sermons o'er lang ; yet there's chiels amang ye that'll gae awa up to Lunnun, and listen to Billy Pitt, Charley Fox, and Neddy Burke, ay, for five and sax hours at a time, and ye winna hear me for twa or three."   Another elderly minister, whom we will call the Rev. Dr. Scott, listened very gravely at a Presbytery dinner to a number of his junior brethren, who bitterly declaimed as to the decline of reverence, and especially among the young.   " Weel," said he, " I dinna think sae.   The youngsters are juist as gude as they used to be."   To confirm his assertion he went on : " I was gaein' the ither day into Margery Musclady's Public [tavern] : twa Lunnon chiels were stannin' recht in the duirway, and they were sweerin' maist dreedfully.   I stopped and admonished them ; and whether it was the caulm yet dignifeed mainner in whilk I rebuked them, or whether it was the pooer o' the word itself, I dinna exactly ken, but ane o' them turned quick roun' to me and said, ' *Thankee, ould boy.* ' " The people, too, were *racy*, as well as the clergy. " I wonder what'n the minister is greetin' aboot," said one old critic to another, while the preacher was weeping over a very foolish sermon. " Gin ye were whaur he is, and had sae little to say for yersel', ye'd greet as mickle as he does."

As it was in Scotland, so it was in New England. The clergy and the laity were quaint and racy. " I have had many a painful occasion," said old Mr. Howe of Hopkinton, Mass., preaching a quarter-century sermon to his people—" I have had many a painful occasion to administer rebuke to you from this pulpit ; but I must do you the justice to say, that you had always the common sense to know that you richly deserved it." A minister who had preached a very long and not very lively sermon, thinking his eloquence gave him a title to complain of his fatigue, said, on coming down from his pulpit, to his deacon, " O Deacon, but I *am* so tired !" " And have ye no pity for us ?" replied the deacon. " Why," said one parishioner to another, coming out of Sunday-morning service, " did our minister preach on the *secret* decrees of the Almighty. Wasn't he aware that half a dozen of the most tattling gossips of the county were present, and that before the afternoon the whole matter will be all over town ?" " So you, they tell me," said an elderly theologian in petticoats to a quiet young man, " are a Universalist preacher !" " Yes, madam, I am," was the calm reply. " And you don't b'lieve in the eternity of hell's torments ?" " No, madam, I don't." " O, horrible ! And do you b'lieve the wicked will suffer at all in the future state ?" " Yes, madam, I do." " How long do you suppose ?" " O, possibly a length of duration which no created imagination can measure or conceive." " Well," groaned out the old lady, partially comforted, " *well, that's something.*"

We are persuaded that gatherings might be made from New England life to fill a volume larger than Dean Ramsay's—and Dean Ramsay's we recommend with all our heart to all who love local knowledge, national enthusiasm, innocent hilarity, and mirth that leaves no stain upon the memory.

We close with two short observations; one as to the humor of the book, and the other as to the humor of the nation. Most of the humor of the book is in some degree clerical, or associated with the religious habits of the people. This is natural; first, because the popular life of deepest and most universal interest was connected with religious habits and religious institutions; secondly, because the clergy were the most marked representatives of that life; and thirdly, because the author, being himself a clergyman, would gather his knowledge a good deal within the sphere of his profession.

As to the humor of the nation, it is, upon the whole, grave, caustic, critical, analytic, logical—more the product of strong common-sense, of keen and observant intellect, than of ready sympathy, quick sensibility, and exuberant imagination. This estimate would not satisfy the author; we doubt if it would satisfy any Scotchman. We would say, however, that we do not mean to disparage Scotch humor; we merely wish to distinguish and define it. We consider it a humor very brilliant and very rich. Besides, we write rather of the popular humor of Scotland than of its literary humor. Unquestionably, Smollett, Burns, Scott, Galt, and Wilson were great masters of humor, but even in these the national characteristics which we refer to are strongly marked. As Scotchmen, they had these characteristics; but as men of genius, they had greatly more. It is by comparing nation with nation in their popular life that we can discriminate their simplest spontaneous tendencies. No one that knew aught of mind, or that ever read history, has denied to the Scotch wit and humor earnest imagination and profound enthusiasm. But the root of these is in the soil of logic, and when the root does not grow bravely upward, and by the sap of thought and passion abundantly effloresce and fructify, it is apt to dry into a stunted and barren literalness. Accordingly, satirists and wags lay hold, in bitterness or fun, on this side of Scotch character, as they do on the weak side of Irish character, when they taunt it with bragging, bulls, and blunders. Our author's sensitiveness against such strictures shows something of the literalness which satirists and wags ridicule. Sydney Smith used to say, " It requires a surgical operation to get a joke well into a Scotch understanding." And this our author treats as if the immortal Sydney meant it seriously—Sydney, who had read Burns, lived with Jeffrey, and was at home with Scott and Wilson ! It was a mirthful extravagance, and had no more intention of reality than a surgical operation would have had adequacy to the cutting of a joke into a Scotchman or any other man. And Charles Lamb is also taken to task. " I wish," said he, at a festival given to the son of Burns, " it had been the father instead of the son ;" upon which four Scotchmen present with one voice exclaimed, " That's impossible, for *he's dead.*" So the author sets himself to prove that, after all, his countrymen were not so much out of the way, for a great many at the time didn't know that Burns was dead. This is what Lamb would have most loudly laughed at. Farmers were not long ago in England who hardly knew that George the Third was dead, and farmers in Pennsylvania supposed for years that General Jackson was still their President. The idea of taking Lamb at his word would have been to him the most amusing of all absurdities. Lamb was told of a man whose arms were shot off in a sea-fight, and, as the poor wretch was lifted to be carried to the cockpit, his legs were also shot off : and " Did he live ?" said Charles.   " No," said the narrator.   " What a pity !" said the melancholy wag, " he'd have been such an ornament to society !"   This might as well be taken for a specimen of Lamb's humanity and æsthetics, as his banter about Burns for a deliberate estimate of Scotch character and talent.   The Scots have all to boast that history can give to claims of noblest glory —independence, liberty, genius, and achievement.   They can, therefore, well afford to bear with the sneers of satirists and the laugh of wags ; to be charitable, also, to nations of not less intellect or bravery than themselves, though not so successful.